The Cambridge Companion to the

The Cambridge Companion to the Italian Novel provides a broad-ranging introduction to the major trends in the development of the Italian novel from its early modern origin to the contemporary era. Contributions cover a wide range of topics including the theory of the novel in Italy, the historical novel, realism, modernism, postmodernism, neorealism, and film and the novel. The contributors are distinguished scholars from the United Kingdom, the United States, Italy, and Australia. Novelists examined include some of the most influential and important of the twentieth century inside and outside Italy: Luigi Pirandello, Primo Levi, Umberto Eco, and Italo Calvino. This is a unique examination of the Italian novel, and will prove invaluable to students and specialists alike. Readers will gain a keen sense of the vitality of the Italian novel throughout its history and a clear picture of the debates and criticism that have surrounded its development.

THE CAMBRIDGE
COMPANION TO
THE ITALIAN NOVEL

EDITED BY

PETER BONDANELLA

AND

ANDREA CICCARELLI

Indiana University

CAMBRIDGE
UNIVERSITY PRESS

PUBLISHED BY THE PRESS SYNDICATE OF THE UNIVERSITY OF CAMBRIDGE
The Pitt Building, Trumpington Street, Cambridge CB2 1RP, United Kingdom

CAMBRIDGE UNIVERSITY PRESS
The Edinburgh Building, Cambridge, CB2 2RU, UK
40 West 20th Street, New York, NY 10011–4211, USA
477 Williamstown Road, Port Melbourne, VIC 3207, Australia
Ruiz de Alarcón 13, 28014 Madrid, Spain
Dock House, The Waterfront, Cape Town 8001, South Africa

http://www.cambridge.org

First published 2003

Printed in the United Kingdom at the University Press, Cambridge

Typeface Sabon 10/13 pt.   *System* LaTeX 2$_\varepsilon$ [TB]

A catalogue record for this book is available from the British Library

Library of Congress Cataloguing in Publication data
The Cambridge Companion to the Italian Novel / edited by Peter Bondanella and
Andrea Ciccarelli.
p.   cm. – (Cambridge Companions to Literature)
Includes bibliographical references and index.
ISBN 0 521 66018 1 – ISBN 0 521 66962 6 (pbk.)
1. Italian fiction – History and criticism.   I. Bondanella, Peter E., 1943–   II. Ciccarelli,
Andrea.   III. Series.
PQ4170.C36 2003
853.009 – dc21   2002041706

ISBN 0 521 66018 1 hardback
ISBN 0 521 66962 6 paperback

For Julia and Amanda

CONTENTS

CONTRIBUTORS

MANUELA BERTONE is the Cultural Attaché of the Embassy of France in Rome, co-editor of *Carlo Emilio Gadda: Contemporary Perspectives* (1994) and the author of *Tomasi di Lampedusa* (1995).

PETER BONDANELLA is Distinguished Professor of Italian and Comparative Literature at Indiana University and past President of the American Association for Italian Studies. He is the author of the *Cassell Dictionary of Italian Literature* (1996); *The Cinema of Federico Fellini* (1992); *The Films of Roberto Rossellini* (1993); *Umberto Eco and the Open Work* (1997); *Italian Cinema: From Neorealism to the Present* (3rd rev. ed, 2001); and *The Films of Federico Fellini* (2002).

JOANN CANNON is Professor of Italian at the University of California – Davis and the author of *Italo Calvino: Writer and Critic* (1981) and *Postmodern Italian Fiction: The Crisis of Reason in Calvino, Eco, Sciascia, Malerba* (1989).

ROCCO CAPOZZI is Professor of Italian at the University of Toronto and the author of numerous studies of contemporary Italian narrative, including *Homage to Moravia* (1990) and *Reading Eco: An Anthology* (1997).

ROLANDO CAPUTO is a Lecturer in the Department of Cinema Studies, La Trobe University (Melbourne, Australia). He has published on Italian cinema and film generally in journals such as *Spunti e Ricerche, Screening the Past, Art and Text*, and *Metro*.

GIOVANNI CARSANIGA is Professor Emeritus of Italian at the University of Sydney, and the author of *Giovanni Leopardi: The Unheeded Voice* (1977) as well as other essays on nineteenth-century Italian literature.

REMO CESERANI is Professor of Comparative Literature at the University of Bologna. Besides a satirical novel – *Viaggio in Italia del Dottor Dapertutto* (The Journey to Italy of Doctor Everywhere, 1996) – he is the author of numerous books on contemporary and comparative literature, including *Treni di carta: l'immaginario in ferrovia* (Paper Trains: The Imaginary on Rails, 1993) and *Raccontare il postmoderno* (Recounting the Postmodern, 1997).

ANDREA CICCARELLI is Chair of the Department of French and Italian and Director of the College Arts and Humanities Institute at Indiana University. He is the author of numerous essays on modern Italian literature and *Manzoni: la coscienza della letteratura* (Manzoni: The Consciousness of Literature, 1996).

ROBERT DOMBROSKI was Distinguished Professor and Director of Italian Graduate Studies at the City University of New York. He was the author of *Properties of Writing: Ideological Discourse in Modern Italian Fiction* (1994) and *Creative Entanglements: Gadda and the Baroque* (1999). Professor Dombroski died in 2002.

ALBERT N. MANCINI is Professor Emeritus of Italian at the Ohio State University, Editor of *Italica*, and past President of the American Association of Teachers of Italian. He has written numerous essays on early modern Italian literature and is a contributor to *The Cambridge History of Italian Literature* (1996).

PIERLUIGI PELLINI is Professor of Italian at the University of Siena, and author of *Naturalismo e verismo* (Naturalism and Realism, 1998).

NICOLAS J. PERELLA is Professor Emeritus of Italian at the University of California – Berkeley, translator of Collodi's *The Adventures of Pinocchio* (1992) and Palazzeschi's *Man of Smoke* (1992), and the author of numerous books and articles on Italian and comparative literature, including *The Kiss Sacred and Profane* (1969).

OLGA RAGUSA is Da Ponte Professor Emeritus of Italian Literature at Columbia, former head of the Department of Italian there, and longtime (1968–84) editor of *Italica*. Her publications include *Comparative Perspectives on Manzoni* (1986) and *Narrative and Drama: Essays in Modern Italian Literature from Verga to Pasolini* (1975).

LUCIA RE is Professor of Italian at the University of California – Los Angeles and the author of *Calvino and the Age of Neorealism: Fables of Estrangement* (1990).

SHARON WOOD is Professor of Italian at Leicester University, editor of *Italian Women's Writing* (1993), co-editor of *A History of Women's Writing in Italy* (2000), and author of *Italian Women's Writing 1860–1990* (1995) and *Woman as Object: Language and Gender in the Work of Alberto Moravia* (1990).

PREFACE

This companion to the Italian novel provides a general introduction to the major authors and critical problems associated with the rise of this genre within Italian culture. It aims, whenever possible and useful, to connect developments in Italy with currents, movements, and literary theories from other relevant traditions. Any such single volume on such a broad and important question must, of necessity, make choices requiring editorial selections. Our contributors deal with most of the major Italian writers but besides those already well known to the English-speaking public (which is our primary audience), they frequently make reference to and analyze other lesser-known figures or topics that may not yet have attracted the wider attention of critics but have already been identified by the most astute of contemporary literary critics as crucial to the development of the Italian novel.

The early epic, lyric, and short prose works by Dante, Petrarca (known in English as Petrarch), and Boccaccio became internationally known models for their genres all over Europe. Their enormous success created within Italian literary tradition a preference for works in these genres, and subsequent centuries continued the peninsula's predilection for poetry or short stories over prose. When the European novel emerged as a new and independent genre in the seventeenth century, Italy was at the time divided into numerous states controlled primarily by foreign countries. In addition, unlike European countries that had achieved political unity much earlier than 1861, Italy was late in becoming a nation state, and its literary language was still in the process of formation.

This situation was recognized by the greatest of all literary historians, Francesco De Sanctis (1817–83), whose final pages of his *Storia della letteratura italiana* (*History of Italian Literature*, 1870–1) notes that with the publication of Alessandro Manzoni's masterpiece, *I promessi sposi* (*The Betrothed*), Italy finally had the historical novel but did not yet have history and the novel, implying that Italy had not yet produced an intellectual class of novelists similar to those already active for decades in England or France.

Nonetheless, with a shorter history than other European nations, the Italian novel has made important contributions to the historical novel (Manzoni, Tomasi di Lampedusa), to European naturalism (Verga), to women's writing and to feminism (Aleramo, Deledda, Banti, Maraini), to modernism (Svevo, Pirandello, Gadda), to Holocaust literature (Bassani, Primo Levi), to realism (Silone, Pavese, Pasolini, Vittorini), to existentialism (Moravia), and to postmodernism (Calvino, Eco, Tabucchi). Our anthology covers these subjects but also points toward new and not yet completely formed directions in twenty-first-century Italian prose (Baricco, Camilleri, Lucarelli). Moreover, one essay is devoted to literature of the frontier and migration, focusing upon either native Italians or foreign-born novelists whose work, although written in Italian, deals with multicultural experiences in an increasingly diverse nation.

ACKNOWLEDGMENTS

Our thanks to our editor, Linda Bree, who believed in the project and had the patience to see it through. As we prepared the final manuscript for submission to the Press, we learned of the death of our colleague and friend Robert Dombroski, whose loss saddens everyone connected with the field of Italian studies.

NOTE ON TRANSLATIONS

Italian novel titles are given first in the original language title with an English translation and the date of publication in parentheses. If the English title is printed in italics – *La coscienza di Zeno* (*The Confessions of Zeno*, 1923) – this indicates that the listed title is also the published title in English translation. If the English title is printed in roman type – *La mossa del cavallo* (The Knight's Move, 1999) – this indicates that the book has yet to receive an English translation.

CHRONOLOGY OF THE DEVELOPMENT
OF ITALIAN PROSE FICTION

1827	Alessandro Manzoni, *I promessi sposi* (*The Betrothed*); Francesco Domenico Guerrazzi, *La battaglia di Benevento* (*Manfred, or the Battle of Benevento*)
1832	Silvio Pellico, *Le mie prigioni* (*My Prisons*)
1833	Massimo d'Azeglio, *Ettore Fieramosca o la disfida di Barletta* (*Ettore Fieramosca or the Challenge of Barletta*)
1834	Tommaso Grossi, *Marco Visconti* (*Marco Visconti, a Romance of the Fourteenth Century*)
1840–2	Alessandro Manzoni, *I promessi sposi* (revised edition)
1843	Giovan Battista Niccolini, *Arnaldo da Brescia* (*Arnold of Brescia*)
1850	Alessandro Manzoni, *Del romanzo storico* (*On the Historical Novel*)
1867	Ippolito Nievo, *Le confessioni di un italiano* (*The Castle of Fratta*)
1868–9	Carlo Rovani, *Cento anni* (One Hundred Years)
1869	Igino Ugo Tarchetti, *Fosca* (*Passion*)
1870–1	Francesco De Sanctis, *Storia della letteratura italiana* (*History of Italian Literature*)
1879	Luigi Capuana, *Giacinta* (Giacinta)
1881	Giovanni Verga, *I Malavoglia* (*The House by the Medlar Tree*)
1883	Carlo Collodi, *Le avventure di Pinocchio: storia di un burattino* (*The Adventures of Pinocchio: Story of a Puppet*)
1884	Matilde Serao, *Il ventre di Napoli* (In Naples' Belly)
1886	Edmondo De Amicis, *Cuore* (*Heart: A Schoolboy's Journal*)
1888	Emilio De Marchi, *Il cappello del prete* (The Curate's Hat)
1889	Giovanni Verga, *Mastro-don Gesualdo* (*Master Don Gesualdo*); Gabriele d'Annunzio, *Il piacere* (*The Child of Pleasure*)
1893	Italo Svevo, *Una vita* (*A Life*)
1894	Gabriele d'Annunzio, *Il trionfo della morte* (*The Triumph of Death*); Federico De Roberto, *I viceré* (*The Viceroys*); Neera, *Anima sola* (*The Soul of an Artist*)
1895	Antonio Fogazzaro, *Piccolo mondo antico* (*The Little World of the Past*)
1898	Italo Svevo, *Senilità* (*As a Man Grows Older*)
1899	Emilio Salgari, *Il corsaro nero* (The Black Corsair)
1900	Gabriele d'Annunzio, *Il fuoco* (*Flame*)
1901	Luigi Capuana, *Il marchese di Roccaverdina* (The Marquis of Roccaverdina)
1903	Grazia Deledda, *Elias Portolu* (Elias Portolu)

1904	Luigi Pirandello, *Il fu Mattia Pascal* (*The Late Mattia Pascal*)
1906	Giosué Carducci wins the first Italian Nobel Prize for literature; Sibilla Aleramo, *Una donna* (*A Woman*)
1910	Filippo Tommaso Marinetti, *Mafarka il futurista* (Mafarka the Futurist)
1911	Aldo Palazzeschi, *Il codice di Perelà* (*The Man of Smoke*)
1913	Grazia Deledda, *Canne al vento* (Reeds in the Wind)
1915	Luigi Pirandello, *Quaderni di Serafino Gubbio, operatore* (*The Notebooks of Serafino Gubbio: [Shoot!]*)
1920	Grazia Deledda, *La madre* (*The Mother*)
1923	Italo Svevo, *La coscienza di Zeno* (*The Confessions of Zeno*); Benedetto Croce, *Storia d'Europa nel secolo decimonono* (*History of Europe in the Nineteenth Century*)
1926	Luigi Pirandello, *Uno, nessuno e centomila* (*One, No One, and a Hundred Thousand*)
1927	Grazia Deledda wins the Nobel Prize for literature
1929	Alberto Moravia, *Gli indifferenti* (*The Time of Indifference*)
1930	Corrado Alvaro, *Gente in Aspromonte* (*Revolt in Aspromonte*)
1934	Luigi Pirandello wins the Nobel Prize for literature; Carlo Bernari, *Tre operai* (Three Workers)
1937	Ignazio Silone, *Pane e vino* (*Bread and Wine*)
1938–40	Riccardo Bacchelli, *Il mulino del Po* (*The Mill on the Po*)
1941	Elio Vittorini, *Conversazione in Sicilia* (*In Sicily*); Cesare Pavese, *Paesi tuoi* (*The Harvesters*)
1944	Alberto Moravia, *Agostino* (*Agostino*)
1945	Carlo Levi, *Cristo si è fermato a Eboli* (*Christ Stopped at Eboli*)
1947	Italo Calvino, *Il sentiero dei nidi di ragno* (*The Path to the Nest of Spiders*); Vasco Pratolini, *Cronache di poveri amanti* (*A Tale of Poor Lovers*); Anna Banti, *Artemisia* (*Artemisia*)
1949	Renata Viganò, *L'Agnese va a morire* (Agnese Goes to her Death)
1950	Cesare Pavese, *La luna e i falò* (*The Moon and the Bonfires*)
1955	Pier Paolo Pasolini, *Ragazzi di vita* (*The Ragazzi*)
1957	Carlo Emilio Gadda, *Quer pasticciaccio brutto de via Merulana* (*That Awful Mess on Via Merulana*); Alberto Moravia, *La ciociara* (*Two Women*); Italo Calvino, *Il barone rampante* (*The Baron in the Trees*); Elsa Morante, *L'isola di Arturo* (*Arturo's Island*)
1958	Giuseppe Tomasi di Lampedusa, *Il Gattopardo* (*The Leopard*)

1959	Salvatore Quasimodo receives the Nobel Prize for literature; Pier Paolo Pasolini, *Una vita violenta* (*A Violent Life*)
1960	Alberto Moravia, *La noia* (*The Empty Canvas*)
1961	Leonardo Sciascia, *Il giorno della civetta* (*Mafia Vendetta*)
1962	Giorgio Bassani, *Il giardino dei Finzi-Contini* (*The Garden of the Finzi-Continis*); Umberto Eco, *Opera aperta* (*The Open Work*)
1963	Natalia Ginzburg, *Lessico famigliare* (*Family Sayings*); Carlo Emilio Gadda, *La cognizione del dolore* (*Acquainted with Grief*)
1965	Italo Calvino, *Le cosmicomiche* (*Cosmicomics*)
1968	Beppe Fenoglio, *Il partigiano Johnny* (Johnny the Partisan)
1972	Italo Calvino, *Le città invisibili* (*Invisible Cities*)
1974	Elsa Morante, *La storia* (*History: A Novel*)
1975	Eugenio Montale receives the Nobel Prize for literature; Dacia Maraini, *Donna in Guerra* (*Woman at War*); Oriana Fallaci, *Lettera a un bambino mai nato* (*Letter to a Child Never Born*); Primo Levi, *Il sistema periodico* (*The Periodic Table*)
1979	Italo Calvino, *Se una notte d'inverno un viaggiatore* (*If on a Winter's Night a Traveler*)
1980	Umberto Eco, *Il nome della rosa* (*The Name of the Rose*)
1981	Andrea De Carlo, *Treno di panna* (*The Cream Train*)
1983	Stefano Benni, *Terra!* (*Terra!*)
1985	Antonio Tabucchi, *Piccoli equivoci senza importanza* (*Little Misunderstandings of No Importance*)
1986	Primo Levi, *I sommersi e i salvati* (*The Drowned and the Saved*)
1988	Italo Calvino, *Lezioni americane: sei proposte per il prossimo millennio* (*Six Memos for the Next Millennium*); Umberto Eco, *Il pendolo di Foucault* (*Foucault's Pendulum*)
1990	Dacia Maraini, *La lunga vita di Marianna Ucrìa* (*The Silent Duchess*)
1992	Paola Capriolo, *Vissi d'amore* (*Floria Tosca*); Antonio Tabucchi, *Requiem* (*Requiem: A Hallucination*)
1994	Susanna Tamaro, *Va dove ti porta il cuore* (*Follow Your Heart*)
1995	Pia Pera, *Il diario di Lo* (*Lo's Diary*)
1996	Alessandro Baricco, *Seta* (*Silk*); Andrea Camilleri, *Il cane di terracotta* (*The Terra-Cotta Dog*)

1997	Dario Fo receives the Nobel Prize for literature; Carlo Lucarelli, *Almost Blue* (*Almost Blue*)
1999	Andrea Camilleri, *La mossa del cavallo* (The Knight's Move)
2002	Andrea Camilleri, *La paura di Montalbano* (Montalbano's Fear)

I

REMO CESERANI AND PIERLUIGI PELLINI

The belated development of a theory of the novel in Italian literary culture

Resistance to theory

The Italian literary establishment has always had a difficult relationship with the novel, and even more with the theory of the novel. "They do not have any novels as their English and French counterparts do": so wrote Mme de Staël, in her essay *De la littérature considérée dans ses rapports avec les institutions sociales* (*On Literature Considered in its Relationship with Social Institutions*, 1800). For this reason when de Staël published "Sulla maniera e l'utilità delle traduzioni" ("On the Manner and Usefulness of Translations," 1816)[1] in the *Biblioteca italiana*, she invited Italians to read foreign writers, especially English and German ones, advice that caused irate reactions in the tiny Italian literary world. In defending Italian literary tradition, some Italians argued that the absence of novels was a reason for pride, not embarrassment, as Mme de Staël suggested.

During the eighteenth century, in fact, the novel was commonly blamed in Italy for committing three unforgivable sins. Morally, novels contained sentimental stories that might corrupt a public of readers made up of idle people, mainly women. Aesthetically, the novel was considered an inferior genre, since it was unknown to the golden centuries of Italian literature and did not enjoy the same dignity, conferred by rigorously codified forms, as epic or tragedy. Linguistically, the novel rejected the selected vocabulary of the Petrarchan tradition and opened the doors of literature to coarse subjects and language; moreover, as it was thought to be of foreign origin, it favored the corruption of the Italian language, particularly by the French language. During the eighteenth century in Italy the genre of the novel had been left to a few professional writers, to a public of low or middle-low

---

[1] See Madame de Staël, *De la littérature considérée dans ses rapports avec les institutions sociales*, ed. Paul Van Tieghem (Geneva: Droz, 1979), vol. I: p. 174; and Anna Luisa Staël-Holstein, "Sulla maniera e l'utilità delle traduzioni," in Egidio Bellorini, ed., *Discussioni e polemiche sul Romanticismo (1816–1826)* (Bari: Laterza, 1943), vol. I: pp. 3–9.

social extraction, and to women: these three groups were treated by literary society with supreme contempt. There were some exceptions, but the general opinion of Italian men of letters was decidedly opposed to the new genre. Not only were all successful novelists rigidly excluded from any classical canon of literature, but also the novel itself was considered foreign to the Italian cultural tradition, and as such was never taken seriously in philosophical or aesthetic debates.

Similar opinions can be found in other European countries, but there the high reputation of illustrious models (some going back to the seventeenth century), the weaker influence of neoclassicism, and, most of all, the presence of a middle-class reading public that was more numerous and self-conscious than in Italy, succeeded in most countries in granting legitimacy to the novel in the literary world. Elsewhere, the novel was given the chance to demonstrate that it could be transformed from a work of simple entertainment into a nobler kind of literature: it could become an instrument of education, a weapon for ideological or political battles, a vehicle for philosophical meditations, and the modern epic of the new bourgeoisie.

The first Italian novel that appealed both to a large public and to the literary establishment was an epistolary novel, *Ultime lettere di Jacopo Ortis* (*The Last Letters of Jacopo Ortis*, first edition 1802; revised edition 1816) by Ugo Foscolo (1778–1827). In his speculations on the novel, Foscolo wavers between a strong defense of his cultural endeavor and an act of repentance for the harmful effects that novels like his or Goethe's *Werther* might have had on some excitable readers, liable to identify themselves with their suicidal protagonists. In successive narrative experiments, and especially when he decided to create a character like that of Didimo Chierico, a counterpart to Jacopo Ortis, Foscolo embraced an ironic, humorous, metaliterary style that had its model in the writings of Laurence Sterne. In England, the Sternian type of antinovel could parody a long tradition of eighteenth-century sentimental novels, but in Italy, on the contrary, the novel and antinovel were born almost at the same time and were created by the same author. They would continue to develop in Italy along parallel lines.[2]

In a letter to Lady Dacre written in 1823 while living in England, Foscolo tells an interesting anecdote, claiming to have written, at least in part, a new novel and to have given it to an Italian friend for an evaluation. According to Foscolo, the friend found in the manuscript "sufficient originality and liveliness to catch the readers' attention," but an imperfect style in need of more care. By this, he meant that while Foscolo's plot was attractive, his

---

[2] See Giancarlo Mazzacurati, ed., *Effetto Sterne. La narrazione umoristica in Italia da Foscolo a Pirandello* (Pisa: Nistri-Lischi, 1990).

linguistic performance did not match the perceived standards of the classical Italian tradition. The friend concluded that an English translation would be welcome but that the Italian original would not do. The English reading public considered story or plot as a value in itself; Italian readers were still more concerned with linguistic style. In his letter to Lady Dacre, Foscolo condemns such a rigid formality of Italian rhetorical expectations, but he seems to have been too pleased with his reputation as a great exponent of Italian poetic style to defy the prevailing national canons of good taste, and he never sent this novel to the printers.[3]

The "questione della lingua"

From its origins, Italian culture has been characterized by a running debate called the *questione della lingua*, which has involved every man of letters from Dante and Machiavelli to Manzoni. This debate has focused upon the problem of which dialect, among the numerous possibilities in Italy, should be generally adopted in literary writing and as a means of communication between people of learning and the leading elite of the country. Antonio Gramsci (1891–1937) once declared that each time in Italian history the debate on language rekindles, other important issues are at stake, such as the socioeconomic structure of the country, a new balance of power, or a struggle for cultural hegemony.[4] The history of the theory of the novel can thus also involve a history of the debates on the language of the novel. In the first decades of the nineteenth century, Alessandro Manzoni (1785–1873), the prominent novelist of the time, played an essential role in the debate on Italian language. In opposition to the program of the so-called "purists" who favored a pure literary language, faithful to the great models of the golden age of Italian literature, the Trecento (the fourteenth century) of Francesco Petrarca (1304–74) and Giovanni Boccaccio (1313–75), Manzoni advocated a universal language that could simultaneously serve as the language of the novel and of his novel, *I promessi sposi* (*The Betrothed*, 1840), and as the language for ordinary communication between educated citizens of a new nation. His choice fell on the Florentine speech utilized by the cultured higher strata of the population: he used this as a corrective for the Italianized Lombard of his first edition of *I promessi sposi* (1827) and employed it more systematically in the 1840 edition that eliminated almost all Lombard expressions. His decision was to weigh heavily on the results of the debate

---

3 Ugo Foscolo, *Epistolario*, ed. Francesco Silvio Orlandini and Enrico Mayer (Florence: Le Monnier, 1936), vol. III: pp. 109–10.
4 Antonio Gramsci, *Quaderni del carcere*, ed. Valentino Gerratana (Turin: Einaudi, 1977), vol. III: p. 2346.

about the standard of literary language in Italy and also on the educational policy of the national school system after 1860 in the new united kingdom of Italy. The language of *I promessi sposi* (a conversational tone, combined with a dignified and somewhat stiffened style indebted in its basic structure to Italian literary tradition) was perfectly suited to the narrative voice of his novel, an omniscient narrator who confronts the mystery of a providential design with a fragmented reality. However, amidst the turmoil and contradictions of the Risorgimento period, around mid-century, Manzoni's type of narrator began to show its inadequacy in dealing with an entirely different kind of social reality.

An internal, pseudo-autobiographical, programmatically semi-educated narrator such as Carlino, the protagonist of *Le confessioni di un italiano* (*The Castle of Fratta*, composed 1857–8) by Ippolito Nievo (1831–61), a novel in which the contradictions of the times were successfully represented, was bound to resort to a more flexible language, to insert words and expressions from the regional dialects of Lombardy and Friuli, and to vary the dominant conversational and serious register with humorous comments or strong expressionistic outbursts. Nievo's interesting compromise, however, exerted little influence on the immediate development of the Italian novel: Nievo's masterpiece was published posthumously in 1867 and passed almost unnoticed.

The prose works of Giacomo Leopardi (1798–1837) contributed little to the modernization of the Italian language: his *Zibaldone* (*Notebook*, last entry made in 1832) would have been a good model because of its varied and modern style, its extreme ductility, and its capacity to adapt language and style to various objects, thoughts, and themes, but it too was published posthumously only at the end of the century. The only Leopardian prose that could influence his contemporaries was the very elegant but austerely classical Italian of the *Operette morali* (*The Moral Essays*, 1824), but this great work did not enjoy favorable critical acclaim for many years.

In the first decades after Italian Unification, in addition to numerous imitations of the linguistic model for the novel proposed by Manzoni, an anti-Manzoni line appeared among writers from Piedmont and Lombardy favoring a humorous and expressive stylistic preciousness closer to the Sternian antinovel. These writers, who were the Italian counterpart of the French *Bohème*, were called the *Scapigliati* (which meant "disheveled" or "unkempt"). Such writers included Igino Ugo Tarchetti (1830–69), Carlo Dossi (1849–1910), Arrigo (1842–1918) and Camillo Boito (1836–1914), and Cletto Arrighi (Carlo Righetti, 1830–1906).

Any Italian novelist wishing to write a realistic novel that kept pace with literary developments in the rest of Europe had first to find a solution to the problem of a literary language. The literary movement called *verismo* (the Italian term for naturalism) that developed in those years was immediately confronted with the problem of which language to use in treating the harsh conditions of the lives of the poor and the social backwardness of the South, as well as representation of the body, physical diseases, or of sexuality, all themes that had no legitimate presence in the conservative Italian literary tradition. Without any systematic attempt to work out a theory of the novel and its proper language, the *veristi* proposed an empirical solution: at times they would imitate foreign (mainly French) models; on other occasions, they retained a prose style close to local dialect, at least in their syntactical constructions, if not in their individual vocabularies. In *I Malavoglia* (*The House by the Medlar Tree*, 1881) by Giovanni Verga (1840–1922), for instance, the impersonal narrative voice adopts the technique of indirect free discourse in a more systematic fashion than is found in Verga's French models, such as Emile Zola. Verga's syntax follows closely the structure of spoken Sicilian; the vocabulary, however, with very few exceptions, is standard Italian. Employing Sicilian dialect would have made the text virtually unreadable in the rest of Italy. This empirical solution, praised and followed by Luigi Capuana (1839–1915) and others, nevertheless prompted heated debates among the writers and critics of the time. Another writer, Antonio Fogazzaro (1842–1911), reached a rather awkward compromise to the linguistic question. In several very popular novels (*Daniele Cortis* [*Daniele Cortis*], 1885; *Piccolo mondo antico* [*The Little World of the Past*], 1895), Fogazzaro allowed lower-class characters to express themselves in the local dialect while those of higher social standing, including the narrator, spoke standard Italian.

At the turn of the century, writers representing a new aestheticism – primarily Gabriele D'Annunzio (1863–1938), his followers, and writers identified as "decadents" – opposed *verismo* and favored the *bello stile* (elevated literary style) against what they felt was the corrupted language of the *veristi*. D'Annunzio, whose novels both popularized and trivialized themes from the dominant tradition of the European novel from Flaubert and Maupassant to Tolstoy and Dostoevsky, nevertheless succeeded in conquering a huge readership among the new bourgeoisie of Italian society, even though his linguistic and stylistic choices were certainly less daring and experimental than those of the naturalists. His goal, spelled out in the dedicatory letter to the *Trionfo della morte* (*Triumph of Death*, 1894),[5] was to write an "ideal book of modern prose... as musical as a poem." In opposition to the polyphony of the

---

[5] Gabriele D'Annunzio, *Trionfo della morte*, in *Prose di romanzi* (Milan: Mondadori, 1988), vol. I: pp. 639–44.

great European bourgeois novel, built upon the conflict between different characters and points of view, D'Annunzio's novel stages "a single dramatis persona"; in opposition to the well-made plot with its effects of suspense, surprise, and recognition, he proposes a prose that registers "the slightest fleeting waves of thoughts...and feelings"; most of all, in opposition to the employment of "words of impure origin" that are "corrupted by vulgar usage," D'Annunzio resorts to "the treasures slowly amassed from one century to another" by the Italian literary tradition – the golden age of the Italian Trecento rather than the models of Dickens or Zola.

The restoration of traditional literary language could never be accepted by the major modernist novelists, such as Italo Svevo (1861–1928) and Luigi Pirandello (1867–1936), who continued to write in the common, everyday language of the *veristi* and, for this reason, were accused by the critics of "writing badly," a major reason for Svevo's exclusion from the Italian literary canon for many years. But many Italian writers shared D'Annunzio's opinion, deplored any reliance upon foreign models, and viewed the novel disparagingly as a genre devoted primarily to popular entertainment.

During the course of the twentieth century, and in spite of the recurrent waves of interest in *prosa d'arte* (artistic prose) or in a precious or expressionistic prose style, Italian literature nevertheless experienced the slow development of a narrative prose capable of a variety of linguistic registers. This transformational process influenced the Italian school system only with great difficulty, since the reading lists there reflected a persistent tendency to privilege texts of poetry or prose works composed in the high, elevated style, and such an aesthetic tendency survives even today, in spite of the enormous enlargement of the school population, the advent of television, and the diffusion of American cultural models. Some writers have attempted to introduce contemporary juvenile slang, as well as the special languages of the political counterculture or of the portions of the Italian population marginalized from the mainstream by contemporary industrial society. Yet even in the 1980s the gap between the language of the novel and that of real life in Italy was certainly not completely bridged. Nevertheless, during the last decade of the twentieth century, many younger writers have developed a consciously antiliterary way of writing, mixing juvenile speech and TV jargon. Their linguistic models are no longer the school textbooks but the cinema, comic strips, and American novels. Their training seems more typical of schools of creative writing than the curriculum of the traditional *liceo classico*. Naturally, such writers have been attacked for their ignorance and their linguistic presumption. But if Gramsci's observation about the *questione della lingua* is correct, then it is obvious that Italian society has experienced major social changes and these changes are slowly being incorporated into the fabric of the Italian novel through linguistic experimentation, and tend to produce a truly postmodern climate for narrative prose.

The disputed necessity of translations

The translation of foreign novels has traditionally been blamed for the corruption of the Italian language in the nineteenth as well as the twentieth century by a substantial number of Italian intellectuals. Yet all major innovations in the history of the Italian novel are linked to the influence of foreign models. Manzoni's decision to write a novel and the literary solution he proposed in *I promessi sposi* – to consign historical figures to the background and to occupy the foreground of his novel with a fictive plot – would not have been possible without the example of the historical novels of Walter Scott, which Manzoni read in French translation just as they were beginning to be rendered into Italian around 1820. Scott's influence was decisive for the birth of the modern novel in Italy. All historical novelists of any importance in the early nineteenth century, from Tommaso Grossi (1790–1853) to Massimo D'Azeglio (1798–1865) and Francesco Domenico Guerrazzi (1804–73), were forced to reckon with the Scottish novelist's example.

Subsequently, the French novel began to circulate in Italy and offered as models for imitation not only Honoré de Balzac but in particular the masters of the *roman feuilleton* such as Alexandre Dumas *père* and Eugène Sue, who were condemned by the critics but widely read and imitated by novelists. Around 1850, the fashion for the historical novel was supplanted by that for what was called "letteratura rusticale" or "letteratura campagnola," which embodied a romantic and idealized representation of the simple and uncontaminated life among peasants in the country. The French novels of George Sand, as well as the German works of Berthold Auerbach, served as inspiration for this kind of literature, and the Italian writer who achieved the best results in this genre was Ippolito Nievo in his collection of short stories entitled *Il novelliere campagnolo* (The Country Storyteller, 1855 and later) and in the novel *Il conte pecoraio* (The Shepherd Count, 1857). A few decades later, Capuana and Verga turned to French naturalism, while other writers of the late nineteenth century selected Charles Dickens as a more moderate and humorous realist. D'Annunzio's poetic prose relied not only on the musical model of Wagner, but also upon the great European novelists of the time: *Giovanni Episcopo* (Giovanni Episcopo, 1891) was explicitly written in the manner of Dostoevsky.

During the second decade of the twentieth century, writers associated with the Florentine literary journal *La Voce* were extremely open to foreign influences, including European expressionism. Alberto Savinio (1891–1952), close to the avant-garde movement of surrealism, had a French education, and it would not be inaccurate to state that until the 1930s the Italian novel looked toward Paris for its inspiration, in spite of the fact that during the Fascist regime the official policy was cultural self-sufficiency. Even during that period, the Florentine literary monthly *Solaria* aimed at reviving the Italian novel and published two special issues dedicated to two great Italian modernists, Italo Svevo and Federigo Tozzi (1883–1920), who had been underrated by the critical establishment. It also made known the works of Proust, Gide, and Hemingway. It was mainly through an increasing interest in American literature and film that Italian literature began to be more concerned with the fictional representation of an Italian reality – a period identified with the term *neorealismo* (neorealism). Such a desire was fostered during the 1930s by such young writers as Cesare Pavese (1908–1950, the translator of Melville, Sinclair Lewis, and John Dos Passos) and Elio Vittorini (1908–66) whose 1941 anthology, *Americana*, fell under Fascist censorship but was a crucial document in the diffusion of American literature in Italy before the end of the war.

In the postwar period, French and especially American models had a parallel influence on Italian literary culture; gradually Latin American and Central European novels came to be important sources of inspiration. The French *nouveau roman* of Alain Robbe-Grillet and Michel Butor influenced both Italo Calvino (1923–85) and Umberto Eco (1932–). Calvino even joined the Oulipo (Ouvroir de littérature potentielle, or Workshop of Potential Literature) group in Paris, which included among its members Raymond Queneau (later translated by Eco) and Georges Perec. Oulipo was devoted to experimentation in prose fiction, especially in the invention of complicated, mathematical plots. The Italian novel during the twentieth century's last decade has been influenced not only by films, comic strips, TV serials, and popular detective or horror novels, but also by the classic American novel by J. D. Salinger, *The Catcher in the Rye* (1951). Portuguese and South American writers have particularly influenced Antonio Tabucchi (1943–). During the postwar period, the Italian publishing industry was in the forefront of producing numerous translations from other national literatures.

The history of the Italian novel is not exhausted by the history of the imitation of works translated from other languages. It must also include the history (or, rather, the geography) of a series of "mental translations." The standard literary language of the Italian novel was based upon the Tuscan dialect, and Italy's publishing industry has traditionally been concentrated in the North (Milan and Turin). But a large number of Italy's modern novelists came either from the South, especially from Sicily (Verga, Capuana, De Roberto, Pirandello, Vittorini, Tomasi di Lampedusa, Sciascia), or from parts of Italy that were only marginally Italian, such as Trieste, which was part of the Austrian Empire for many years and where the two main languages were German and Triestine, not standard Italian. Yet Trieste produced many important Italian writers: Svevo, Slataper, Saba, Giotti, Quarantotti-Gambini, Magris, and others. Many Italian writers were compelled to emigrate toward the cultural capitals of the country and to write in a language that they did not consider truly their own and into which they had mentally to translate their own native and personal idioms. Southern naturalists moved first to Florence, then to Milan; Pirandello went to Germany, then to Rome; Tozzi remained isolated even after he moved from his native Siena to Rome; sixty years after Verga, Vittorini moved first to Florence and then to Milan. Italian critics and the educational establishment in the newly unified Italian state systematically undervalued and even ignored regional differences as they imposed a linguistically unified canon upon the Italian novel, a canon from which many writers today considered the greatest novelists of the century were banned.

The tradition of the antinovel

It is a peculiar, almost paradoxical, feature of Italian literature that the antinovel, instead of being a whimsical and lighthearted reaction to the romantic and melodramatic modes, was born and developed parallel to the novel. Foscolo had just written the *Ortis* when he started writing the parodic pieces of prose signed by Didimo. Manzoni resisted the lure of writing anything in the style of Sterne and in successive editions of *I promessi sposi* he deleted humorous, digressive, and metafictional elements that were present in his first draft, which was entitled *Fermo e Lucia* (Fermo and Lucia). But even Manzoni renounced narrative prose after the publication of his masterwork, and from that moment on he abandoned the attempt to intermingle fiction and reality, which was the most important feature of the European historical novel. The Lombard and Piedmontese *Scapigliati* never ceased paying homage to, and at the same time parodying, Manzoni's *I promessi sposi*, and acted as if Manzoni's work had exhausted all the possibilities of the novel as a genre. On the other hand, the moderately fortunate reception of the naturalistic movement in Italy can also be explained at least in part by its antifictional stance, since literary naturalism's purpose (at least in theory, if not in practice) was not to reflect upon or to parody the fictionality of fiction, but was, instead, aimed at providing the reader with documents of truth and reality, avoiding the usual artifices of fiction. Pirandello took a different stance, wrote a treatise on literary theory entitled *L'umorismo* (*On Humor*, 1908), and adopted some of the strategies of the antinovel in order

to deconstruct the epistemological certitudes of nineteenth-century philosophy and psychology, representing the modern loss of identity with what he
called the "feeling of the contrary" and which might well be translated by
Kenneth Burke's phrase, "perspective by incongruity."[6]

In the second half of the twentieth century, reaction against neorealism and
its aspirations to a didactic objectivity gave rise to a new type of metanovel,
a sort of "novel of the novel," that followed the example of the French
nouveau roman, employed some of the narrative proposals of structuralism
and semiotics, and at the same time revived the Italian Sternian tradition, as
well as the surrealistic experiments of Savinio and others. Examples of this
tendency include several works by Giorgio Manganelli; Edoardo Sanguineti's
parodic disassembly of traditional narrative forms in a variety of work; or
the camp style of Alberto Arbasino. Many such writers became identified
with a group calling itself Gruppo 63 (so called because the group met first
in Palermo in 1963) and are also identified in Italian literary history as the
"neoavanguardia" (the neo-avant-garde). Since the majority of such writers
were poets and not novelists, they had little effect upon the development of
the novel, even though they loudly attacked such popular novelists of the
time as Carlo Cassola (1917–87), Alberto Moravia (1907–90), and Giuseppe
Tomasi di Lampedusa (1896–1957). They denigrated those writers and called
them the "Lialas" of Italian literature. (Liala was the pseudonym of Amalia
Negretti Cambiasi, an enormously successful author of sentimental novels
for young ladies, and the Italian counterpart to Barbara Cartland.) The neo-
avant-garde's attacks were aimed primarily not at high modernist literature
but, rather, at well-made fictional plots indebted to the nineteenth-century
realist novel. However, they did help to bring Italian literature into the postmodern era by popularizing foreign theories of fiction or experimental prose
from other national literatures. One of their number, Umberto Eco, became
the century's best-selling Italian author and Italy's most popular exponent of
postmodern fiction. Eco's response to the tradition of the antinovel and its
refusal to compromise with the narrative experiences of fictionality was to
revisit in a postmodern vein traditional, nineteenth-century literary genres,
such as the detective story or the historical romance.

Belatedness of the theory

Almost none of the literary theories that have dominated Italy, from the
Romantic age to postmodernism, have reserved a place of importance in the

[6] Kenneth Burke, *Permanence and Change: An Anatomy of Purpose* (New York: New
Republic, 1935; 3rd edn Berkeley: University of California Press, 1984), pp. 91 and ff.

literary canon for the novel. In spite of his own experiment with *I promessi sposi*, Manzoni's essay *Del romanzo storico* (*On the Historical Novel*, 1850) rejected any novel belonging to the "mixed genre of history and invention," in effect rejecting the very notion of the novel itself that could never be a substitute for the truth of history. Few Italian writers systematically tackled the theoretical problem of the novel as a literary genre. Few Italian novelists (except for Italo Calvino or Umberto Eco) managed either to write high-level literary criticism of the novel or to explore its technical and rhetorical problems in the same manner as such writers as Henry James, Marcel Proust, or E. M. Forster have done. All too often, Italian writers do not consider such problems as worthy of serious attention.

Among the major critics the only relevant exceptions to the general indifference toward the novel were those of Francesco De Sanctis and Giacomo Debenedetti (1901–67). De Sanctis was fascinated by the contemporary novel, and his magisterial *Storia della letteratura italiana* (*History of Italian Literature*, 1870–1) can even be read as a novel, a *Bildungsroman* that has as its protagonist the rising national consciousness of Italian writers. His strong ethical and educational concerns, as well as his keen interest in the relationship between literature and society, drove De Sanctis to favor realism and naturalism in literature and even, in his later years, to appreciate the novels of Zola. Unfortunately, De Sanctis – now considered the founding father of literary criticism in Italy and generally considered the greatest literary historian of any national literature – was isolated within Italy during his lifetime. In the universities, the dominant philological school ("scuola storica") was more concerned with erudition and analysis of the early centuries of Italian literature. Many of these scholars were either suspicious of novels or were, as in the case of Giosuè Carducci (1835–1907) and Arturo Graf (1848–1913), poets and not novelists. When the lesson of De Sanctis was finally rescued from oblivion in the twentieth century, it was divorced from the historian's particular insight into the development of the novel. The influential interpretation of De Sanctis by Benedetto Croce (1866–1952) in the early decades of the century paid very little attention to his original essays on naturalism. Croce's most dogmatic followers ignored the complexity of his philosophical system and reduced his literary theory to a sort of catechism: the theoretical distinction between "poetry" and "non-poetry" – true literature was lyrical in the sense of the absolute perfection of lyrical intuition. The novel could be relished only in its fragmentary moments of poetical glowing, while the complexities of its diegetic and mimetic development and the richness of its various discourses were considered alien to art and rejected. It was not by chance that the young writers, gathered during the second decade of the century around the journal *La Voce*, preferred the short piece of artistic prose (*prosa d'arte*). The very title of a collection of essays, *Tempo di edificare* (Time to Build, 1923) by Giuseppe A. Borgese (1882–1952) argued for the necessity of recapturing the complex structures of the great novels of the nineteenth century. But his proposal found few followers, and even his own personal attempt at creating a modern novel in *Rubé* (*Rubé*, 1921) was only partially successful.

La Ronda, the journal that took the place of *La Voce* in the restorative climate of the early 1920s showed again a clear preference for poetry or ventured to suggest, as an example of perfect prose, the recaptured elegant classicism of Leopardi's *Operette morali*. The novel itself returned to the front of cultural debate and literary practice with the new Florentine journal *Solaria* (1926–34), which published not only prose by Moravia but also works by Alvaro, Jovine, Vittorini, and Pavese. After 1945, these writers were considered to be the precursors of Italian neorealism, but this reading of their first works obscured both the experimental quality of their writing and their links with the grand tradition of European modernism. In the postwar period that witnessed the first publication of the works of Antonio Gramsci, Marxist critics and writers were concerned with the question of "realism," but their emphasis was an ideological one, focusing upon the relationship between intellectuals and society rather than on the techniques of the representation of reality in literature. Italian critical debates on the theory of the novel suffered from such ideological blinders until the advent of the neo-avant-garde in the 1960s opened a number of perspectives upon the novel by popularizing foreign critics, theories, and writers. It is not by accident that the single most important book written in Italy on the novel was *Il romanzo del Novecento* (The Twentieth-Century Novel) by Giacomo Debenedetti, published posthumously in 1971.[7] It was a transcript of lectures given at the University of Messina in the early 1960s. Debenedetti, who had been associated with *Solaria*, was a brilliant critic who never achieved a permanent university position. He had been responsible for introducing critical methodologies (Freudian psychoanalysis, as well as the methods of the French disciples of Freud and ideas taken from anthropology, linguistics, etc.), which had been banned from the Italian cultural scene by the orthodoxies of Crocean idealism or Gramscian Marxism in the postwar period. Debenedetti's comparative openness toward the great European literatures of the century was shockingly innovative to the eyes of the Italian critical establishment. Retracing the story of the Italian novel from *verismo* to the 1930s, Debenedetti created what amounts to a literary canon of Italian modernist prose,

---

[7] Giacomo Debenedetti, *Il romanzo del Novecento. Quaderni inediti*, with a preface by Eugenio Montale (Milan: Garzanti, 1971; new edn 1987).

calling attention to writers that had been systematically undervalued, such as Tozzi, and giving forceful and convincing interpretations of figures such as Svevo or Pirandello. He was battling against prejudices that were still strong: the belletristic prejudice of much academic criticism, given to philology, stylistics, and the worship of poetry; the linguistic prejudice that was hostile to works linguistically impure and alien to the national tradition; and the ideological prejudice of the Crocean–Marxist tradition that was suspicious of any expression of bourgeois "decadence" and of any "literature of crisis."

The belated recognition of the Italian modernist novel has repeated itself, perhaps even more forcefully, in the postmodern period that brought the century to a close. Numerous Italian writers recognized the economic and cultural upheaval that took place around the end of the 1950s in the industrially advanced part of the world. However, the cultural and literary establishment, once again, substantially ignored the transformation taking place in the collective imagination of the time, to the point that the word "postmodernism" itself is frequently used in a disparaging fashion and can rarely be found, even in Italian studies of Calvino, Eco, and Tabucchi, all three of whom are considered to be key postmodernist writers by theorists and critics outside of Italy. Moreover, since postmodernism is characterized by a revitalized and strengthened interest in the problems of narration and representation, as well as by a cultivated revisitation of literary genres once considered too popular or kitschy (such as the detective novel, science fiction, or the sentimental novel), the absence of a serious debate in Italy on these aspects of contemporary literature runs the risk of keeping the novel in its subordinate position. On the other hand, interesting signs of a renewed interest in the study, if not the theory, of the novel have come from Italian universities where newly opened disciplines of comparative literature and literary theory have directed critical attention in that direction.

Paradoxes of the canon

The dominant prejudices and strictures of Italy's literary establishment have had important consequences upon both the formation and the conservation of a novelistic canon in Italy. One can say without exaggeration that there is one and only one novel that has always been considered a classic in Italian literature: Manzoni's *I promessi sposi*. Not a single novelist after Manzoni – with the possible exception of D'Annunzio, whose fame was mainly due to his poetry within Italy, although his novels were voraciously read in translation abroad – has had the immediate, almost unanimous, and even embarrassing praise offered to such modern poets as Carducci, Ungaretti, Montale, and Quasimodo. Nievo's great novel had to wait until the second half of the twentieth century to be acknowledged by the critical establishment as a masterpiece. By borrowing the techniques of the popular novel (misplaced identities, melodramatic scenes, portentous adventures) and combining them with the high literary tradition, Nievo achieved an astounding modernity but condemned himself to a long critical disregard. To add a great novel like *I viceré* (*The Viceroys*, 1894) by Federico De Roberto (1861–1927) seems impossible, since the book still suffers the consequences of a disparaging judgment by Croce. This masterpiece, a pitiless allegory of the historical and existential malaise of the world, does not leave any space for a reading in a lyrical key. Even Verga, grudgingly admitted by the canon, is affected by Italian culture's penchant for the lyrical over the prosaic: between his two major works, critics generally prefer *I Malavoglia* because it can be read (sometimes mistakenly) as a work reflecting the identification of the author with the humble fishermen of Aci Trezza, and as a work of romantic nostalgia with an idyllic nature that features the symbolic transfiguration of Sicilian reality. The coherent pessimism of *Mastro-don Gesualdo* (*Master Don Gesualdo*, 1889), which was close to the models of Flaubert, could not win the favor either of the Crocean critics (who searched only for lyrical fragments), or of the neorealists (who desired positive and progressive messages), or even those who privileged linguistics or stylistics (who appreciated the fine narrative technique of *I Malavoglia* but rejected the more traditional structure of the second work). Naturally, the popular novel – especially when sentimental and feminine, as was the case in the works of Matilde Serao (1856–1927), or, in recent years, in *La storia* (*History*, 1974) by Elsa Morante (1912–85) – has been another victim of Italian canon. Both women novelists and the major writers of the nineteenth century are often systematically ignored by the reading lists of Italian schools or overlooked by the backlists of Italian publishers.

Svevo's first two novels, linked in an original way to the tradition of European naturalism, went completely unnoticed in a cultural context that was dominated by the aestheticism of D'Annunzio or the spiritualism of Fogazzaro. His third novel and masterpiece, *La coscienza di Zeno* (*The Confessions of Zeno*, 1923), published after a long creative silence and influenced by the most advanced experiments of Central European culture (Freudian psychoanalysis), found Italian criticism completely unprepared for its originality. It became known only after James Joyce spoke of the work to Valéry Larbaud and other critics and writers in Paris. Svevo's literary reputation was made almost exclusively abroad and blossomed in Italy only after the war. Pirandello reached a large audience not with his novels but with his short stories and plays. Tozzi was considered a minor writer until Debenedetti reevaluated him.

The reception of Verga's novels summarizes many of the contradictions that we have pointed out. Disregarded by the critics of the first decades of the century, Verga nevertheless remained a point of reference for the novelists of the same period (Svevo, Pirandello, Tozzi), who took him as an example of a literary style made of "things" and not merely of "words," as was the case with D'Annunzio – the distinction was introduced by Pirandello.[8] Verga was recovered in the 1940s and 1950s by the critical establishment, motivated primarily by interest in his lower-class subjects and by the debates inspired by the publication of Gramsci's *Quaderni del carcere* (*Prison Notebooks*, 1948–51), as well as by Gramsci's celebrated thesis on the social failure of the unitary revolution of the Risorgimento. At about the same time, two excellent stylistic critics – Giacomo Devoto and Leo Spitzer – offered analyses of Verga's peculiar use of free indirect discourse in *I Malavoglia*, but until very recent times the narrative techniques of *verismo* and its links to European naturalism, elements required for an understanding of Verga's masterpieces, passed virtually unnoticed by the Italian literary establishment.

The polarization in the critical opinion on Verga, divided between ideological and stylistic approaches to his prose, presents an accurate picture of the general tone of the debate on the novel in Italy during the first few years after the end of the Second World War. On one side, the critics of the Gramscian School, sometimes influenced by the cultural politics of the Italian Communist Party, continued down to the very end of the 1950s to uphold a model of politicized neorealism, which subjected any specific aspect of literature to a program of cultural hegemony. Thus, in 1956, when *Metello* (*Metello*) by Vasco Pratolini (1913–91) appeared, one of the "official critics" of the Communist Party, Carlo Salinari (1919–77), saluted this mediocre novel as representing the long-awaited passage from neorealism to a true and full "realism." Today this discussion sounds terribly provincial. Within the ranks of the critics from the left, there were some independent minds, which found themselves in accord with the theories of Georg Lukács or the Frankfurt School, but they remained a small minority. On the other hand, a sensitive critic such as Gianfranco Contini (1912–90), who combined philological expertise with stylistics and a great capacity for reading, proposed a canon for the novel that was the opposite of the one proposed by neorealism. Contini's canon was based upon originality of linguistic expressionism and had its distant origins in the medieval and Renaissance periods, with Dante or Folengo. In the modern period, it ran from the *Scapigliati* in the nineteenth century to Carlo Emilio Gadda (1893–1973) in our times.

---

[8] Luigi Pirandello, "Giovanni Verga," in *Saggi, poesie, scritti varii*, ed. Manlio Lo Vecchio Musti (Milan: Mondadori, 1960; new edn 1977), pp. 389–406.

Subsequently, Italian structuralist critics proposed the inclusion of the under-rated novels of Beppe Fenoglio (1922–63) in this new expressionistic canon. But since Contini insisted that "Gadda's art is completely lyrical,"[9] he implicitly returned to the traditional Italian prejudice that an Italian masterpiece must have a poetic, not a narrative, character – even if it is a novel.

Gadda and Fenoglio have meanwhile been enduringly, if grudgingly, admitted into the canon of the twentieth-century Italian novel, while many once-popular neorealists have been devalued and excluded. In general, the cases of belated recognition of merit and eventual canonization, or of marked differences in value judgment between what the reading public and the critics prefer, or what Italian critics and/or readers like as compared to what foreign critics and/or readers admire in Italian literary culture, continue to be surprisingly numerous. Moravia or Calvino enjoy or enjoyed tremendous prestige abroad, but within Italy they have not always been so popular. A particularly revealing case is that of *Il Gattopardo* (*The Leopard*, 1958). Following the great success of the film made from the novel by Luchino Visconti, with Burt Lancaster in the role of Don Fabrizio, this novel by Giuseppe Tomasi di Lampedusa, with its extraordinary protagonist and talented blend of what some critics perceived as "high-level kitsch," succeeded in conquering the reading public of the entire world. In Italy, however, the novel encountered the opposition of the Marxists for obvious reasons; but those who supported the expressionistic tendency in the novel, as well as the neo-avant-garde, also attacked it.

Even more oddly contradictory has been the Italian critical reception of Eco's *Il nome della rosa* (*The Name of the Rose*, 1980). Hailed abroad, especially in Germany and the United States, as a masterpiece of postmodern literature, and as such studied in the universities and commented upon in endless articles, books, and conferences, *Il nome della rosa* in Italy, on the contrary, is often considered a curious, inexplicable case of editorial success.

What seems to be typical of all these strange literary judgments that have gone into the formation of a contemporary canon of Italian novels is the absence of any explicit discussion on a sophisticated theoretical level. Choices are too often made without any serious theoretical debate. It is difficult to find in Italy anything like the recent American revisions of the literary canon based upon political, gender, or cultural grounds. Even interesting internal conflicts among Italian intellectuals, such as a recent debate arising from a book that attacked the cold, abstract, combinatory art of Italo Calvino in favor of the existential and expressionistic art of Pier Paolo

---

[9] Gianfranco Contini, *Quarant'anni di amicizia. Scritti su Carlo Emilio Gadda (1934–1988)* (Turin: Einaudi, 1989), p. 20.

Pasolini (1922–75),[10] are inevitably reduced to journalistic chatter. People may be asked to provide a list of their top ten favorite Italian novels, but a true discussion of the meaning and the functioning of the Italian novelistic canon has so far been sadly lacking. Were such a serious debate to be staged, it would be obvious that the two main lines of the development of the Italian novel that are supposedly juxtaposed by warring critical camps – the defenders of the Manzonian realist canon and the proponents of the Gaddian expressionistic anticanon – are not really in conflict, but represent two aspects of the same literary tradition. From its origins, in fact, Italian literature has embodied the multilinguistic style of Dante as well as the stylistic selectivity preferred by Petrarca and Petrarchism. The basic difference is that while Dante needed a variety of styles to narrate his adventurous encounters during his imaginary journey through Hell, Petrarca did not require such linguistic variety to write his love poems. Both canon and anticanon can therefore be traced back to a high literary tradition, and they inform both the Manzonian and the Gaddian narrative threads. In like manner, both Calvino and Pasolini were perfectly integrated, although in different ways, into the Italian literary establishment.

In search of a public

"In less than twenty days, more than 600 copies have been sold": so wrote, with wonder and pride, Manzoni's daughter Giulietta to the Parisian friend of her father Claude Fauriel (1777–1844).[11] *I promessi sposi* was the great best-seller of Italian literature in the nineteenth century. Yet the numbers are not so extraordinary: 600 copies in twenty days! Nievo did not sell. Verga was commercially unsuccessful with his masterpiece: *I Malavoglia*, he wrote, was "a fiasco, a complete and total fiasco."[12] Svevo's first novels were practically unread outside Trieste. The history of the novel in Italy is also the history of a dull market, in which customs barriers hindered the circulation of books until national unification. It is also the history of an often difficult relationship between writers and publishers and of a mediocre public that preferred the much more enticing products of foreign literatures, while the sophisticated and cultivated reading public disparaged the novel altogether.

Even in the twentieth century, the transformation of the Italian publishing world into a true industrial activity was slower than in most Western

---

[10] Carla Benedetti, *Pasolini contro Calvino. Per una letteratura impura* (Turin: Bollati Boringhieri, 1998).

[11] Quoted by Alberto Cadioli, *Il romanzo adescatore. I lettori e il romanzo nel dibattito del primo Ottocento* (Milan: Arcipelago, 1988), pp. 184–5.

[12] Gino Raya, *Carteggio Verga-Capuana* (Rome: Edizioni dell'Ateneo, 1984), p. 111.

countries. In Italy, the small one-man or family publishing business was much more common than in other industrialized nations. In some cases (Einaudi of Turin, for example), these small enterprises have developed into large capitalist enterprises. One reason for the relatively small size of Italian publishers was that the reading public was smaller and the retail market still very backward. The first true Italian best-seller was really *Il Gattopardo* in 1958, more than a century after Manzoni! The book sold more than a hundred thousand copies in a few months. A new record was reached with Eco's *Il nome della rosa*, which sold two million copies in Italy alone in less than a decade. Significantly, both of these texts belong to the genre of the historical novel: the first moves elegantly within the limits of the midcult, while the second employs postmodern techniques of double coding and can be read on several intellectual levels, ranging from the simple "whodunit" to an intricate intellectual and philosophical exercise. Both works have encountered great difficulty in obtaining critical recognition and canonization. Even Eco, once a member of the neo-avant-garde, wrote disparagingly of Lampedusa, although now that he has become a successful novelist he seems to have a better opinion of successful writers. As for so-called "popular" literature – assuming that such a term is still useful today – the highest sales figures have been reached in the 1990s by the sugary works of Susanna Tamaro (1957–), such as *Va dove ti porta il cuore* (*Follow Your Heart*, 1994), or by the more talented crime novels of Andrea Camilleri (1925–), which now occupy the best-seller lists on a regular basis in Italy. Camilleri's case is interesting, for it marks the appearance on the Italian literary scene of the kind of novelist that has always been missing in the Italian tradition: a writer who knows how to tell exciting and amusing stories, who is first of all a real narrator, and who knows how to attract both the middlebrow public and the more exacting highbrows. Still, the history of his success is filled with a long list of rejected manuscripts, returned by all the leading northern publishing houses, and supercilious reactions on the part of some of Italy's leading literary critics. Camilleri's literary success was minimal until his work fell into the expert hands of a small and refined publisher from Palermo: Elvira Sellerio.

It seems that, in the early twenty-first century, the novel – both native Italian products and numerous translations from other national literatures – has at long last found a large and stable literary public in Italy. In addition, the Italian publishing industry appears to have aligned itself, for better or worse, with the standards of the other major European nations. However, the theory of the novel seems more at risk than ever. The laws of the publishing industry and the cultural market have drastically reduced the space and role of possible critical mediation between writers and their public. The opportunities for public debates and discussions on the nature and future of the novel seem less and less numerous. It remains to be seen if the Italian novel can develop into the new century in interesting and original ways without such a healthy theoretical underpinning.

Further reading

Barański, Zygmunt G. and Lino Pertile, eds. *The New Italian Novel*. Edinburgh: Edinburgh University Press, 1993.

Calabrese, Stefano. *Intrecci italiani. Una teoria e una storia del romanzo (1750–1900)*. Bologna: Il Mulino, 1995.

Dombroski, Robert S. *Properties of Writing: Ideological Discourse in Modern Italian Fiction*. Baltimore: Johns Hopkins University Press, 1994.

Guglielmi, Guido. *La prosa italiana del Novecento II. Tra romanzo e racconto*. Turin: Einaudi, 1998.

Lavagetto, Mario. *L'impiegato Schmiz e altri saggi su Svevo*. Turin: Einaudi, 1975; new edn 1986.

Lucente, Gregory L. *Beautiful Fables: Self-Consciousness in Italian Narrative from Manzoni to Calvino*. Baltimore: Johns Hopkins University Press, 1986.

Mazzacurati, Giancarlo. *Pirandello nel romanzo europeo*. Bologna: Il Mulino, 1987.

2

ALBERT N. MANCINI

The forms of long prose fiction in late medieval and early modern Italian literature

An overview of the early Italian novel might well begin with the observation that Italian writers never felt too comfortable with the novel as a literary form before the nineteenth century. Therefore, many literary historians came to the inevitable conclusion that the birth of the Italian novel takes place in 1827 with Alessandro Manzoni's *I promessi sposi*.[1] Such an assessment makes sense only if it implies that detecting a unified pattern of development in the Italian premodern novel leading to the "rise" of the "modern" novel would be very difficult. To put it another way, the Renaissance Boccaccian *novella* does not "evolve" into the bourgeois novel of the eighteenth century. In the Italian canon, there is no *Astrée* after Sannazaro's *Arcadia*, and the historical novel of the seventeenth century does not constitute an antecedent of the early nineteenth-century historical novel. Yet so vast a literary output cannot fail to stimulate the curiosity of the reader interested in the history of the genre and in the relationship between literature and the society that produced it.

The fourteenth century

Giovanni Boccaccio is generally considered to be the founder of modern narrative as it emerged in postmedieval Europe. He stands out in the history of modern European culture as a reviver of the literary tradition, of the pastoral allegory and biography as well as the various forms of fiction: the *novella*, the longer narrative poem, and long prose fiction. Just as his friend Francesco Petrarca created the language of the new lyric, so Boccaccio, gathering up the entangled but vigorous threads of the medieval tale and novel, established the types and prose style of European narrative. Although he is best known for *The Decameron*, his major contributions to the

[1] *Il Settecento. Storia letteraria d'Italia*, vol. II (Milan: Vallardi, 1964, 6th edn), p. 409.

early modern novel are two vernacular works: the *Filocolo* (*Filocolo*, 1336) and the *Elegia di Madonna Fiammetta* (*The Elegy of Madonna Fiammetta*, 1343–4).

The *Filocolo*, composed during the young author's sojourn in Naples between 1336 and 1338, is a long prose novel in five books, based upon the legend of Florio and Biancofiore, a romantic tale known to Boccaccio through two French versions of the twelfth century and a later popular Italian version. The two protagonists grow up together at the court of Spain and fall in love. The king and queen, believing the orphaned girl to be of low birth, send Florio, heir to the throne, away and treat Biancofiore cruelly. Accused of attempting to poison the king, she is condemned to be burned at the stake, but, after being rescued by Florio, she is sold to merchants who trade with the Orient. The core of the narrative relates the adventures of Florio in quest of his beloved. Before setting out on his search, Florio assumes the name of Filocolo, a compound of the Greek words for "love" and "labor." During his wanderings he stops at Naples where he is admitted into the inner circles of the local nobility. At one of the society games, known as "questions of love," Fiammetta, the daughter of the king of the region (but also Boccaccio's lady love whose name appears here for the first time), is named "queen" and each participant proposes a problem. There are thirteen such questions. Finally, after many adventures at sea and on land, Florio, aided by the ancient pagan gods, succeeds in freeing Biancofiore from captivity in the tower in Alexandria where her Arab master keeps her; finally reunited, the two young people can marry. Later on, Florio, his companions and family, are converted to Christianity, the religion of his beloved, who is recognized as the child of descendants of Scipio murdered during a pilgrimage to Spain. At the death of his father, Florio and Biancofiore are crowned king and queen.

The main reason for the *Filocolo*'s success among the writers of the Renaissance is young Boccaccio's daring attempt to fuse romance with classical erudition and even Christian allegory. With its persistent references to Virgil's *Aeneid*, Ovid's *Metamorphoses*, and Dante's *Divine Comedy*, the *Filocolo* constitutes a *summa* of medieval storytelling and the Western novelistic tradition. The scope of the *Filocolo*, constructed around a simple love story supposedly set in early Christian times, is amplified by ambiguous experiential and autobiographical material, crammed with lengthy allusions to convoluted episodes of contemporary history (e.g. the Angevin dynasty's conquest of the Realm of Naples; the founding of Certaldo, the author's birthplace), and encumbered by the insertion of extraneous information about geography, science, and folklore. The *Filocolo* has never been regarded as Boccaccio's masterpiece. Yet twentieth-century criticism has recognized its originality and significance, even acclaiming it as one of the important novels "that change the face of fiction."[2]

Boccaccio's second prose novel, the *Elegia di Madonna Fiammetta*, dates from the first years after the author's return to Florence. Centering on the broken relationship of Fiammetta, a married woman, and a young man, Panfilo (one of the names recurrent in Boccaccio's fictions meaning the one who loves all and, therefore, the one who cannot be faithful), the story is narrated in the first person from the woman's point of view. Fiammetta first sees Panfilo in a church. She is attracted by him and at social gatherings takes pleasure in luring him to love her. Their love attains sensual fulfillment, but soon afterward Panfilo's father calls him back to Florence. Panfilo promises to come back, but some time later Fiammetta hears that he has married. Considered the predecessor of the modern psychological novel, the *Elegia* was, and to date remains, the most popular as well as the most controversial of Boccaccio's early works. Recent scholarship tends to deny its autobiographical nature and places more emphasis on his classical sources and his imitation of Ovid's *Heroides*. Fiammetta is thus remembered as the heroine of ill-starred love and unconditional faithfulness. Alternatively, some critics read the text as a tale of erotic frustration, a parody of the whole courtly love tradition, a comedy rather than a tragedy. Others still, in quite a different reading, have seen Fiammetta as a proto-feminist because it is rare in premodern literature to have such an active and outspoken female protagonist.

The fifteenth century

The influence of all of Boccaccio's fiction is quite evident in the *Paradiso degli Alberti* (The Paradise-Garden of the Alberti), an interesting prose narrative composed in the early part of the fifteenth century by Giovanni Gherardi da Prato (c. 1367 – c. 1444). The work circulated widely in manuscript form and went through thirty-four editions between 1472 and 1594. It is an amalgam of the *Filocolo* and *The Decameron*, a mixture of genres and styles held together by a frame narrative of social gatherings featuring cultural events and games which have as protagonists prominent Florentine figures. Book I describes an imaginary journey by the author along the coast of Italy and Sicily to Cyprus, with many digressions on mythological lore and learned conversations on love. Book II takes us back to Tuscany in 1389 with some

---

[2] Margaret Anne Doody, *The True Story of the Novel* (New Brunswick, NJ: Rutgers University Press, 1996), p. 193.

references to the ancient Etruscans and the sacred places of Saint Francis, but above all to a prolonged sojourn of a select group of travelers at the court of the counts of Poppi. In the remaining three books the main characters return to Florence where their gatherings are held at the villa "Paradiso" of Niccolo' degli Alberti. In the *Paradiso* sessions, storytelling modeled on *The Decameron* alternates with philosophical and political-historical arguments that proved of crucial interest to the Renaissance.

Explicit and conscious links with both the *Filocolo* and the *Fiammetta* can also be found in one of the three major romantic novels written at the end of the fifteenth century, the *Libro del Peregrino* (The Book of Peregrino) by Iacopo Caviceo (1443–1511). Dedicated to Lucrezia Borgia, the novel first appeared in Parma in 1508, reached at least nineteen editions in the first half of the sixteenth century, and was translated into Spanish (1520) and French (1528 and 1535). In it, the author relates the tragic love story of the dead protagonist, Peregrino, who appears to him in a dream. After years of forced separation from his chaste beloved Ginevra and a venturesome search for her, which takes him to the Orient and everywhere else including the underworld (visited in a prophetic dream), the lover-pilgrim manages to win her in marriage, only to lose her shortly after she gives birth to a son. Incapable of a sustained effort in long narrations, Caviceo feels more at ease in dealing with his privileged topic of love. The book could be read as the author's autobiography, and perhaps its main value for modern readers is the picture it gives us of the contemporary northern courtly circles the author knew so well, and the type of romantic fiction the readership of his times preferred. He gave this narrative form a breath and fullness previously unknown.

If the *Peregrino* seems to be conceived as fashionable reading aimed at upper-class, largely female, readers who were the principal consumers of romantic fiction in late fifteenth-century Italy, the esoteric narrative *Hypnerotomachia Poliphili* (*The Strife of Love in a Dream of Poliphilus*, 1499), attributed to the Dominican monk Francesco Colonna (1433–1527), was directed at a more selective readership of humanist scholars and art connoisseurs. The novel contains two very different parts. In book I Polifilo, "the lover of Polia," in a long allegorical sequence dreams of being lost in a forest, meeting his beloved, and traveling with her to Cythera (the realm of Venus). In book II, a much shorter narrative, he recounts the story of his love for Polia. The two lovers renew their vows, but Polia disappears when Polifilo, now awake, tries to embrace her. The language of the novel is an eclectic hybrid of Italian and anti-Ciceronian Latin, mingled with dialectal Venetian elements and riddled with newly coined words. It is a wholly artificial language, as expansive as the many classical and vernacular technical sources upon which it draws. Colonna is consistently better at description than narration, and more sensitive to the task of reproducing meaning by exploiting the visual properties of language, as demonstrated by the innumerable detailed descriptions of gardens, buildings, sculptures, and inscriptions that inspired generations of artists.

Hypnerotomachia Poliphili, published by Aldus Manutius in Venice in 1499, is famous as the most richly illustrated book of the Renaissance, containing almost two hundred woodcuts. Yet, from the point of view of fiction, by far the most important book composed at the end of the period is the pastoral novel *Arcadia* (*Arcadia*, 1505) by the Neapolitan humanist poet Jacopo Sannazaro (*c.* 1458–1530). Its authorized redaction of 1505 consists of a prologue, an epilogue, and twelve prose selections intercalated with an equal number of poems, written in various meters. The main story is related in the first person by the author's textual persona, Sincero. The subject of the connecting frame tale is the love story of the protagonist narrator who travels to Arcadia, the mythical scene of almost all classical bucolic poetry, to escape from the memories of an unreciprocated love. Sincero participates in the daily life of the Arcadian shepherds; he shares in their games, their singing and dancing contests, their religious rituals and funeral ceremonies, but he is troubled by a premonition of impending calamities. With the help of a friendly nymph who escorts him through caverns under the sea, he manages to return to Naples only to find his beloved dead. Structurally, it must be noted that while in the first part of *Arcadia* the poetry seems to be more relevant, the author's focus shifts to the narrative, beginning especially with the seventh prose passage. In part II, a shift of tone is also noticeable, from the scenes of pastoral merrymaking and the tranquil life of the carefree shepherds to a more pronounced evocation of grief and despondency. Sannazaro, like his contemporaries, wrote in other literary forms and was highly conscious of classical and previous vernacular works. The artificial language of *Arcadia* with its classicizing phrasing, complex syntax, and Latinate diction may not appeal to modern readers, but it was appreciated as being well suited to the pastoral in the humanist environment of the late fifteenth century. There were sixty-six editions of the work in Italy alone during the Cinquecento and seventeen more during the first half of the seventeenth century, not to mention the numerous imitations at home and abroad. The *Arcadia* was translated into all major European languages, and its popularity helped spread the pastoral mode throughout the early modern period. In this respect it has an enormous experimental importance in the history of both fiction and drama.

The sixteenth century

The traditional forms of long prose narrative were still popular in the sixteenth century, but the best and most influential products of fiction writing
were the chivalric romance in the style of Ludovico Ariosto (1474–1533) in
the first half of the century and the classicizing heroic poem of the last part of
the century in the style of Torquato Tasso (1544–95). Thus the sixteenth century cannot claim a major or influential novelist. Most of the practitioners
of this form were lesser writers, but nonetheless men of considerable culture
and keen observers of the contemporary scene and tastes, who could compete
at times for an appreciative readership. The extent to which they were read is
demonstrated, for example, by the enormous popularity of the anonymous
Compassionevoli avvenimenti di Erasto (The Piteous Adventures of Erasto,
1542), a modern rewriting of the medieval Italian and French versions of the
famous *Historia septem sapientium* (Book of Seven Wise Men): twenty-six
editions in the sixteenth century and eight more in the seventeenth century.
It was translated into French (1564), Spanish (1573), and English (1674).
The plot is thin and recounts the tragic story of the love of the lustful stepmother Aphrodisia, wife of the emperor Dioclitian, for her stepson Erasto.
The chaste and wise youth, accused of raping her, is saved from execution by
his seven teachers who continue to tell stories. The bulk of the work consists
of a string of intercalated *novelle*.

Much less popular was the *Philena* (Philena, 1547) of Niccolò Franco
(1515–71), first friend and later rival of Pietro Aretino (1492–1556) and
victim of the Inquisition. The 935-page work, an imitation of Boccaccio's
Fiammetta, contains twelve books. At the beginning of the work, the protagonist Sannio has a dream in which Amore shows him a beautiful woman;
his search to find her takes him to Venice, where he falls in love with Philena,
already married and a mother. In despair he flees to Milan and later to Casale,
where in another dream Amore finally delivers him from the burden of carnal
love so that he can turn to God. In the preface, Franco encourages the readers
of his novel to view the writer and the hero of his novel as interchangeable.
But the text offers only superficial autobiographical underpinnings, and the
looseness of its texture is further undermined by the intrusion of erudite digressions, social satire, speeches, and reflections on love, that interrupt the
development of the psychological novel.

Two other novels of the second half of the sixteenth century reflect types
of prose fiction clearly related to the love and adventure romance, although
differing in some respects from their models. In the *Cortigiano disperato* (The
Desperate Courtier, 1592), Gabriele Pascoli uses a fictional narrator who
interacts with the nominal protagonist as part of the narrative. A young

Italian nobleman travels to Barcelona where he hears an account of the love story of Gioseffo and Panfilia. The tragic story of passion, jealousy, and revenge is related to him in flashback by the protagonist. It is set in a specified historical period, some time after the battle of Lepanto (1571), and in a specified ambience (the ducal court of Barcelona). Contemporary courtly life and mores are evoked with some measure of consistency and realism. Alvise Pasqualigo's *Lettere amorose* (Love Letters, 1563) offer an original variation to sixteenth-century love fiction in the form of the epistolary novel. The narrator's presence is consistent, but self-reflection evolves in the course of his work, providing it not only with a substance and an impetus that are discretely autobiographical, but also with a high measure of narrative self-consciousness, thereby exploiting the letter's potential as a vehicle apt to express the trials and contrivances of a long and turbulent adulterous affair.

Recent critics have renewed interest in another aspect of sixteenth-century prose fiction: the novel written for the moral benefit of the reader and intended to contain useful teachings in compliance with the moralizing efforts of the Catholic Reformation. Some of these works, written at the end of the century and structured around the theme of metamorphosis, warrant more consideration than they have received to date. The *Metamorphosi cioè trasformazione del virtuoso* (The Metamorphosis or the Transformation of the Virtuous, 1582) by the Franciscan monk Lorenzo Selva (d. 1593) was reprinted six times between 1583 and 1616. Its young hero, Acrisio, is forced to leave his beloved Clori and is sent to Naples by his greedy mother. Here he falls victim to magic and is transformed into a serpent. After many vicissitudes of fortune and perils, the metamorphosed youth manages to return to his hometown where he resumes his human form, but Clori, bitten by a spider, dies shortly afterwards. Numerous moral and philosophical digressions and thirteen exemplary *novelle* are included in the work.

Metamorphosis and travel also mark the *Brancaleone* (Brancaleone, 1610) of the Milanese Giovanni Pietro Giussani (*c.* 1548 or 1552–1623), a work reprinted five times during the seventeenth century. Its protagonist, a man transformed into an ass, reaches the land of the lion, king of the forest, after numerous changes of strict masters. Profiting from what he has learned from overhearing the stories narrated by the humans and animals encountered in his adventures, the hubristic man-ass befriends the lion under the assumed name of Brancaleone. The many exemplary narratives, referred to as *novelle*, are as striking as the framework within which they are told. Giussani presents us with a world of violence, foul play, misguided intentions, and deceit in Spanish-dominated Italy. These evils erupt in the character of the hero, the ass turned tyrant, who in the end usurps the power of the king of animals, and establishes a reign of terror, only to be assassinated by peasants in revolt. Giussani draws from Apuleius's *Golden Ass*, but also from an array of folkloristic materials, and brings into play the strategies of the apology, the aphorism, and the Aesopian animal fable. Echoing the guiding spirit of the post-Tridentine Catholic church, the author, a physician and a priest, loses few opportunities to underline the message of his politico-moral fable: act with prudence and be content with your lot.

Novels from Greek or Latin literature enjoyed particular success in Italy and influenced the production of prose fiction in the vernacular. Often they were adapted and rewritten in an elegant and learned style by preeminent men of letters for a wider audience. The *Metamorphoses* by Apuleius (*c*. AD 125–80), already translated by Matteo Maria Boiardo (*c*. 1440–94), was again modernized by Agnolo Firenzuola (1493–1543) between 1515 and 1525, and subsequently published in Venice in 1550 with the title *Asino d'oro* (*The Golden Ass*). Niccolò Machiavelli (1469–1527) wrote a poetic version of Apuleius's novel during the last years of his life, leaving it incomplete. Francesco Angelo Coccio (no sure date) rendered *Leucippe and Cleitophon* by Achilles Tatius into Italian in 1551. Heliodorus's *Aethiopica* (*c*. AD 230) was translated into Italian in 1588 by Leonardo Ghini (d. 1589) with the title *La dilettevole historia di Heliodoro* (The Entertaining History of Heliodorus). The translation-adaptation of the *Daphnis and Chloe* of Longus the Sophist (*c*. AD 160) by Annibal Caro (1507–66) was published posthumously in 1786, but had circulated widely in manuscript form long before that time. The novelist Giovan Battista Manzini (1599–1664) published another rendition of Longus's novel, *Gli amori innocenti di Dafni, e della Cloe* (The Innocent Loves of Daphne and Chloe) in 1643.

The seventeenth century

During the seventeenth century, the novel began to develop as an autonomous literary genre and to assert itself as the most prestigious narrative mode. In the preface to his novel *Il Cretideo* (Cretideo, 1637), Manzini provided a tentative definition of the *romanzo* (novel) – the term for the genre that became accepted near the mid-seventeenth century – by attempting to distinguish it from the other genres with which it overlaps. He considers the genre "called *romanzo* by the moderns," as he puts it, the most difficult to practice; it is superior to history because of its association with epic poetry, and superior also to the noble epic poem because of its independence from Aristotelian rules. The *romanzo* is "therefore the most astonishing and glorious construct that human ingenuity can devise." However, the seventeenth century did not produce full-fledged theoretical treatises on the novel, for questions concerning narrative genres were still inextricably tied to discussions involving epic poetry. The most important of such discussions was the debate during the mid-fifteenth century on the relationship between the chivalric romance of Ariosto (designated as a *romanzo* by the theorists) and Aristotle's *Poetics*, or the argument during the late sixteenth century over the comparison of Ariosto and Tasso and what constituted the most acceptable form of the vernacular epic poem. Not surprisingly, while the prefaces to the novels and certain passages in them provide some clues to the writers' motivating principles and aspirations, the seventeenth-century novel was characterized by a high degree of experimentation in line with the poetics of the "marvelous" as practiced by the baroque master Giambattista Marino (1569–1625) and in accord with the trends towards generic and cultural heterogeneity during the baroque period.

The number of editions and reprints of novels published in the seventeenth century underscores the genre's popularity. More than 180 novels were published in Italy during the century, most of them in Venice but also in other cities with less active presses (Genoa, Bologna, Rome, and minor provincial cities). Many of these novels went through more than thirty editions or reprints. Moreover, a good number of them were translated into other major European languages. The sixteen most popular novels account for 250 editions, with a cumulative total reaching almost 900 printings. The pace of production quickened in the 1630s, reached its peak in the 1640s, and dropped dramatically in the 1660s due to changes in taste. Printers and booksellers were dependent upon the approval of a wide public, and in their works novelists consciously reflected the ideas and tastes generally held, a tendency consonant with the fundamental tenet of Italian baroque poetics that the reader's approval, not adherence to a set of abstract aesthetic values, make for the success of literary efforts.

Arcadia felice (Happy Arcadia, 1605) by Lucrezia Marinella (1571–1653) is a little-known but interesting pastoral novel that introduces substantial innovations into the form as practiced in the late sixteenth century, and shows how such a work could be put to new uses to conform with contemporary sociocultural concerns and literary tastes. The large-scale surge in the production of novelistic narrative, the "deluge of *romanzi*" to quote the satirists, does not take place until later in the 1620s and 1630s. The Dalmatian historian Giovan Francesco Biondi (1572–1644), who lived in England most of his life and was knighted by James I, provided the first landmark for the Italian baroque heroic-gallant novel. His successful trilogy, *Eromena* (Eromena, 1624), *La donzella desterrata* (The Banished Virgin, 1627), and *Coralbo* (Coralbo, 1632), was clearly indebted to the neo-Latin novel *Argenis* (1621) by Scottish humanist John Barclay (1582–1621), whose popular book was the unquestionable international best-seller of the first half of that century.

These long stories are built upon a double plotline – one amatory, the other political – interwoven in such a way that the events involving the one supply support to the other. Structurally, they rely heavily on suspense and the marvelous in both content and in style, and they stress rhetorical amplification and flourishes, elevated and ornate prose, and painterly effects rather than character portrayal and adroitness of construction. The heroic novel thus develops in Italy as an outgrowth of earlier narrative forms – namely, the romantic Greek novels, the *novella*, the pastoral, but above all the Renaissance chivalric poem. The major characters are generally conquering knights and beautiful heroines exposed to a multitude of dangers. The main plot, as well as the secondary plots, often begin with the separation of a pair of lovers and follow each of the two partners on their separate odysseys. The standard components of these wanderings include adventures on land and sea, attacks by pirates, abductions, battles, duels, jousts, palace intrigues, and mistaken identities. The story achieves closure with the reunion of the two lovers.

The success of Biondi's novels strengthened the vogue of heroic-gallant fiction especially among his fellow members of the Venetian Academy of the Incogniti (1630–61), founded by Giovan Francesco Loredano (1614–61), a celebrated patron of literature, a novelist, and a translator of foreign novels, whose promotion of the new genre contributed to making Venice the most important printing center of prose fiction in Italy. Loredano's own contribution to the form, *La Dianea* (Dianea, 1635), was very well received and enjoyed more than twenty printings during the seventeenth century throughout Europe. Part of its popularity was undoubtedly due to the veiled references to historical events and prominent political figures of the time of the Thirty Years War. Aspects of the heroic novel, such as the concern to unite romantic fantasy and a realistic portrayal of current mores and politics, are present in the many novels by fellow Incogniti members written in the 1630s and 1640s: *Ormondo* (Ormondo, 1638) by Francesco Pona (1595–1655); *Gli accidenti di Cloramindo principe della Ghenuria* (The Misfortunes of Cloramindo, Prince of Ghenuria, 1639) by Francesco Belli; and the *Istoria del Cavaliere Perduto* (The Story of the Lost Knight, 1644) by Pace Pasini (1583–1644).

While Biondi and Loredano introduced heroism into modern narrative, a more abstract and sublime form of heroism is depicted in Giovan Ambrogio Marini's *Calloandro* (Calloandro), the recognized masterpiece of the heroic novel that remained popular in Italy well into the mid-nineteenth century. Part I of the novel first appeared in 1640, part II was published in 1641; and the revised version titled *Calloandro fedele* (The Faithful Calloandro) was published in 1653. Marini (*c.* 1594 – *c.* 1667), a Genoese priest and religious essayist, spent over a decade improving the coherence and structural unity of the narrative and toning down or deleting episodes and details contrary to the idealistic expectations, especially fidelity in love, of the readers. The influence of the epic-romantic tradition can be seen in the eastern Mediterranean setting, the timelessness of the action, and the mechanism of plot anticipation. The protagonists, Calloandro and Leonilda, are superhuman beings caught in a intricate web of amazing adventures and concerned more with finding their own identity and preserving their reputation as models of chivalric heroism than with either contemporary history or politics. Even more revealing for an understanding of the baroque vision of life is Marini's preference for such themes as the relation of appearance and reality, the instability of all things subject to the whims of Fortune, and his predilection for open-ended structure and a focus on suspense, metamorphosis, and masking.

Love and devotion, among the most important components of chivalric heroism, gain an even more prominent place in the heroic and sentimental works of Marini's fellow Ligurian novelists Luca Assarino (1602–72) and Bernardo Morando (1589–1656). Assarino's *La Stratonica* (Stratonica, 1635) reached almost forty reprints in the seventeenth century and deals with the traditional theme of love sickness. Adopted from classical sources and a *novella* by Matteo Bandello (1485–1561), the basic story of the young Prince Antioco's passion for his stepmother Stratonica contains fundamental changes: the queen loves Antioco, and King Seleuco is willing to give up his beautiful queen in order to save his son's life. Compared to the *Calloandro*, *La Stratonica* seems a model of conciseness and psychological penetration, features that were to be recognized as the distinctive mark of the psychological novel as it developed in the eighteenth century.

Yet the new religious climate effected changes even in a novel of exotic adventures like Morando's *Rosalinda* (Rosalinda, 1650), a novel that enjoyed over twenty reprints. Lealdo and Rosalinda, both children of Catholic Genoese merchants living in England, fall in love; but Rosalinda is also courted by the Protestant Eldemondo of Essex and promised in marriage to the sinister Crisauro. Forced to flee, the young lovers are separated and subjected to trials including shipwrecks, attacks by pirates, and captivity that threaten their life and chastity. Eventually the couple are reunited, but stoic constancy and strict religious observance help them conquer sexual urges, and they choose the cloister instead of marriage. Despite his usually less pretentious narrative style, Morando, a prolific man of letters of mercantile background, loses few opportunities for emotional or rhetorically molded outbursts, and a generous use of lyric poetry and dramatic devices.

In other works of the time, the moral and edifying intent is so pervasive as to justify the term of "religious novel," a subgenre that played a vital role in the spiritual revival of the post-Tridentine period. In this type of narrative, particularly popular among Ligurian and Bolognese novelists, virtue and religious zeal are made to triumph, while moments of eroticism are justified as the exposing of vice for the benefit of the reader. In this context, the *Maria Maddalena, peccatrice e convertita* (Mary Magdalen, Sinner and Converted, 1636) by the Genovese Anton Giulio Brignole-Sale (1605–62) stands out as a prototype of the genre because of its characteristic themes and mixture of religious mysticism and sensuality. Various types of religious narrative continue, of course, throughout the century. Biblical characters and saints illustrate a heroic ideal offered to the educated minority in the baroque age as an alternative to the protagonists of the heroic-chivalric novels. This form of prose fiction deserves to be better known for its centrality to seventeenth-century religious sensibility and our understanding of it. It is represented historically by works as diverse as the ornate lives recorded in *Il Giuseppe* (*Joseph*, 1637) and *La Susanna* (*Susanna*, 1638) by the libertine Ferrante Pallavicino (1614–44); or in the sententious accounts of historical events – *Le battaglie d'Israele* (The Battles of Israel, 1634) and *Le turbolenze d'Israele* (The Commotions of Israel, 1633) – by the pious Luigi Manzini (1604–57). Such fiction reaches its peak in narratives dealing with contemporary subjects and figures, narratives that encouraged their readers to observe the militant revivalism of the Counter-Reformation. Noteworthy for its success in this regard is *Il cappuccino scozzese* (The Scottish Capuchin, 1644) by Bishop Giovan Battista Rinuccini (1592–1653). Rinuccini's novel enjoyed more than twenty-six reprints in the seventeenth century, was translated into French and Spanish, and was reissued in a somewhat revised version as late as 1863.

Normative didacticism and proselytizing enthusiasm cannot be found in the vast oeuvre of Girolamo Brusoni (1614–86), who was a historian, short-story writer, novelist, and journalist. His most interesting narrative work is a Venetian trilogy: *La gondola a tre remi* (The Three-Oared Gondola, 1657); *Il carozzino alla moda* (The Fashionable Carriage, 1658); and *La peota smarrita* (The Lost Boat, 1662). These three novels feature no knight-errantry but do provide a portrayal of contemporary Venetian *dolce vita*. Their protagonist, Glisomiro, a learned patrician and an irresistible Don Juan, is an autobiographical projection of the author. The narrative is replete with anecdotes, sketches, descriptions, refined conversations, and academic discussions that focus on the sociocultural milieu rather than individual characters. The trilogy is indicative of the end of the high season of the baroque heroic novel and evinces an evolution of prose fiction in the direction of a realism grounded in a greater situational and psychological verisimilitude. And yet, what might pass for realism is still invariably heightened by the baroque taste for sensational attitudes and situations, and by an excessive reliance on metaphors and conceits. Chronologically, the emergence of this narrative trend coincides with that of the intellectual current of seventeenth-century libertinage.

The reader of Glisomiro's trilogy misses the daring vindication of intellectual or moral freedom of Brusoni's younger friend and Loredano's protégé, Ferrante Pallavicino, who was beheaded at Avignon for his anti-papal pamphlets. Resentful of any kind of authority and unsubmissive in spirit, this rebellious monk's narrative interests ranged from the heroic novel *Taliclea* (Taliclea, 1636), and the erotic narratives *La pudicitia schernita* (Modesty Scorned, 1638) or *La rete di Vulcano* (Vulcan's Net, 1640), to satirical fiction such as the *Il corriere svaligiato* (The Post-Boy Robbed, 1641) and the *Il divorzio celeste* (The Celestial Divorce, 1643). The latter work is a virulent satire on contemporary mores and political authority, as well as an attack upon sexuality and religion employed as a hypocritical mask.

More representative of the rationalist and scientific antiauthoritarian tendencies prevailing among many members of the Venetian Academy of the Incogniti is *La lucerna di Eureta Misoscolo* (Eureta Misoscolo's Lamp, published in 1625 and placed on the Index in 1627) by the noted physician Francesco Pona, who had also translated Barclay's *Argenis* in 1629 as well as the first book of Ovid's *Metamorphoses* in 1618. His novel draws on the tradition of the novel of transformation, but it is structurally patterned after another ancient model, the satiric dialogue of Lucian. The Lamp of the novel has in many other previous existences experienced innumerable reincarnations: as an innocent girl; a prostitute; historical characters such as Sulla, Cleopatra, and Ravaillac; animals such as a flea, a mouse, a horse, a bee, or a cricket. On four consecutive evenings, the Lamp instructs its current owner and interlocutor, the student Eureta, with fantastic tales inspired by Boccaccio, Aretino, Bandello, and Barclay, among others. The *Lucerna* is a collection of novelistic narratives focusing for the most part on the dark, even pathological, sides of human ethos and behavior. Its unity lies not only in the continuous presence of its author, felt both in ideological and technical or in stylistic terms, but also in the frame story that gives these materials their structural relevance: the Lamp as narrator, protagonist, and commentator.

Clearly influenced by Pona's *Lucerna*, the *Cane di Diogene* (Diogenes' Dog, 1687–9) by Francesco Fulvio Frugoni (1620 – *c.* 1686), author of the religious novel *La vergine parigina* (The Parisian Virgin, 1661) and the historical novel *L'eroina intrepida* (The Fearless Heroine, 1673), is important also as a cultural source because it displays so many different aspects of late seventeenth-century culture. As its title implies, a dog reminiscent of the picaresque hero of other such novels, whose name is Saetta (Dart), narrates his life with the Cynic philosopher Diogenes and many other masters in twelve episodes. Frugoni's daring ethicosocial and cultural judgments and encyclopedic digressions go well beyond the scope of the narrative framework. Over forty-three hundred pages in length, Frugoni divides the novel into seven volumes or "barks," all structured on the baroque metaphor of the world turned upside down. Frugoni's world is a disjointed one; his irony is grim and tinged with gripping baroque *desengaño* inspired by the irredeemable wickedness and stupidity of men.

The *Cane di Diogene* represents the last stage in the transition of the seventeenth-century novel from idealistic fictions to narratives rejecting a fictional mask in favor of a more explicit connection with a readily recognizable contemporary reality. The *Esploratore turco* (Turkish Explorer, 1684) by Giovanni Paolo Marana (1642–93) brings us to the threshold of the Enlightenment. The extant manuscript text in Italian, which comprised only thirty-three letters, is a small part of the enormous multilingual corpus comprising between five and seven hundred letters, known commonly by the French and English titles *L'espion turc* (1686) and *The Turkish Spy* (1691–4). The work became one of the best-sellers of late seventeenth-century and early eighteenth-century European literature and inaugurated yet another subgenre of modern fiction: the pseudo-foreign letter or spy novel. The first 102 letters attributed to Marana, a Genoese historian and political exile living in Paris, already clearly define the principal thematic and structural characteristics of this variety of epistolary novel. The fictitious letter-writer Mahmut, dispatched to Paris under the alias of Abbot Tito of Moldavia, addresses his observations on European politics, religion, and mores to his superiors but also to friends and relatives in a straightforward, direct style. Marana uses a Turkish "informant," his fictional alter ego; with shameless cynicism this character accepts the moral disorder of late seventeenth-century European society. Furthermore, in the work's preface, the author makes sure to claim that he has merely translated a manuscript originally written in Arabic. Marana's satirical pseudo-Oriental novel stands in marked contrast to the seventeenth-century heroic romances. It combines a number of heterogeneous elements in its formal and thematic structure: the picaresque; fictionalized biography of important personages; historical chronicle; social and political satire; popular anecdotes; court gossip; as well as information on the Ottoman sultanate and Moslem beliefs or customs. The book produced numerous imitations based on its apparently serious confrontation of Occidental and Oriental customs, and it helped to inspire at least one European masterpiece, Montesquieu's *Lettres persanes* (*Persian Letters*, 1721).

Who actually read such original and translated narratives? Which segment of the Italian reading public received them with the enthusiasm alluded to by the most enterprising printers of the time–printers who were themselves instrumental in promoting and supplying the demand for novels? In the preface to his devout novel *Cavaliere d'honore* (The Honorable Knight, 1673), the theologian Giovanni Maria Versari admits that the novel's readership is quite diverse and includes learned as well as average people and even the ignorant.[3] In seventeenth-century Italy, the novel, especially of the heroic-gallant kind, was popular primarily with a provincial aristocracy that did not gravitate around a court or the salons of a national capital such as London and Paris. But long prose fiction was also popular among a group of readers of average education. Such an audience was intellectually not too discriminating and lacked a high degree of sociopolitical consciousness. It was thus incapable of the kind of active participation in the shaping of a new narrative style for the genre of the novel that the rising middle class was enjoying elsewhere in Europe.

The eighteenth century

Toward the end of the seventeenth century, the prestigious Academy of Arcadia (founded in 1690) promoted with success the restoration of a more sober conception of literary expression and led the reaction against what became viewed as the bad taste of the baroque. As a result, even the inflated rhetorical style of prose writers, particularly of fiction writers, came under attack and ceased to enjoy favor among the literati. In the middle of the eighteenth century, the spread of the Enlightenment aided greatly in the reawakening of Italian culture and helped to diffuse the knowledge of foreign literature, then considered a complement to one's own national and regional culture. By the mid-seventeenth century, the novel had already achieved a pronounced international character and had become a means of cultural exchange. The rapid expansion of translations and adaptations of novels, particularly from France, and more indirectly from England, encouraged Italian writers to follow the example of foreign novelists.[4]

The Abbé Pietro Chiari (1712–85), the chief rival playwright of Carlo Goldoni (1707–93), found himself to be the most successful novelist and translator of novels of his time after an initial disapproval of novel writing. His first novel *La filosofessa italiana* (The Woman Philosopher, 1753), presented as the autobiography of an adventurous heroine, enjoyed some nine reprints in a few years. In the over forty novels attributed to him, Chiari's writing is dull, the pace of his stories slow and diffuse, and his narrative style repetitious, based on the binary structure of action and comment. Yet,

---

[3] See Lucinda Spera, "Un consuntivo tardo-secentesco sul romanzo," *Studi Secenteschi* 35 (1994), pp. 145–65.

[4] See Maria Rosa Zambon, *Bibliographie du roman français en Italie au XVIII siècle* (Florence: Sansoni, 1982).

in spite of the criticism leveled at his works, Chiari remains a prototypical figure of great interest. The depiction of the contemporary scene and its values was doubtless what gave his huge novels their special popular appeal. Their chief novelty was the introduction of female protagonists, and the presentation of the actions of nonaristocratic individuals (particularly those from the middle class), to replace those of higher social standing in the courtly baroque novel of adventure. His trilogy on the theater is important in this respect: *La ballerina onorata* (The Honorable Dancer, 1754), *La cantatrice per disgrazia* (The Unlucky Singer, 1754), *La commediante in fortuna* (The Fortunate Actress, 1754–5). Modern society is represented in all its color and eccentricity in novels such as *La francese in Italia* (The Frenchwoman in Italy, 1759) and *La bella pellegrina* (The Fair Pilgrim, 1761). In the earlier *La giocatrice del lotto o sia le memorie di Madama Tulot* (The Lady Lottery Player or the Memoirs of Madame Tulot, 1757), Chiari deals with the role of chance with an original infusion of grim and satirical humor. The independent and resourceful heroines of these pseudo-autobiographical stories, narrated in the first-person singular, introduce a type of female character quite new to the Italian literary canon.

To his credit, Chiari admitted that the private circumstances of his life forced him to write novels because they were the only books that would sell.[5] In the Venice of the mid-eighteenth century, academic writers considered novel writing beneath their dignity. The dramatist Carlo Gozzi (1720–1806) warned the readers of his *Memorie inutili* (*Useless Memoirs*, 1797–8) that the members of the prestigious Venetian Accademia dei Granelleschi (founded in 1747) held Chiari's works in disrepute, but unfortunately they were to be found everywhere: on the dressing tables of the ladies, the desks of the gentlemen, the benches of the shopkeepers and artisans, in the hands of strollers, in public and private schools, in colleges, and even in monasteries.[6]

The emphasis Chiari placed on extraordinary and improbable adventures is equally prominent in the early novels of the Venetian Antonio Piazza (1742–1825), a successful journalist frequently presented as Chiari's natural successor. Among Piazza's most popular works in this vein were *L'ebrea, istoria galante scritta da lei medesima* (The Jewish Woman, A Gallant Story Written by Herself, 1769) – notable for the realistic rendering of its social milieu and the swift pace of the narration of its heroine's calamities; and *I Zingani* (The Zingani, 1769), the travel adventures of two likable confidence men loosely related to a picaresque model. Piazza's late production revolves

---

5 *La francese in Italia* (Parma: 1763), vol. I: p. 8.
6 "Occasione di scrivere queste memorie, e motivi ragionevoli di pubblicarle," from *Memorie inutili* in *Scritti*, ed. Ettore Bonora (Turin: Einaudi, 1977), p. 197.

more often around stories of passionate love. The author introduced in them the kind of effusiveness and sentimentality that anticipates the romantic novel of the early nineteenth century. One of these novels, *Deliri dell'anime amanti* (Raptures of Loving Souls, 1782), was Piazza's most popular novel. A similar novel, but more ambitious and less successful, was *L'amor fra l'armi* (Love among Arms, 1773). Here the title suggests the flavor of the entire book: a love story related against the background of the anti-French rebellion by the Corsicans (1752–68) led by their national hero, Pasquale Paoli.

As a genre placed in a competitive and historically unfavorable position with established literary forms, the novel had to assert itself through continued reliance on contemporary taste and the expectations of the reading public. Two main veins for novel writing emerge clearly in Italy during the second half of the century. While chastising the proliferation of mediocre, "popular" novels predicated upon requirements other than purely artistic ones, such as the novels created by Chiari and Piazza, academic writers were trying with their own original narrative efforts to meet the imaginative needs of the more sophisticated segment of the readership, already familiar with European foreign imports then widely translated into Italian.

The leading popularizer of the ideas of the French Enlightenment in Italy, Francesco Algarotti of Venice (1712–64), published a short novel, anonymously entitled *Il congresso di Citera* (The Congress of Cythera, 1745), that was heavily indebted to the *Temple de Gnide* (The Temple of Gnide, 1724) by Montesquieu (1689–1755). In it, Cupid summons three famous heroines representing Italy, France, and England to the island of Venus to discuss love and customs in high society. Addressed to the habitués of eighteenth-century aristocratic salons, the novel is permeated with a rococo spirit and manner, and is consequently more frivolous and witty than prurient in its ambiguous eroticism and anti-Petrarchan satire.

The contributions of the Milanese nobleman Alessandro Verri (1741–1816), the younger brother of Pietro (1728–97), were more ambitious. Associated with the progressive journal *Il Caffè* (The Coffeehouse, 1764–6), Alessandro translated Shakespeare's *Hamlet*, Homer's *Iliad*, and Longus's *Daphnis and Chloe*, in addition to producing three long prose fictional works: *Le avventure di Saffo poetessa di Mitilene* (The Adventures of the Poetess Sappho of Mitylene, 1782); *Notti romane al sepolcro degli Scipioni* (*The Roman Nights at the Tomb of the Scipios*, part I, 1792; part II, 1804; part III, 1967); and *La vita di Erostrato* (The Life of Erostrato, 1815). Verri's reputation as a novelist rests on *Notti romane*, composed in Rome over a period of twenty years. In a series of imaginary conversations on Roman history and a variety of current intellectual and political topics, held during eight nights by the author-character with the shades of great Roman figures in the shadow of the tombs of the Scipios, the aged Verri managed to combine with artistry the funereal gloom and sepulchral melancholy of one of his main sources, *Night Thoughts* (1742–5) by Edward Young (1683–1765), with a heightened interest in reflections on the greatness of ancient Rome and of the Christian tradition. Verri's *Notti romane* kept its place as a classic well into the nineteenth century. Between 1792 and 1886, it ran through more than one hundred editions; between 1796 and 1850, it received sixteen translations into most European languages, with three published in England, and one in America.[7]

In general, however, the late eighteenth-century Italian novel reflects two opposing tendencies: a strand of autobiographical or memorialistic narratives; and another strand of satirical or philosophical fiction. Between 1749 and 1764, the Venetian Zaccaria Seriman (1708–84) published an interesting satirical novel in four sizable tomes, *I viaggi di Enrico Wanton alle terre incognite australi ed ai regni delle Scimmie e dei Cinocefali* (The Travels of Henry Wanton to the Unexplored Southern Lands and the Kingdoms of the Apes and the Dog-faced People), a book that owes a debt to Jonathan Swift's *Gulliver's Travels* (1726). Although beginning and ending in London, the bulk of the first-person narrative is structured as a utopian imaginary travel account. The protagonist Enrico and his companion, Roberto, shipwrecked on a desert island, visit, among other exotic localities, the cities of the Mathematicians, the Grammarians, the Poets, and the Antiquarians. As a narrator, Enrico loses credibility as his innumerable adventures develop around all of European, and more especially Venetian, civilization. Seriman's prose is often an accumulation of quotidian minutiae, further weakening the already illogical plot and loose storyline. What is striking in the novel is the depth of the author's moral indignation for the decline in current social and moral values.

The satirical energies of the novel are better expressed in fiction more overtly comical in intent, such as in *La mia istoria, ovvero memorie del sig. Tommasino scritte da lui medesimo. Opera narcotica del Dott. Pifpuf* (The Story, or Memoirs of Sig. Tommasino Written by Him. Narcotic Work by Dott. Pifpuf, 1767) by Francesco Gritti (1740–1811). This novel, left incomplete, treats the wanderings of a young Venetian, Tommasino, and his servant Zofolo throughout Europe as they undergo numerous adventures in a world populated by extravagant characters: wild men, women of loose morals, quixotic innkeepers, avid readers of the songs of Ossian, and the

---

[7] See James T. S. Wheelock, "Verri's *Notti romane*: A New Edition and Some Old Translations," *Italica* 46.1 (1969), pp. 58–68.

like. Gritti's vigorous satire is marked by a gentle sense of humor. In addition to his satirical talents, the author also possesses a notable gift for realistic observation, and when required he can write with a sharp wit. Because Gritti's work can be seen as an attack on what its author views as outmoded forms of prose fiction, it includes metanarrative elements in its pseudo-autobiographical adventure novel and a parody of literary language and techniques.

Another eccentric Venetian writer of the period that sought a niche as a novelist was Giacomo Girolamo Casanova (1725–98), the legendary lover and adventurer who wrote four novels in Italian. Two are adaptations from the French: *Lettere della nobil donna Silvia Belegno* (The Letters of the Noblewoman Silvia Belegno, 1780), a romantic epistolary novel; and *Di aneddoti viniziani militari e amorosi del secolo XIV* (Venetian Military and Amorous Anecdotes, 1782). A more original narrative, *Il duello ovvero saggio della vita di G. C. veneziano* (The Duel or Essay of the Life of G. C., a Venetian) holds a special place in Casanova's oeuvre, as it provides an autobiographical account in the third person of his duel with the Polish count, Francis Braniski, over a ballerina. The minute description of this event is meant to be a continuation of his narrative of the escape from the state prison of Venice in 1756, related in his *Histoire de ma fuite* (History of my Escape, 1788). Another original work, *Né amori né donne, ovvero La stalla* (Neither Loves nor Women, or The Stable, 1782), is a *roman à clef* written by Casanova to take revenge against some Venetian noblemen who had offended him. Such attempts to produce a novel did not enjoy a great popularity with Casanova's contemporaries, but they are interesting as an anticipation of his massive twelve-volume autobiography, *Histoire de ma vie* (*The History of my Life*), clearly his narrative masterpiece written between 1790 and 1792 and published in its entirety only in 1960–2. Casanova's autobiography follows, in many respects, the generic rules of several kinds of period fiction (the adventure novel, the satirical novel, the amorous novel, etc.).

The novel *Abaritte* (Abaritte, 1790), published by Ippolito Pindemonte (1753–1828), another major Italian writer of the second half of the eighteenth century, also presents a mixture of autobiography and satire modeled on such works as Samuel Johnson's *Rasselas* (1759) and Montesquieu's *Les lettres persanes*. Like Pindemonte, who from 1788 to 1790 journeyed abroad, the young author-figure Abaritte spends considerable time traveling through Russia, Prussia, Austria, France, and England, partly in search of knowledge, partly out of a desire to acquire experience of life and love, before returning to his native country Tangut (i.e. Italy) and marrying his betrothed Ema. The fictional form of this *roman à clef* is the travel memoir, but the driving force behind the narrative is its author's keen interest in political and social institutions, and his novel invites the reading public to come to grips with the pressing Italian social and political problems of the period before the French Revolution. This civic and patriotic theme was to play a central role in the important epistolary novel *Le ultime lettere di Jacopo Ortis* by the poet and literary critic Ugo Foscolo. The historical novels of the Romantic period during the first half of the nineteenth century continued this political goal of awakening the spirit of freedom in Italy and arousing national pride by bringing to life past periods of national greatness. In Italy, as elsewhere in Europe, literature – in particular the popular novel and the newspaper – contributed to the formation of a new concept of a national language and national literature in the Romantic period.[8]

The relationship between the fashionable new fictional form and the traditional genres, especially history, was often the focus of heated debates among writers. In his *La frusta letteraria* (The Literary Whip), the critic Giuseppe Baretti (1719–89), Samuel Johnson's friend, castigated the proliferation of mediocre novels and criticized Chiari's output as recommended reading for house servants and women. In so doing, he set a pattern for the adverse criticism of the popular novel in Italy that prevailed until recent times and prevented a genuine historical appreciation of the role the Abbé Chiari played in the prehistory of modern Italian narrative and culture.[9] As late as 1818, Foscolo could boast with obvious pride in his *Essay on the Present Literature of Italy*:

> Chiari and Piazza, and other common writers, had before published some hundreds of romances, which had been the delight only of the vulgar reader; for those of a more refined taste had resorted to the foreign novels. *The Letters of Ortis* is the only work of the kind, the boldness of whose thoughts, and the purity of whose language, combined with a certain easy style, have suited it to the taste of every reader.[10]

The two main trends of opposition affecting the genesis of the modern novel in Italy can be traced from this period. First of all, historical and literary considerations associated with the revivalist spirit of both the Arcadian movement in the earlier part of the century and the fin-de-siècle neoclassic program created a similar aversion to experimentation and influenced the

---

[8] Timothy Brennan, "The National Longing for Form," in Bill Ashcroft, Gareth Griffiths, and Helen Tiffin, eds., *The Post-Colonial Studies Reader* (London: Routledge, 1995), p. 172.

[9] Giuseppe Baretti, *Opere scelte*, ed. Bruno Maier (Turin: UTET, 1972), vol. I: p. 435.

[10] Ugo Foscolo, *Opere*, ed. Cesare Foligno (Florence: Le Monnier, 1958), vol. XI: part II, p. 470.

negative attitude of Italy's most prestigious literary figures towards the novel, which was then considered an anomalous and unpredictable form of narration with its blending of romantic and realistic elements. Second, the debate on the novel as an autonomous form of narration centered quite significantly, especially in the 1770s and 1780s, on the ethical function of the genre, on its morally pernicious and socially dangerous influences, and on its potential didactic usefulness for readers – especially women, the principal consumers of romantic fiction.[11] The spread of the rationalistic ideas of the Enlightenment aided greatly in promoting among readers of fiction a marked preference for the actual and the contemporary. Popular long prose narrative, once available, offered a challenge and a guarantee of readership to writers who wished to exercise their talent. Yet even the most loyal contemporary practitioners of the form, such as Chiari and Piazza, do not make much of a claim for their novels on strictly literary grounds. Theirs was the language and style of other contemporary genres with which the modern novel overlaps: the diary, the memoir, the imaginary voyage, and the newspaper. One searches in vain for an unrecognized masterpiece, but the role eighteenth-century novelists played in the emerging modern world of print culture cannot be denied. Burdened by the need to please readers of varying social class and hard-pressed by the demands created by the industry that had grown up around the production of popular fiction, these writers became well-known contributors to the cultural life of their times as their works reached an increasingly wider mass readership, especially in northern Italy.

After almost two centuries of scholarly neglect, recent critics and literary historians have begun to pay attention once again to the antecedents of the modern Italian novel from the fourteenth through the eighteenth centuries, with particular emphasis upon novels during the Enlightenment. In this new favorable critical climate, many important texts, particularly of the seventeenth and eighteenth centuries, have been reprinted in modern editions and made available for the first time in decades or even centuries. Moreover, even the critical literature on the early novel before Manzoni has been rapidly increasing, with a significant number of studies that challenge and redefine the traditional view held about the Italian modern novel's origins and goals. On the other hand, it is also a fact that this aspect of literary culture, so little known outside of Italy, has yet to be favored with much enthusiastic study by Anglo-American scholars and critics. Part of the explanation may lie in the traditionally biased critical views of Italian literature outside of Italy,

---

[11] On women as average readers of novels in the eighteenth century, see Elvio Guagnini, "Rifiuto e apologia del romanzo nel secondo Settecento italiano. Note su due manifesti (Roberti e Galanti)," in *Letteratura e società* (Palermo: Palumbo, 1980), vol. I: pp. 291–309.

views that move foreigners to create a somewhat mythical map of Italian culture after the end of the Renaissance, implying that little of interest occurs between then and the dawn of the Romantic period and the appearance of Alessandro Manzoni. Premodern long prose fiction in Italy thus figures as a wasteland and the nonspecialist reader is rushed directly from Boccaccio to Manzoni, with no stops along the way, except for quick peeks at oddities such as Sannazaro or Colonna. Another explanation of this critical neglect may perhaps be that critics specializing in British and French literatures have been the most important influence upon Anglo-American academic criticism of the novel. Italian works for the most part have been left out of the histories of the European development of the genre.

Further reading

Asor Rosa, Alberto. "La narrativa italiana del Seicento." In *Letteratura italiana. Le forme del testo*, vol. II: *La prosa*. Ed. A. Asor Rosa. Turin: Einaudi, 1984, pp. 715–57.

Brand, Peter and Lino Pertile, eds. *The Cambridge History of Italian Literature.* Cambridge: Cambridge University Press, 1996.

Bruscagli, Riccardo. "Il romanzo del Cinquecento." In *Storia della letteratura italiana*, vol. IV: *Il primo Cinquecento.* Ed. Enrico Malato. Rome: Salerno Editrice, 1996, pp. 888–907.

Calabrese, Stefano. "Funzioni del romanzo italiano del Settecento." In *Intrecci italiani. Una teoria e una storia del romanzo (1750–1900).* Bologna: Il Mulino, 1995, pp. 47–107.

Capucci, Martino. *Romanzieri del Seicento.* Turin: UTET, 1974.

Clerici, Luca. *Il romanzo italiano del Settecento: il caso Chiari.* Venice: Marsilio, 1997.

Kirkham, Victoria. *Fabulous Vernacular: Boccaccio's "Filocolo" and the Art of Medieval Fiction.* Ann Arbor, MI: University of Michigan Press, 2001.

Madrignani, Carlo A. *All'origine del romanzo in Italia: Il "celebre Abate Chiari."* Naples: Liguori, 2000.

Marini, Quinto. "La prosa narrativa." In *Storia della letteratura italiana*, vol. V: *La fine del Cinquecento e il Seicento.* Ed. Enrico Malato. Rome: Salerno Editrice, 1995.

Portinari, Folco, ed. *Romanzieri del Settecento.* 3 vols. Turin: UTET, 1988.

Varese, Claudio. "Il romanzo." In *Storia della letteratura italiana*, vol. V: *Il Seicento.* Ed. Emilio Cecchi and Natalino Sapegno. Milan: Garzanti, 1967, pp. 619–702.

3

OLGA RAGUSA

Alessandro Manzoni and developments in the historical novel

The nineteenth-century historical novel

Since the time of Napoleon's collapse, the historical novel has been an extremely popular genre. A type of narrative literature in prose, a fictional story set in a documented or documentable context which may also include actual persons who lived at the time, this genre has one foot in fact and the other in fiction, one in a kind of scholarship or erudition and the other in a kind of entertainment. Its purpose is to instruct and to divert. The heterogeneity of historical novels produced over time and in response to various audiences militates against a narratological, technical approach. The historical novel humanizes history and rediscovers land- and cityscapes.

In the history of Italian literature, historical fiction – whether in poetic and dramatic forms or in prose – preceded Manzoni's *I promessi sposi* (1827 and 1840). One can refer to Manzoni's own tragedies, *Il Conte di Carmagnola* (The Count of Carmagnola, 1820) and *Adelchi* (Adelchi, 1822), whose completion had been interrupted by the beginning of the novel, and to works originating in his Romantic circle in Milan: Tommaso Grossi's *Ildegonda* (Ildegonda, 1820) and *I Lombardi alla prima crociata* (The Lombards in the First Crusade, 1826), both set at the time of the Crusades; or *I profughi di Parga* (The Exiles of Parga, 1823) by Giovanni Berchet (1783–1851), set in Albania during the struggle between the Turks and the English. One might also cite the earlier *Platone in Italia* (Plato in Italy, 1804–6) by Vincenzo Cuoco (1770–1823), who imagines that he has found a manuscript in which the Greek philosopher reported on a trip to Italy in pre-Roman times; or Alessandro Verri's *Notti romane al sepolcro degli Scipioni*, a work indebted to the excavations that in 1780 brought to light two funerary inscriptions from the time of Scipio Africanus. But the interest of these works as antecedents of the nineteenth-century historical novel in Italian is to a large extent archaeological, for *I promessi sposi*, although in some respects a representative of its genre, is unique in terms of conception, achievement, and reception.

Upon publication in a three-volume edition, known as the *ventisettana* (that is, published in 1827), *I promessi sposi* was an immediate success, measurable in the large number of unauthorized reprintings throughout the as yet separate Italian states and in numerous translations. Its audience consisted not only of the reading public but of the many illiterates, both among the peasants and the middle classes, to whom it was read. Many of its characters – chief among them Don Abbondio – became proverbial. Many of its episodes refer to recurrent situations in real life in which the strong are pitted against the weak, the oppressors against the oppressed. A similar dynamic was at work during the many years that *I promessi sposi* was a required text in schools. Up to a generation or so ago, it was not unusual to find Italians able to recite from memory long passages from the most famous pages of the novel.

None of the great number of properly historical novels that followed *I promessi sposi* during the Risorgimento – the name given to the drive for national independence in nineteenth-century Italy – could be said to rival Manzoni's masterpiece, although they were tremendously popular and read well into the twentieth century. Only with *I Malavoglia* did a novel appear that eventually enjoyed a comparable prestige among literary historians. But Verga was a *verista*, an off-shoot of Zola and French naturalism and linguistically anti-Manzonian. Only in a very restricted meaning of the term historical novel (where history would be interpreted as "facts") could his works be considered historical. In the trajectory between the original historical novel by Manzoni and Verga are to be found the major developments of the genre: *Cento anni* (One Hundred Years, 1857–8) by Giuseppe Rovani (1818–74); and *Le confessioni di un ottuagenario* (The Confessions of an Octogenarian, 1867) by Ippolito Nievo, its title later restored to *Le confessioni di un italiano*, a change that suggested the exemplariness of its protagonist.

The uniqueness of *I promessi sposi*

The stature of Alessandro Manzoni as a literary and cultural force in nineteenth-century Italy, and the history of his extraordinary novel itself, examined in every detail by several generations of Italian scholars, have made *I promessi sposi* a canonical text on which critical discourse has never ceased. Writing from the perspective of a very different literary milieu than Manzoni's had been, the novelist Anna Banti (1895–1985) characterized Manzoni in 1959 as "no professional scribbler who chanced upon a means for making a living and gaining fame, but an intellectual and moral philosopher, by vocation a historian, who devoted more or less his whole life to *I promessi sposi*, a work he continued to consider irrational and incoherent, neither fish nor fowl."[1] Manzoni was characterized by a restless intellectual curiosity, a highly developed critical faculty, and a rationalist pursuit of truth to the very threshold of the certitudes of revealed faith. He experienced personally the transition from the Enlightenment to romanticism when he lived in Paris between 1805 and 1810. As he matured, his ability to compare and contrast, to draw conclusions from examined facts and to assert these conclusions, not to speak of the persistence with which he sought to resolve his doubts, refined his intuitions and corrected, modified, and implemented the expression of his convictions. These experiences reinforced the originality of his thinking, making him very much aware of the difficulty in gaining consensus for what is truly new rather than a superficial novelty. As a result, Manzoni's representation of the historical novel in Italy came into being "fully armed" – that is, equipped with the tools for its own analysis. In a letter Manzoni wrote to his French correspondent, Claude Fauriel on 29 May 1822, Manzoni remarks that his own introduction to the novel he was then in the act of writing might well stop at that very point in the composition, since Manzoni believed everything critics might ever have to say about the novel was already contained in that part of it.

The process that led to the refinement of Manzoni's narrative techniques and to the conquest of the subject matter of his novel was a long one. It cannot be adequately described by invoking the concepts of influence and imitation, although contemporaneous cultural and intellectual developments played an important part. Neither Manzoni's acquaintance with the novels of Sir Walter Scott nor his participation in the discussions about romanticism in the wake of Mme de Staël's 1816 article, "Sulla maniera e l'utilità delle traduzioni," can be cited as the "origin" of his own historical novel, whose first draft dates from 14 April 1822. Manzoni had begun writing poetry at school as part of instruction in versification. On his own, he read Giuseppe Parini (1729–99), Vittorio Alfieri (1749–1803), and Vincenzo Monti (1754–1828). His youthful production was typical for the time, although there are traces in it of a more personal and reflective bent than in the usual neoclassical poetry of the day. He moved to Paris in 1805 to be with his mother, whose long-time companion Carlo Imbonati, a member of the enlightened Milanese aristocracy, had died. Through his mother he met the group of the *idéologues*, anti-Napoleonic heirs of the Enlightenment in France and survivors of the Revolution. From them, Manzoni derived

---

[1] Anna Banti, *Opinioni* (Milan: Il Saggiatore, 1961), pp. 189–90 (author's translation).

his empiricism, his logical rigor, and his model for a new kind of historical writing combining the best of the strict factualism of the scholarship of Lodovico Antonio Muratori (1672–1750) and the interpretive sweep of the historical philosophy of Giambattista Vico (1668–1744). But the most important event of the Paris years, not only in personal terms but for the direction his later work was to take, was his religious conversion following his marriage to the Swiss Enrichetta Blondel (1791–1833). Her conversion from Calvinism to Catholicism was accompanied by his own return to religious practice with what has been perceived as its distinctive Jansenist slant and coloring, derived from the seventeenth-century theological movement centered in France at Port-Royal and important for its doctrinal content but also for its association with Racine and Pascal. Almost concurrent was a literary "conversion," foreshadowed by his growing impatience with new versions of pastoral poetry and updated invocations of the Muses. His first *inno sacro* (sacred hymn) with Christian subject matter and in a new poetic form dates from 1812, while his first *canzone civile* (ode on a contemporary political event), known as "Aprile 1814" ("April 1814") was written after the fall of Napoleon and just before the Austrian invasion of 1815.

The circumstances of his life and the works referred to established the range of Manzoni's intellectual contacts and his readiness to abandon one form of expression for another under the impact of new suggestions. Manzoni did not live in an ivory tower but was at all times engaged in a collective cultural project such as he had become acquainted with in France. In the *sala rossa* ("red parlor") of his home in Milan, the ultra-Romantic circle of that city congregated. Through Manzoni's far-flung correspondence, of which the exchanges with Claude Fauriel provide the best insights into his work-in-progress, he communicated with the European literary world. An observation by Emilio Cecchi (1884–1966) comes to mind:

> Aside from much else, the exceptional, in a certain sense unique, nature of a novel such as *I promessi sposi* is also the result of this: that its genesis and elaboration seem – I say seem – to do without those conditions of solitude, mystery, freedom and complete inner isolation that would appear to be indispensable for the creation of a work of art. From 1820 to 1840 Manzoni seems to have worked *in public* with a crowd of advisers, referees, etc.[2]

Cecchi's comment goes a long way to explaining why works begun, completed, or left unfinished during this period (1820–40), being roughly the years from conception to final edition, create an interrelated whole, none

---

[2] Cited from Emilio Cecchi's *Taccuini* (Milan: Mondadori, 1976), p. 603 (author's translation).

completely independent of the others. At the same time, the form taken by *I promessi sposi*, with its third-person omniscient narrator framed by the fiction of a rediscovered manuscript, gave Manzoni uncommon flexibility in a democratic technique of communication that invites the reader's collaboration in establishing its meaning and gaining assent from his audience.

I promessi sposi: theoretical questions, characters, plot, setting, and meaning

In his "Lettre à M. Chauvet sur l'unité de temps et de lieu dans la tragédie" ("Letter to Monsieur Chauvet on the Unity of Time and Place in Tragedy"), published together with Fauriel's translation of Manzoni's tragedies that appeared in the French capital in 1823, Manzoni distinguishes between the domain of the poet and that of the historian with an impassioned definition of what poetry (that is, invention) can add to facts, without sinking to the level of the *romanesque* (the invention of "historical" facts) from which he at all times distanced himself. If history gives us events, what men have done as seen from the outside, the poet adds what they thought and felt, the measure of the success or failure of their projects, and even the words that revealed their passions and will. Manzoni declared "All that is strong or mysterious in human desire, religious and deep in misfortune, the poet can guess; or, better, perceive, comprehend and give back." Manzoni's exceptionally strong awareness of the difference between reality and fiction or, in his terms, truth and verisimilitude, is a leitmotif in his thinking on problems of aesthetics until the contrast became irreconcilable in *Del romanzo storico* (published in 1850 but already begun in 1827). At the time of *I promessi sposi*, however, the complexities inherent in the very term "historical novel" (a "mixed" genre for classicist poetics, precisely because of the coming together of fact and fiction) were overlooked.

I promessi sposi has a frequently omitted subtitle: "A Milanese Tale of the Seventeenth Century Discovered and Made Over by Alessandro Manzoni." It hints at the theoretical impasse previously mentioned, while at the same time capitalizing on the double meaning of the Italian word *storia*: "tale" as well as "history." And in an almost perfect reversal, the title of the novel's companion piece, *Storia della colonna infame* (*The Column of Infamy*, 1842), restores the meaning of "history" in designating the long digression Manzoni felt coming to him "on the tip of his pen," as he put it, while at work on the episode of the plague of 1630 in the first version of *I promessi sposi*, known as *Fermo e Lucia*.[3] The column in question once stood as a reminder

---

[3] See Olga Ragusa, "Due digressioni: Ancora sull'unità dei *Promessi Sposi*," *Forum Italicum* 19 (1985), pp. 284–97.

and a warning on the site where the unjustly accused, tortured, and executed *untori* (spreaders of the plague) had lived. It had been demolished only after the publication of *Dei delitti e delle pene* (*Of Crimes and Punishments*, 1764) by Cesare Beccaria (1738–94) and *Osservazioni sulla giustizia* (Observations on Justice, 1777) by Pietro Verri had brought about dramatic reform in criminal legislation. Manzoni was not so much interested in legislation, although he quotes the laws at length. Instead, he focuses upon the motives and feelings of the judges in a miscarriage of justice that was historically avoidable. The *Storia della colonna infame*, first published as the final installments of the 1840–2 edition of *I promessi sposi* but omitted from almost all later translations or editions (in particular, those for school use), has an intimate relationship to Manzoni's conception of the historical novel as giving new life to the "obscure actors" of history, both individuals who actually existed and those "invented" by the author. It reinforces his conviction that literature must serve the common good by examining "the desires, the fears, the suffering, the general condition of that immense number of men who had no active part in the events, but who felt their consequence . . . an immense multitude of men . . . that passes on earth, its earth, unobserved, without leaving a trace." This important statement is to be found in one of Manzoni's preparatory works for *I promessi sposi*, the *Discorso su alcuni punti della storia longobardica in Italia* (Essay on Some Points of the History of the Lombards in Italy, 1822), a work that contains a description of the Lombard nation at war with Charlemagne.

The action of *I promessi sposi* is set in motion by an obstacle placed in the way of a marriage slated to occur the following day, and finds its closure when the obstruction is removed and the marriage is celebrated. Thus, it is not the typical love story ending in tragedy but a love story leading to the cares and pleasures of the every-day. Renzo (originally named Fermo in Manzoni's first draft) and Lucia, the parish priest Don Abbondio, Lucia's mother Agnese, and Don Abbondio's servant Perpetua no doubt belong to the "familiar characters" Manzoni pulled out of his desk drawer every morning, as he was to tell one of his sons-in-law many years later, setting them before him "like so many puppets" and writing down what they did and said. Together with a host of others, named and nameless, speakers or walk-ons, they belong to the village-life setting on the shores of Lake Como in the early part of the novel. A different category of characters, still belonging to the same apparently idyllic region, is represented by Padre Cristoforo (whose biographical sketch is based on the life of Saint Francis of Assisi) and Don Rodrigo (an evil figure from Gothic fiction), known locally more for his shoddy deeds than for any personal achievements as a member of the Spanish ruling class. Padre Cristoforo and Don Rodrigo represent respectively the defender of the humble and the exploiter of the weak. To a still different social order belong the Cardinal Federigo Borromeo (1564–1631) and the Innominato (the "Nameless One"): this latter character is granted the divine grace of conversion from evil-doing to good through his meeting with Lucia ("giver of light"). In this group should also be placed Gertrude, the nun of Monza, whose unhappy fate as youngest child of an unidentified prince leads to a life of sin, including complicity in murder.

Interaction between the characters would not in itself have required an elaborate historical setting. Plot and psychology could have sufficed. Nor would the fact that the characters belonged to different social classes, each with its own function and mode of expression, have of necessity contributed to the linguistic revision known as the *risciacquatura in Arno*, the "rinsing out" by Manzoni during the late summer of 1827 of his story in the Florentine idiom that was on its way to becoming the standard literary language of a united Italy. In his 29 May 1822 letter to Fauriel, Manzoni had already described the subject of the novel in whose writing he was immersed, not in terms of characters and plot but in terms of the setting as recorded in "the documents that remain to us of that epoch." One of these documents was Giuseppe Ripamonti's seventeenth-century *Storia di Milano* (History of Milan), where a passage concerned the laws against the criminal activities of the *bravi* (hired henchmen of local lords) – including interference with marriage, the kind of crime that opens Manzoni's novel. A frequently repeated comment on *I promessi sposi* implies that Manzoni chose the setting of Milan under its long Spanish domination (1559–1748) in support of the anti-Austrian conspiracies common in the Lombardy of the Restoration, as well as to make a statement of support in defense of the independence movement of the Risorgimento. There is no question that Manzoni was a patriot, convinced that the future of Italy lay in national unity. But the specific historical setting of his work (1628–31) was chosen primarily because the apex of the historical action coincided with a situation in which human motivations and responses could be portrayed and judged – as though in a scientific experiment – in an extreme moment of crisis: "finally a plague which offered room for the exercise of the most accomplished and shameless wickedness, the most absurd prejudices, and the most touching virtues etc. etc... there is enough to fill a canvas."

In the novel, the historical action makes its first appearance in Don Abbondio's encounter with the *bravi*, in the evidence of hard times in chapter III (Fra Galdino's request for alms), and more emphatically in chapter IV (the landscape of human suffering through which Padre Cristoforo hurries on his way to the house of Agnese and Lucia). Historical action reappears, slightly expanded, in the second major narrative sequence of the novel (chapters XI–XVII). Here, Manzoni describes Renzo's adventures in Milan in the midst of a bread riot brought about by the short-sighted measures of the Milanese Grand Chancellor Ferrer during the Thirty Years War and the siege of Casale. The historical action is almost completely absent (except for the presence of Cardinal Federigo) in the chapters that free Lucia from Don Rodrigo as a result of the great spiritual (and therefore suprahistorical) crisis experienced by the sinister character known as the Innominato, while history erupts with full force once again into the narrative with the return to the war over the capture of two outposts, east and west on the border of the Duchy of Milan, in chapter XXVII. The war brings the greater evil, the plague, in its wake, and it is the plague that leads to the *dénouement*: the death of Don Rodrigo and Padre Cristoforo, the reunion of Renzo and Lucia, and the torrential rain that providentially puts an end to the pestilence. This plague cut the population of Milan in half, but it also provided Manzoni with the occasion to compose some unforgettable pages. Critics have always praised his description of the *monatti*, men entrusted with the burial of the dead in the decimated city, as well as the episode concerning the mother of the dead child Cecilia (chapter XXXIV).

The final formulation of the judgments expressed and implied throughout the novel on private and public decisions, on the motives and rationalizations, the impulses and the reflections of the actors, single and collective, is entrusted to the illiterate Lucia and contains the "moral of the tale." She counters Renzo's summary of what he has learned from experience with her own, and while his list is made up of the recollection of discrete episodes, each with its separate and practical lessons learned, she is able to generalize, to rise to a different level of understanding, from the particular to the universal. And whereas in fusing with his character in the novel's great lyric page "Addio, monti" ("Farewell, mountains," chapter VIII), Manzoni had lent *his* language to Lucia, so now the same omniscient author accepts *her* mode of expression: "troubles often come to those who ask for them, but the most cautious and innocent life is not sufficient to keep them away; and when they come, through one's fault or without, trust in God moderates them, and makes them useful for a better life." The sentiment is close to that expressed by the author to the "invented character" at the beginning of the second volume of *Fermo e Lucia*, an imaginary interlocutor who provided Manzoni with a built-in critic of his own modus operandi. The "invented character" had questioned Manzoni's reluctance to portray passionate, romantic love in describing Renzo's separations from Lucia in a manner so "dry, undernourished, succinct," so matter-of-fact. The defense had been two-pronged. On the one hand, Manzoni invoked the power of understatement, of a technique that Proust would later refer to as *raturer à l'avance* ("to erase beforehand") and that Lampedusa would recognize in the sentence "La sventurata rispose" ("The unfortunate woman replied"), the sentence that Manzoni employs in chapter X to cut short Gertrude's intrigue with her seducer Egidio. On the other hand, he defended the ethical purpose of literature, that of fulfilling a more useful social function than serving an author's popularity or providing entertainment for frivolous readers. But at the very end of the novel Manzoni has done with reasoning; his message stands, and with a bow to the audience he joins together the recorder and the rewriter of the tale in a low-key appeal in favor of the individual conscience guided by the long tradition of Western Christianity in the never-ending battle against the forces of destruction and degradation.

Historical novels of the Risorgimento

In typical novels of the Risorgimento the regeneration of Italy takes precedence over literary discussions, and the recovery of the past, nourished by documentation, serves the political passions of the moment. Such novels have been variously classified. But one generalization needs to be made of them all: nowhere in the work of the historical novelists who follow Manzoni in the nineteenth century do we find a narrative complexity, a critical self-awareness to the universal function of literature, a constructive intelligence, or the kind of irony comparable to those found in *I promessi sposi*.

Francesco Domenico Guerrazzi was a Tuscan from Livorno, a center of radical politics. The two historical novels for which he is remembered were incidents in a busy life as a man of letters engaged in public issues, including prison terms for incitement to rebellion and a short term in office in the government of Tuscany. *La battaglia di Benevento* (*Manfred, or The Battle of Benevento*, 1827), dealing with the thirteenth-century struggle between imperial and papal power in southern Italy, is closer to Lord Byron's kind of romanticism than to Manzoni's – emphatic and exaggerated in style rather than down-to-earth and analytical. *L'assedio di Firenze* (The Siege of Florence, 1836) is set during the siege of the city in 1530, which put an end to republican aspirations and reestablished the domination of the Medicis. Fictional characters and historical figures hold the stage, and the author echoes Mazzini's republican ideas on the Unification of Italy. Guerrazzi's identification with the background is so pervasive that his prose acquires a strong Renaissance patina – an excellent example of what some traditionalists might have preferred to find in *I promessi sposi*.

The novels of Tommaso Grossi and Cesare Cantù (1804–95) stand in sharp contrast to Guerrazzi's works. Grossi and Cantù were both born on the shores of Lake Como. Grossi became such a close friend of Manzoni that for many years he lived at his house and his literary career, from dialect poetry in Milanese through the genres of the verse *novella* and the epic poem to the historical novel *Marco Visconti* (*Marco Visconti, a Romance of the Fourteenth Century*, 1834), followed closely in the steps of Manzoni. This novel is set in fourteenth-century Lombardy and is based on chronicles of the period. A complicated love story is intertwined with familiar historical events: the struggle between Papacy and Empire, the invasion of Lombardy, the siege of Milan. Its landscapes and descriptions are reminiscent of Manzoni's. Grossi's exceptional popularity led to his novels being turned more than once into operas. Cantù was an extremely prolific political and literary historian, author of a history of the city and diocese of Como (1829–31), of a commentary on *I promessi sposi*, and of a fundamental work of historical popularization, the thirty-five-volume *Storia universale* (Universal History, 1838–46). His novel *Margherita Pusterla* (Margherita Pusterla, 1838) was composed while its author was in prison. The book's villain is Luchino Visconti, brother and successor of Marco Visconti (the protagonist of one of Grossi's novels), who is bent on seducing the virtuous wife of one of his wealthiest and most powerful subjects. This book is crowded with subsidiary plots, scenes of violence, and pathos, and remained in print until well into the twentieth century.

The Piedmontese Massimo D'Azeglio, son of Cesare D'Azeglio – the individual to whom Manzoni had addressed his "Lettera sul romanticismo" ("Letter on Romanticism," 1823) and later husband of one of Manzoni's daughters – had spent his early years in Rome and his life there as an artist in the 1820s had turned him into a notable painter of historical subjects. His novel *Ettore Fieramosca o la disfida di Barletta* (*Ettore Fieramosca or the Challenge of Barletta*, 1830) was preceded by a painting on the same subject: the challenge in 1503 made by thirteen Italian knights in the service of Spain to a like number of Frenchmen during the war between those two countries for control of southern Italy. The pictorial origin, albeit complemented by historical research contributed by D'Azeglio's cousin Cesare Balbo, no doubt accounts for the vivacity of its all-action narrative, while the modern, Manzonian Italian in which it is written gives it a freshness that most other historical novels of the time lack. *Niccolò de' Lapi* (*Niccolò dei Lapi*, 1841) has a more bookish origin, going back to the same siege of Florence that had been Guerrazzi's subject, this time with emphasis on the enmity between the followers of the religious reformer, the monk Girolamo Savonarola (1452–98), and those of the Medicis.

By moving the setting of the historical novel closer to the reader's present, Giuseppe Rovani and Ippolito Nievo belong to a different moment in the development of the genre, although they keep the Italian historical novel's basic ideological thrust intact. But the tension between history and invention, fact and fiction, is so different in Rovani and in Nievo that the usual joining of these two names in surveys throws into relief the contrast between the backward-looking Rovani and the forward-looking Nievo. Rovani became a leading protagonist in Milan's cultural life after his return from fighting in the First War for Italian Independence (1848–9). In 1857, the first installment of his major work, *Cento anni* began to appear and received its definitive edition in 1868–9. It is still a recognizably historical novel, although some of its features are those of what would later be called "un romanzo al passato" ("novel with a touch of the past") – a work that did not attempt to reconstruct a distant past as an example of daring and valor for the present, but a story in which the past simply plays a role. The hundred years are those from the beginning of the Enlightenment in Milan (1748) to the birth of the modern city as the commercial and publishing capital of a new and recently unified Italian nation. The fictional structure of *Cento anni* is a plot centered on a will stolen in 1750 and traces the original protagonists and their descendants through several generations down to the siege of Rome in 1849. In some respects, *Cento anni* could be considered popular rather than serious literature, but it succeeds in holding the reader's attention as a kind of tourist's guide to Milan's historical center and is full of factual information and curious anecdotes about the landmarks in and around the center of the city where its action takes place.

Nievo's premature death not only cut short a literary career but also impeded a more vigorous after-life for his work. Even today, he continues to hover between the designations of "major" and "minor" writer, seen as either the complex and original artist he was or as the emblematic Risorgimento "poet soldier" lost at sea on his return from Garibaldi's expedition to Sicily in 1861. *Le confessioni di un italiano* are the memoirs of the fictional Carlo Altoviti, who summarizes the meaning of life in his first sentence in terms of the traditional historiographical perspective of the many "little" Italies followed by the united nation: "I was born a Venetian on 18 October 1775, the Day of Saint Luke the Evangelist and I shall die, by the Grace of God an Italian, when the Providence that mysteriously controls our world shall ordain it." Born in Padua and educated at its university, Nievo through his maternal grandfather knew the Venetian countryside in his childhood. It is there at the Castello di Colloredo in the Friuli that he became acquainted with the still feudal life that he later transferred to the Castle of Fratta in the justly celebrated early sections of his novel, especially the famous description of its cavernous kitchen. From that vantage point, Carlo Altoviti experiences Napoleon's betrayal of Venice with the Treaty of Campoformio (1797) and the first disturbances that eventually culminate in the Italian Wars of Liberation. As in Foscolo's earlier *Le ultime lettere di Jacopo Ortis*, Nievo intertwines a love story with his depiction of political events. Its female protagonist, Altoviti's cousin La Pisana, with whom Carlo grew up, later shares many of his adventures up and down the Italian peninsula from Naples and the Abbruzzi to Genoa, and even follows him into exile in London. She is an unparalleled heroine in Italian literature, at once capricious and sentimental, impulsive and constant, and she exudes an aura of eighteenth-century amorality that does not diminish either the young author's confident optimism or his octogenarian alter ego's trust in Providence. At the end of the book, narrated time and the time of narrating converge to cancel out the distance that at the beginning of the evolution of the genre had seemed a stumbling block. When the book was published posthumously in 1867, it was initially given a new title of *Le confessioni di un ottuagenario* in order to undercut any obvious identification with the Risorgimento. The fascination of Nievo as a writer with a tragic destiny survived into the twentieth century when a descendant of his, Stanislao Nievo, wrote a sequel not to *Le confessioni* but to Nievo's life entitled *Il prato in fondo al mare* (The Meadow at the Bottom of the Sea, 1974). This book is an unusual historical novel, inspired by the deep-sea search for the boat that should have brought Nievo back from Sicily and whose wreck, still visible when divers find it, crumbles into nothingness when it is touched.

The past in the Italian novel

The Risorgimento was to continue to engage historical interest and provide literary subject matter after its political objective was achieved, especially in the outlying areas where regional differences were most pronounced. In the latter half of the nineteenth century, the historical novel seemed to lose critical prestige and public popularity. The key to the past was no longer written documents but, rather, first-hand observation and personal memoirs. This tendency may be found in the novels of Antonio Fogazzaro, Giuseppe Giacosa (1847–1906), Giovanni Verga, Federico De Roberto, and Luigi Pirandello. Fogazzaro's *Piccolo mondo antico*, a novel treating the period 1848–95 on the shore of Lake Lugano between Austria and Lombardy, De Roberto's *I vicerè*, a masterpiece set in Catania among the Spanish nobility progressively displaced in the second half of the nineteenth century, Verga's cycle of novels about defeated protagonists (some published, others only planned but never written), and Pirandello's *I vecchi e i giovani* (The Old and the Young, 1913) are all usually subsumed under other headings for critical discussions, such as naturalism or decadent literature, and this critical commonplace underscores the differences between historical novels in the nineteenth and twentieth centuries rather than focusing upon their underlying continuity. But such works do deal with generic historical topics experienced through the lives of their authors.

If the historical novel seems to decline around the turn of the century, it descends into a virtual critical abyss after World World II with the rise of neorealism. It was into this climate of opinion, hostile to the historical novel itself and marked by constant laments of the "death" of the novel, that the immediate and phenomenal international success of *Il Gattopardo* by Giuseppe Tomasi di Lampedusa burst like an explosion. The deep change in Italian intellectual and political life brought about by the Unification of Italy stands in sharper focus from a comparison between the circumstances that accompanied the production and reception of what are widely considered Italy's two historical novels par excellence: *I promessi sposi* and *Il Gattopardo*. The uniqueness of *I promessi sposi* is paralleled by the singularity of *Il Gattopardo*, a novel that differs from *I promessi sposi* in so many respects that it could perhaps even be called nonhistorical.

The singularity of *Il Gattopardo*

Like *Le confessioni di un italiano*, *Il Gattopardo* was published posthumously. But while at his death at the age of thirty Nievo already enjoyed a literary identity, if not a literary career, at the age of sixty-two Lampedusa had neither. Of the book that won the Strega Prize for the novel in 1959, the general public knew only what it learned from the preface contributed by Giorgio Bassani (1916–2000), who had recommended the book's publication solely on the basis of its aesthetic merits. Its readers were doubtless also aware of the avalanche of discussions appearing in newspapers and periodicals, and driven by opposing ideological positions: the book was denounced as "reactionary" (a *romanzo antistorico*, an "antihistorical novel," as a later formulation would have it); others praised it as "revolutionary" (for example, the French Communist writer Louis Aragon). The singularity of *Il Gattopardo* lies precisely in this: that contrary to what is often the case and was certainly so with respect to *I promessi sposi*, *Il Gattopardo* was not conceived in a circumscribed, professionally recognizable literary environment which would have left its own imprint and facilitated acceptance of the work in a definite and definable classification and tradition. Instead, it appeared suddenly and shockingly, revealing to most Italians, who believed that the aristocracy had disappeared as a class after World War II, that members of the class represented by Lampedusa were still alive. The novel thus served as a testimonial to a forgotten sociohistorical reality, and this trait relates it to the many biographies and autobiographies, memoirs and confessions, reevocations of past circumstances and experiences, and sometimes the mere presence of local color that invaded the space of narrative in the latter part of the twentieth century.

Lampedusa began writing *Il Gattopardo* late in 1954, and its composition reflected an extraordinary literary culture based on the author's lifetime of reading, particularly the classic novels of France and England. When it was first published and became an international best-seller (the first real international best-seller in the history of Italian literature), *Il Gattopardo* was classified at once as a historical novel pure and simple, a judgment underscored by the fact that it appeared in the midst of the celebrations of the anniversary of Italy's Unification, with the backward and forward glances that such an occasion fosters. But how and to what extent can *Il Gattopardo* be considered a historical novel in the traditional sense? It has many of the trappings of the genre, the most obvious its insistence on a firm chronological framework. Each of its eight parts – not chapters, thus emphasizing its episodic rather than epic character – is marked by a date. The time span goes from May 1860 to May 1910, from Garibaldi's landing at Marsala to the end of the history of the protagonist's family, when the stuffed and motheaten body of the protagonist's dog is thrown on the garbage heap, recalling for a brief instant the heraldic figure on the coat-of-arms of the noble Salina family, now only a footnote to history.

Lampedusa's larger-than-life protagonist, whose step made the floor tremble, Don Fabrizio Corbera, the Prince of Salina, is modeled on Lampedusa's own great-grandfather, Giulio Fabrizio (1815–85), by avocation an astronomer, liege to Ferdinand II, last ruler of the Kingdom of the Two Sicilies. The identification of author and character is unusually strong for a third-person narrative such as this. It is almost as though Lampedusa had read himself *into* Don Fabrizio rather than adopting a more objective point of view. It is not surprising that, like Manzoni, Lampedusa should have interrupted his writing early in the process to seek additional documentation. Manzoni did so to study the plague and its consequences for the Lombardy of the seventeenth century during the Thirty Years War. Lampedusa completed research on his own family's history that reached back to the almost legendary times of the Byzantine Empire. While the actual lives of author and character in terms of historical period, family situation, interests, and associations are significantly different, they are linked by a consonance in attitude toward existence itself. Author and protagonist alike share the same values: they experience the inevitability of change as loss; their attitude about what life has to offer reflects a tolerant disenchantment; and, finally, they view their existence as a balance sheet in which the number of joyful hours are infinitesimally small in contrast to a lifetime's many years of tedium and unhappiness.

Neither Lampedusa nor Don Fabrizio can be called Sicilian separatists aspiring to regional autonomy. Lampedusa's concerns are not social institutions or the workings of government but the daily realities of social life as determined ultimately by class rather than economics. In this respect, parts II–IV of the novel are of fundamental importance and go well beyond personal memory toward the construction of a symbolic microcosm. In the subtle changes that the establishment of a new form of government had brought about, the foundation is laid for the marriage between Don Fabrizio's nephew Tancredi and Don Calogero Sedàra's beautiful daughter Angelica. As the marriage takes place, the new republic begins to erode the promise of egalitarian democracy in an election rigged by the same Don Calogero, now mayor of the town of Donnafugata, once the prince's feudal residence. Don Fabrizio's refusal to become a senator in the Kingdom of Sardinia (successor to the Kingdom of the Two Sicilies) seals his withdrawal from the contingent world of politics, a realm described by Tancredi's cynical credo that also implicitly presents Lampedusa's devastating judgment upon the failed aspirations of the Risorgimento: "If we want everything to remain as it is, everything must change." As his world is changing, Don Fabrizio cannot adapt to it as his corrupt nephew Tancredi easily can, and he prepares to meet his death with a sense of relief.

We cannot know, of course, whether Lampedusa's death corresponded to the one he imagined for Don Fabrizio. But the fact that such a question can arise allows a further insight into *Il Gattopardo*'s singularity, and accounts for the work's exceptional after-life, not in terms of numbers of copies sold, but in terms of the kind of interest it elicited outside the strictly literary-critical ones. In the final analysis, the book's significance lies beyond the recovery of a forgotten area of Italy's past and consists of its remarkable ability to portray irrecoverable loss.

The continuation of the historical novel in contemporary literature

History, real and often imagined, has provided an inexhaustible fund of subject matter in the latter half of the twentieth century. The historical genre has become fashionable, spawning biographies, collections of correspondence, diaries, documents, memoirs, the confessions of more or less significant figures from the past, and works of historical popularization. While the critical profile of historical novelists in the recent past remains to be written definitively, a number of significant figures continue to work in this literary genre.

Fulvio Tomizza (1935–97) was born in Giurizzani, one of the villages of the parish of Materada in Istria, at a time when this mountainous peninsula with its ethnically mixed population was part of Italy. The years between 1947 and 1954 saw the exodus of half a million Italians from the area, among them Tomizza's family. This traumatic experience became a dominant element in his fictional and later fictionalized-historical retelling of the fate of his people. *Trilogia istriana* (Istrian Trilogy, 1967) – consisting of *Materada* (Materada, 1960); *La ragazza di Petrovia* (The Girl of Petrovia, 1963); and *Il bosco delle acacie* (The Wood of the Acacia Trees, 1966) – deals with the postwar destiny of innocent victims uprooted from their homes in order to satisfy the geopolitical schemes of the major world powers. *La miglior vita* (The Better Life, 1977) intertwines political history with the humble events in the lives of a rural population watched over by a succession of parish priests from the beginning of the century to the 1970s. The research that went into that book, coupled with the impact of Carlo Ginzburg's *Il formaggio e i vermi* (*The Cheese and the Worms*, 1976), led to a series of documented novels on the infiltration of Protestantism into the peasant culture of northeastern Italy at the time of the Inquisition: *La finzione di Maria* (Mary's Pretense, 1981); *Il male viene dal nord* (Evil Comes from the North, 1984); *Quando Dio uscì di chiesa* (When God Abandoned the Church, 1987); and *Fughe incrociate* (Intertwined Flights, 1990). Tomizza's last novel, *Franziska* (Franziska, 1997), describes a love story between a Slovenian girl and an Italian officer, separated by their ethnic cultural differences that remind the reader of similar cultural and ethnic conflicts not only in Italy but all over Europe.

Lalla Romano (1906–2001), at the other extreme of northern Italy, was born in Demonte (Cuneo), a western alpine center, which has become the setting for her minimalist novels: *Maria* (Mary, 1953); *Il tetto murato* (The Walled-Up Roof, 1957); *La penombra che abbiamo attraversato* (The Darkness that We Crossed, 1964); and, most recently, the collection of jottings entitled *Dall'ombra* (From the Shade, 1999). In all of these works, memory rather than documents provides the medium through which the past is imaginatively recovered by invention. The result often makes the past present where everyday happenings take the place of plotted continuities. This kind of historical view succeeds in erasing the feeling of estrangement from forgotten ways of being with which today's reader must come to terms, unblocking the perennially obstructing present that stands in the way of a more inclusive, tolerant understanding.

Isabella Bossi Fedrigotti (1948–), born in Rovereto in the border region that was Austrian until 1919 and then became, with varying fortunes, Italian, draws upon her family history for a look back into the distant past.

Landscape, buildings, and artifacts, perhaps even more than memory, are inscribed with the characteristic European past of man's steady activity. Her first novel, *Amore mio uccidi Garibaldi* (My Love, Kill Garibaldi, 1980) derives its title from her great-grandmother's wish that her husband, Federigo, hussar in the Austrian army during the 1866 campaign for the "liberation" of the Trentino from Austria, should succeed in defeating Garibaldi so that he can return home safely to her. This is history seen "from the other side," and it is built on letters, portraits, and stories heard in childhood that reveal the human rather than the political side of events. An intimate family story stands opposed to the official, nationalist historiography of the Italian Risorgimento. The same point of view and compositional strategy can be found in later novels by Fedrigotti, including: *Casa di guerra* (The House of War, 1983); *Diario di una dama di corte* (The Diary of a Lady at Court, 1984); and *Di buona famiglia* (From a Good Family, 1991), although their subject matter is more intimate and less dramatic than her first work.

Alberto Vigevani (1918–2000) was born into a comfortable professional Jewish family with an extended circle of friends and relatives in the rest of Europe. He wrote a number of historical novels, including *Il grembiule rosso* (The Red Apron, 1975); *La Lucia dei giardini* (Lucia of the Gardens, 1977); *Un'educazione borghese* (A Middle-Class Education, 1987); *La casa perduta* (The Lost House, 1989); and *Milano ancora ieri* (Milan Even Yesterday, 1996). His books form a *Bildungsroman*: successive chapters in the history of an "education" that includes his father's industrious world of Milanese business in the great period of bourgeois expansion at the turn of the century, remembered friendships, the beginning of his passion for reading the adventure stories of the "Italian Jules Verne," Emilio Salgari (1862–1911), and, finally, his sense of exclusion and difference but also deep belonging to the "places" of his life reminiscent of a literary culture steeped in readings of Marcel Proust. Beyond the paper world of words, however, the "real" (factual, historical) world beckons in Vigevani, inviting the reader to walk down the occasionally quiet, solid, sleepy streets tucked away in European metropolises, be they Paris, London, or Milan. It is indicative of the oversights that occur in the breathless whirl of contemporary publishing that a small masterpiece like Vigevani's story, "Lettera al signor Alzheryan" ("Letter to Mr. Alzheryan") – an imaginary letter addressed to his godfather, a member of the Berlin Jewish community, who upon his death shortly before the advent of Hitler had left his property to that community – should have failed to enter the international canon of fiction devoted to the European Holocaust.

Other less well-known writers of historical novels can be mentioned. The presence of the Middle Ages is evident in Umberto Eco's *Il nome della rosa*

(1980 – treated in another chapter); in *L'invenzione della verità* (The Invention of the Truth, 1988) by Marta Morazzoni (1950–); or in *I dodici abati di Challant* (The Twelve Abbots of Challant, 1981) by Laura Mancinelli (1933–). Other writers place their works in postmedieval settings: *I fuochi del Basento* (The Fires of Basento, 1987) by Raffaele Nigro (1947–) takes place in southeastern Italy between 1784 and 1861; *Cercando l'imperatore* (Looking for the Emperor, 1985) by Roberto Pazzi (1946–) is set in the Russian Revolution and is described as "a philosophical novel masked as an historical one." *Il bastardo ovvero Gli amori, i travagli e le lacrime di Don Emanuel di Savoia* (The Bastard, or the Loves, Travails, and Tears of Don Emanuel of Savoy, 1996), by Gina Lagoria (1922–) portrays an illegitimate historical figure who nevertheless belongs to the class of princes and potentates that Manzoni refused to privilege in his novel, while in Melania G. Mazzucco's *La camera di Balthus* (The Room of Balthus, 1998), different historical periods intersect in "time reversible like a typewriter ribbon," as the book's epigraph from Montale states.

The fact of the matter is that the new millennium has brought with it, after a century of failed "futures," a veritable obsession with the "past" in Italian narrative. Three examples can be cited to underline the historical richness of fiction at the present time: *Un amore inconveniente* (An Inconvenient Love, 1999) by Angela Bianchini (1921–); *L'ombra della luna* (The Shadow of the Moon, 1999) by Elisabetta Rasy (1947–); and *Il mio nome a memoria* (My Name By Heart, 2000) by Giorgio van Straten (1955–). Bianchini's novel recounts an "unsuitable" marriage between an assimilated Italian Jew and an Aryan woman of doubtful social and national descent, and the story goes from pre-World War I Italy to the period after World War II. Rasy's work presents an imaginative retelling of Mary Wollstonecraft's life in revolutionary and postrevolutionary France and of her affair with the American businessman Gilbert Imlay, father of her daughter Fanny. Its theme is the emancipation of women and follows a household servant in France who is last encountered on her way to becoming the headmistress of a school for girls in England. Van Straten's novel may well be the most ambitious and the most "historical" of these three recent and exemplary historical works of fiction. It narrates the history of the van Straten family, descendants of Hartog, son of Alexander, who took a Christian surname in 1811 during the reign of Louis Bonaparte, King of Holland, emancipator of the Jews. Giorgio is the last of his family to appear on the genealogical table that spreads across the back of the front cover and the end paper of the book. The last episode of the epilogue is dated Florence 1999: "I am the stories that I have told, the slow progress of a name. Men and women whom I never met. I am something of their faces and their hands. Small gestures, thoughts.

Survivals in the recesses of time."[4] This is a passage Manzoni could never have written, and its tone underlines just how the historical novel has evolved in Italy since the nineteenth century.

Further reading

Chandler, S. Bernard. *Manzoni: The Story of a Spiritual Quest.* Edinburgh: Edinburgh University Press, 1974.

Ciccarelli, Andrea. *Manzoni: la coscienza della letteratura.* Rome: Bulzoni, 1996.

Della Colletta, Cristina. *Plotting the Past: Metamorphoses of Historical Fiction in Modern Italian Fiction.* West Lafayette, IN: Purdue University Press, 1996.

Gilmore, David. *The Last Leopard: A Life of Giuseppe Tomasi di Lampedusa.* New York: Pantheon, 1988.

Lucente, Gregory. *Beautiful Fables: Self-Consciousness in Italian Narrative from Manzoni to Calvino.* Baltimore: Johns Hopkins University Press, 1986.

Manzoni, Alessandro. *On the Historical Novel.* Translated by Sandra Bermann. Lincoln, NE: University of Nebraska Press, 1984.

  The Betrothed and History of the Column of Infamy. Ed. David Forgacs and M. Reynolds. London: J. M. Dent, 1997.

  Fermo e Lucia, I promessi sposi, 1827, I promessi sposi, 1840. Ed. Salvatore Nigro. Milan: Mondadori, 2002.

Nigro, Silvano. *La tabacchiera di don Lisander.* Turin: Einaudi, 1996.

Orlando, Federico. *L'intimità e la storia. Lettura del "Gattopardo."* Turin: Einaudi, 1998.

Pierce, Glenn. *Manzoni and the Aesthetics of the Lombard "Seicento": Art Assimilated in the Narrative of "I promessi sposi."* Lewisburg, PA: Bucknell University Press, 1998.

Ragusa, Olga. *Comparative Perspectives on Manzoni.* New York: S. F. Vanni, 1986.

Scarano, Emilio, *et al. Il romanzo della storia.* Pisa: Nistri-Lischi, 1986.

Tomasi, Gioacchino Lanza. *Giuseppe Tomasi di Lampedusa: una biografia per immagini.* Palermo: Sellerio, 1998.

Tomasi di Lampedusa, Giuseppe. *Opere.* Ed. Gioacchino Lanza Tomasi. Milan: Mondadori, 1995.

---

4 Giorgio van Straten, *Il mio nome a memoria* (Milan: Mondadori, 2000), p. 299 (author's translation).

4

GIOVANNI CARSANIGA

Literary realism in Italy: Verga, Capuana, and *verismo*

Realism or *verismo*? Basic assumptions and related problems

In late 1894 Giovanni Verga and Emile Zola (1840–1902), who had first met in Paris some twelve years earlier, were guests in Rome of Luigi Capuana. Capuana and Zola discussed literary theory to the veiled annoyance of Verga. When Zola ventured the opinion that Italian *verismo* and French naturalism were the same thing, Verga exclaimed: "*Verismo, verismo . . .* I prefer to call it the truth."[1] Many literary historians, having spent much time and ingenuity in discriminating between the two terms, would dispute Zola's opinion. Zola, Capuana, Verga, and other European nineteenth-century novelists, together with playwrights, poets, and visual artists outside the scope of this work, consciously followed a number of conventions and methodologies loosely called "realism," whose various subcategories, however defined, all assume the artist's intention of modeling the artwork on life as it actually is.

This assumption raises intractable problems. Even if one was willing to take intentions into account, they tend to be undeclared, or obscured by lack of evidence. They may sometimes be reconstructed from the author's work, but to use the work as evidence of the author's alleged intentions in order to take them as material for its evaluation is a vicious circle. Declared intentions are often unrealized or largely at variance with the actual texts – and Verga's, as we shall see, represent a case in point. Second, how does one model literature on life? Life is stranger than fiction: many facts would appear "unrealistic" if told in a story. Actual events are ultimately unfathomable, boundless, and not reducible to any one parameter or even to a multiplicity of parameters. A literary text, on the other hand, is finite, language-bound, historically determined. One can only compare like with like, but life is facts and literature is words, with even less in common with life than the visual arts from which the concept of realism derived (its first important profession

---

[1] Lucio d'Ambra, quoted by Enrico Ghidetti, *Verga. Guida storico-critica* (Rome: Editori Riuniti, 1979), pp. 29–30.

was made by the painter Gustave Courbet in 1855). Visual works share many structural features with their real-life models such as shape, color, volume, and perspective. A text, on the other hand, is not analogous to any factual structure, excepting some elements of the time dimension; and can approximately encode part of an event only if that part is made up of spoken words. The model of a written narrative can only be a spoken narration.

Realism and verisimilitude

On reading a story we often feel we are experiencing something close to "the truth," as Verga put it. And yet, as we read, for example, Verga's *Vita dei campi* (Life in the Fields, 1880), we cannot possibly know the "truth" of nineteenth-century Sicilian peasant life. The question is therefore why, or how, we get an impression of realism, or – more to the point – why we do not get it all the time, considering that most fiction is modeled on life and attempts verisimilitude. Verisimilitude is inherently untestable as a criterion of realism because it depends on how our culture prepares us to observe facts and read texts, not on the alleged resemblance between them. Being prepared to believe a story, or at least to suspend our disbelief, is the basic precondition of being a reader of fiction: prepared to believe, that is, not necessarily that the story is true, but that it is worth reading (and that includes stories not based on fact, such as fairy tales or science-fiction adventures). Our perception of what is believable is historically conditioned. It is shaped and guided not only by our understanding of artistic conventions but also by our personal system of knowledge of the real world – our encyclopedia – enabling us to describe experience through language and to use language instead of experience. Clearly, by relating literature, or the visual arts, to our encyclopedia, we are not comparing anything to "the world out there": we are relating words and images to that part of our cultural experience that we have structured in our memory through language or retained as images. That accounts for the undeniable feeling that most fiction is related to the real world, because our encyclopedia is; and for the fact that the category of realism does not seem to apply, for instance, to instrumental music. Our enjoyment and appreciation of music, while still resting on our understanding of artistic and aesthetic conventions, does not depend upon our nonmusical experience.

We can now assign their proper role to the author's intentions, equally difficult to dismiss. When they are known, or can be inferred, they are relevant not so much to the production of the text, spicing it with realism, as to its consumption by readers who, knowing the author claims to be realistic, allow themselves to be influenced (attracted or repelled) by the claim. Since no true comparison between life and art is possible or meaningful (life is real but only art can be realistic), our impression of realism must be wholly founded on the text, even when it seems to imply a resemblance between the text and the world outside it. We can only compare like with like: a writer's depiction or description techniques and conventions with newer or different techniques and conventions by the same writer, or by other writers. When the author describes what readers believe to be possible, the new set is felt to be "realistic," or more so than the one it supersedes. The description, on the other hand, of impossible, magical, or miraculous events is taken to be a move in the opposite direction (and yet consider science fiction: once we consent to suspend our disbelief, we may grant it a degree of realism if it raises issues beyond the accepted magical-technological conventions of the genre). Thus realism does not consist in the artwork but in the perception by the readership of the difference, however construed, between this and other artworks. Bear all this in mind as we examine Verga's alleged conversion to *verismo*, the position of some of his contemporaries, and the theoretical debates of the time, which concentrated on the production of literature but hardly ever considered its reception by readers.

Literary conversions

Realism in its various shades did not spring onto the Italian literary scene in the late 1870s. The aspiration towards it is rooted in the beginnings of the novel as an art form. Indeed some late nineteenth-century critics went as far as to consider Manzoni not merely the most notable exponent of the Romantic historical novel but also the first and the greatest of all *veristi*. In Italy the term *realismo* was applied to fiction by Torquato Giordana, in the preface to his novel *Il primo amante di Berta* (Berta's First Lover) as early as 1860, when Manzonianism and the ideological novel for the edification of the working classes in Giulio Carcano's style were already losing ground to the anti-Manzonian reaction of the *Scapigliatura*, and various offshoots of Zola's naturalist novels by Cletto Arrighi, Cesare Tronconi (1842–90), and others. By the time Giovanni Verga traveled northwards from Catania to begin his literary apprenticeship in Florence (1865) and aspire to greater maturity in Milan (1872), Francesco Mastriani (1819–91) had already published in Naples most of his copious imitations of Eugène Sue. Verga's Florentine mentor, Francesco Dall'Ongaro (1808–73) was a notable exponent of regional (Friulian) realism, together with Caterina Percoto (1812–87), to whom he presented Verga's *Storia di una capinera* (Story of a Blackcap, 1871).

The category of conversion has been extensively used in speaking of Manzoni's move from deism to Catholicism, not to speak of his other transitions from early classicist verse to Romantic tragedy, from cultured subject matter to popular contents (the universally known myths of religion), and finally from poetry to narrative prose. That is perhaps the reason why it has also been misapplied to Verga,[2] to explain why, after a string of well-received but undistinguished novels (*Una peccatrice* [A Sinner, 1866]; *Storia di una capinera*; *Eva* [Eve, 1873]; *Tigre reale* [Tigris Regalis, 1875]; *Eros* [*Eros*, 1875]), he was able to produce his masterpiece *I Malavoglia*, preceded by the "new-look" *Nedda, bozzetto siciliano* (*Nedda, a Sicilian Sketch*) in 1874. Two problems arise from this account. The first is why Verga, if his "conversion" dates from *Nedda*, continued to write stories, and one more novel (*Il marito di Elena* [Helen's Husband], 1882) with which he was dissatisfied, in his preconversion style. The second concerns the reasons why *I Malavoglia* is so much better than anything else written by Verga, or indeed by any other so-called *verista*.

The preface to *Eva*, with the lip-service it paid to plain unvarnished truth, its typical moralizing strictures on bourgeois hypocrisy, and its references to art as the expression of society, reminds one not merely of Giordana's "realist" preface, but also of Théophile Gautier's preface to *Mademoiselle de Maupin* (*Mademoiselle de Maupin*, 1835) and the Goncourts' preface to *Germinie Lacerteux* (*Germinie Lacerteux*, 1864). Even a cursory look at contemporary reviews shows that Verga's early novels were welcomed, or rejected, as examples of realism. Given that Verga had been practicing *verismo* since the late 1860s, what could he "convert" to in the late 1870s? If *I Malavoglia*, *Mastro-don Gesualdo*, and the Sicilian stories were the first instances of *verismo*, there would be no *verista* except Verga: the novels by his contemporaries are not unlike his 1866–75 productions, and none comes anywhere near his best work. It makes more sense to say that *I Malavoglia, Mastro-don Gesualdo*, and the Sicilian stories are works which, to a greater or lesser extent, break through the mould of *verismo* and what Capuana called "contemporary *-isms*" to stand in a class of their own. And those who place Capuana, De Roberto, or Serao among the Italian practitioners of realism should not neglect to point out that, sooner or later, they all repudiated it. Finally, those who see literary conversions as moves between separable "movements" – for example, classicism, romanticism, *Scapigliatura*, regionalism, *verismo*, psychologism, decadentism, futurism – should remember that to list them as if they were in chronological order is merely a historiographical convention. *I Malavoglia* (1881) shared its publication date with Fogazzaro's *Malombra*

---

[2] In spite of several warnings, including, authoritatively, Alberto Asor Rosa's in "Il primo e l'ultimo uomo del mondo," *Problemi* 7–8 (1968), reprinted in A. Asor Rosa, ed., *Il caso Verga* (Palermo: Palumbo, 1973), p. 11.

(*The Woman*, 1881); and *Mastro-don Gesualdo* with D'Annunzio's *Il piacere* (*The Child of Pleasure*). Svevo's *Una vita* (*A Life*, 1892) preceded by two years De Roberto's *I viceré*. Deledda's *Canne al vento* (Reeds in the Wind, 1913) came out four years after Marinetti's Futurist Manifesto.

Narrators and narrative frames

Narrators are fictional characters. Manzoni did not find and edit a seventeenth-century manuscript; his fictional projection did, who, posing as the rewriter of *I promessi sposi*, speaks with his own voice and has an omniscient grasp of the events, of which he constantly boasts before his twenty-five readers. Some authors masquerade as the writer and/or editor standing outside the story (extradiegetic). Some, to give the story greater immediacy, choose to place narrators as characters within the story (intradiegetic), either as protagonists or secondary participants. Others disguise narrators as mere collectors of letters written by the characters, and produce epistolary novels. In his earnest search for an effective narrative structure Verga tried out all these devices. The narrator of *La peccatrice* is both one of the protagonist Pietro Brusio's friends and the editor of two letters, by him and his lover Narcisa, describing the final stages of their doomed relationship. In the introduction to *Storia di una capinera*, the story of a girl forced to become a nun is said to have been told to the narrator by a woman, but the narrative is developed as an epistolary novel. Some of the girl's final letters are unimaginable as letters or even diary pages, and could only make sense as transcriptions of her final ravings. Both *Eva* and *Tigre reale* are told by an intradiegetic narrator who is a friend of the male protagonists.

Writers thus construct a sort of "narrative frame" around the story by having a narrator either explain how and why the story is being told (when the explanation is elaborate enough it becomes a story in its own right), or describe, in the "present" time of narrating (which is not necessarily the "present" of reading), how the narrator witnessed, or became aware of, the fictional events in the "past" time of the story. This frame mediates between the narrating voice and the reader, and, though it may reflect the encyclopedia of the fictional characters, it usually suits that of the assumed or hoped-for readers. All the narrators of Verga's veristic stories, for instance, eager to offer tantalizing glimpses of the upper-class world in which some of the characters move, scatter here and there knowing references to Dumas's and Sue's novels, Verdi's operas and other popular music, fashion terminology in French, and so on. The Zolian claim to a "scientific" methodology necessarily placed the "experimental novelist" on the same social level as a scientist. Most writers belonged to it anyway, together with their readers; and it could not be otherwise, given that the working classes, particularly in Verga's Italy, were largely illiterate. But did the working classes have a right to the novel?

Popular realism and social Darwinism

That was the question the Goncourts asked in their preface to *Germinie Lacerteux* and answered by narrating the surprising life of their house-keeper Rose Malingre (one of the first examples of urban working-class protagonists). They, and other writers and readers, found the exploration of the lower classes as fascinating "as a journey into unexplored lands." For most Italian educated and urbanized readers the "unexplored lands" were the country, especially the southern regions, or the low-life areas of large towns: hence the rise of regional realism in the style of Dall'Ongaro and Percoto (Friuli), Giovanni Faldella (1846–1928, Piedmont), Renato Fucini (1843–1921, Tuscany), Domenico Ciampoli (1852–1929, Abruzzo), Nicola Misasi (1850–1923, Calabria), Grazia Deledda (1871–1936, Sardinia); or urban chronicles such as those by Remigio Zena (1850–1917, Genoa), Gaetano Carlo Chelli (1847–1904, Rome), Federigo Verdinois (1844–1927, Naples), and others (including Verga himself who practiced in both areas).

The choice of lower-class characters might have been enough to mark the break with the old narrative conventions and the shift to different contents, but did not necessarily demand the development of a suitable form. The Zolian "experimental novel" required writers to place themselves in an ideal laboratory looking patronizingly at their "human documents" as if they were specimens under a microscope, or "poring over reality." This pseudo-scientific stance made it easy for many writers, including Verga, to accept the pseudo-Darwinian theory of social evolution, according to which human refinement, culture, and psychological complexity were directly proportional to class status. It followed that the description of the upper classes offered greater challenges. Indeed by 1879 the question had become, as Edmond de Goncourt put it in the preface to *Les Frères Zemganno* (The Zemganno Brothers, 1879), whether realism would ever achieve its potential, unless it found the strength to deal as confidently with the upper classes as it had with the lower.

Verga, of course, had been attracted by the upper classes long before read-ing Edmond de Goncourt, and was still partly conditioned by his *beau monde* style when he began his first exploratory forays into the Sicilian proletariat. *Nedda*, the alleged turning point, is introduced by a worldly cigar-smoking narrator relaxing in the glow of his fireplace. Its flames remind him of the fires on the slopes of Etna, in his native Sicily, and, by an unexplained association, of a young olive picker, her nasty and brutish life, and her short and ill-fated love for a poor wretch like herself. Surprisingly he tells her story in a language much more simple and direct than the novella-like and cliché-ridden reverie of his introductory "frame." A similar stylistic discrepancy exists between *Fantasticheria* (Reverie, written in 1878, but the idea may arise out of Narcisa's and Pietro's journey to Aci Castello concluding *Una peccatrice*) and *I Malavoglia*. The story, whether meant as an introduction to the novel or to its first draft, offered to Sonnino's *Rassegna Settimanale* and then abandoned, is obviously "framing" the plot of the novel for a bourgeois readership. Verga drafted two prefaces for *I Malavoglia*. His publisher Emilio Treves rejected the shorter one (not unlike *Fantasticheria* and the introduction to *Nedda*), and printed the other, possibly because it read more like a mature writer's artistic program. About 1878 Verga had begun to plan an ambitious saga, of which he now revealed the outline, in accordance to precedents set not only by Balzac and Zola, but also by Rovani (*Cento anni*) and Nievo (*Le confessioni di un italiano*). The cycle, *La marea* (The Tide), a title later changed to *I vinti* (The Losers), was to consist of five novels on the theme of upward social mobility. Society, red in tooth and claw, witnessed the survival of the fittest, who, seeking social betterment, trampled the losers underfoot in their scramble for the highest rungs of the ladder. Human passions were interpreted along positivistic lines as a "mechanism," and their delicacy and complexity were rated according to social Darwinism. After *I Malavoglia*, showing the basic struggle for purely material needs, *Mastro-Don Gesualdo* would deal with middle-class greed; his daughter's story, *La Duchessa di Leyra* (The Duchess of Leyra) would describe aristocratic vanity; *L'Onorevole Scipioni* (The Right Honorable Scipioni) – named after her illegitimate son[3] – would probe into political ambition; and in the final novel, *L'uomo di lusso* (The Man of Luxury), Scipioni's father would sum up all these passions and be destroyed by them.

I Malavoglia, however, is at variance with every single point of this program. The novel is genetically unconnected with the cycle: none of its characters reappear in *Mastro-Don Gesualdo*. The psychology of its fishermen is much more subtle and believable than the antics of Verga's previous and subsequent bourgeois protagonists. The mainspring of the story is not social betterment, since the struggle for material needs is motivated not by ambition but by penury. In fact the moral of the story is that human beings will not realize their dignity through social climbing but only through loyalty to their milieu – through a keener class consciousness (as we would say, not Verga,

---

[3] The name probably comes from one of Sue's characters mentioned in ch. 1 of *Una peccatrice*.

a staunch reactionary who praised Bava-Beccaris's May 1898 massacre of rioters). But, whether fishermen should stick to their boats out of class consciousness or for the convenience of their exploiters, the Malavoglias, under the guidance of Alessi, are certainly not losers. In order to prosper they do not need to emigrate, as Manzoni's betrothed (and countless Italians) had to do.

Impersonality

In the letter-preface to his short story "L'amante di Gramigna" ("Gramigna's Lover," 1880), Verga had described his artistic aim (with due homage to Zola's "scientific rigor" and the naturalistic theory of the "human document") as the complete cohesion of all narrative elements into such an organic whole that the hand of its author would disappear, almost as if the story had written itself. In a letter to Capuana (19 February 1881), Verga called this ideal of an organic work of art a *vecchia fissazione*, an old hobbyhorse of his. Indeed the letter-preface echoes, in its reference to the almost pathological process of emotions, the introduction to *Una peccatrice* of fourteen years earlier. All his "preconversion" novels, therefore, must have been written with this aim in mind: but only in *I Malavoglia* was it successfully achieved. The unidentified narrator tells the Malavoglia story from the same viewpoint as the characters, never going beyond or above their culture and ideology, never saying anything they might not have said themselves or mentioning things they would not have known. Obviously Verga could not write in Sicilian, a dialect incomprehensible to most readers. His innovation was just as momentous as Manzoni's half a century earlier: he used an Italian lexicon with Sicilian syntax, flavoring it with other popular-sounding features (repetitions, stereotypes, proverbs) and indirect free speech (reported speech, structured as unattributed independent secondary clauses).

Verga's main narrative problem was how to reconcile a viewpoint placed on the same level as the characters with the narrator's overall omniscience. His brilliant solution was to make the narrator a sort of village gossip. Though he is not intradiegetic, in the sense of being involved in the action, he is a witness to nearly all the events. He knows even normally hidden facts because nothing is secret in a small village community, where the smells wafting from open windows reveal what people are having for lunch, and the financial standing of everyone is known to the last penny. Verga enables him to have knowledge otherwise hidden from an insider by giving him time to acquire it, and not making his narration follow the end of the story. This is done through a serial manipulation of the time-frames, largely entrusted to the tense structure. The first verb of nearly all the chapters is either an imperfect or a pluperfect, suggesting a beginning of that part of the story in the diegetic "now," rather than in a predetermined and already known chronology: almost like a series of reports about various events taking place shortly beforehand. Other transitions and small flashbacks in the text are also dominated by the imperfect and pluperfect tenses, stressing continuity and state, rather than time sequencing and process. A similar "synchronizing" function is performed by hinting at future events. Anticipations point to the continuity between what is being told and the overall narration, which is, of course, "going on now": they do not distance the narrative "present" from the story's "past," but bring the story's past nearer the narrative present. That makes the narrator's near omniscience acceptable without postulating a kind of collective "chorus" as the main narrative voice, taking over from the single virtual narrator without actually replacing him. The difficulty of accepting the choral hypothesis, or the "chameleon narrator" mimicking each character in turn, is that the narrator is credible largely because of his consistently individual tone, occasionally reflected in asides, anticipations, and pointed comments (authorial comment is totally absent, narratorial comment is not). Verga knew that "impersonality" is a metaphor; that his rejection of a conventional authorial frame, confirmed by the rejection of *Fantasticheria* as an introduction to the novel, was just as much a technical artifice as any other (see his letter to Capuana of 2 February 1881). "Impersonality" does not mean "absence of personality": our narrator may be unidentified or unidentifiable but he has a characteristic voice nevertheless.

This perfect solution, used also in some Sicilian stories (e.g. "Rosso Malpelo" ["Rosso Malpelo"]), would not, however, fit the progress of the builder Gesualdo Motta, from his marriage with the impoverished noblewoman Bianca Trao, through his relentless acquisition of worldly goods, to his demise and death in the house of his granddaughter the Duchess of Leyra. This story could not be told from that single coherent insider's viewpoint that suited the Malavoglias' situation devoid of social mobility. Thus *Mastro-don Gesualdo*, sensitively revised between its publication in installments (*Nuova Antologia*, 1888) and in volume (1889), is a different kind of masterpiece, somewhat less stylistically consistent. In the third novel of the projected series, trying to meet de Goncourt's challenge, Verga was inevitably stuck with a narrator using the educated upper-class language novelists had been using all the time. If writer, narrator, and (presumably) readers all speak with the same voice, how can the writer be made to disappear? That is perhaps why Verga could not proceed beyond the first chapter of *La Duchessa di Leyra* and did not publish anything after the feeble novelization (1906) of his play *Dal tuo al mio* (From Mine to Yours, 1903). Other novels completed the imagined evolutionary path sketched out in the preface to *I Malavoglia*. Federico De Roberto's somber novel, *I viceré*, described the fall of a noble Sicilian dynasty, the Uzeda Francalanza; the politician was described by Antonio Fogazzaro in *Daniele Cortis*;[4] and Gabriele D'Annunzio's *Il piacere* treated the playboy.

Theoretical principles and writing practice

Like Manzoni, Verga stopped writing when he became aware of an insuperable inconsistency between his theoretical principles and his writing practice. This awareness disproves the widespread myth that in Italian *verismo* – which oddly enough turns out in some literary histories to be a movement with only two members – Luigi Capuana was the theoretical mind and Verga his disciple. Undeniably Capuana published a very large body of influential critical works, whereas Verga's principles are contained in three prefaces, an interview, and a few letters. Nevertheless Capuana took his definition of impersonality straight from his friend's writings, and, unlike Verga who wrote at least one masterpiece fully consistent with his artistic ideal, was unable to apply to his own narrative work any of the doctrines contained in his largely unoriginal presentation of French naturalism. Capuana's *Profili di donne* (Profiles of Women, 1877) is a series of portraits of women whose irredeemably conventional and novelettish style belies their pretence of psychological insight. The last version of the repeatedly revised *Giacinta* (Giacinta, 1889) owes much to Verga's best work without achieving any of its quality. *Profumo* (Perfume, 1890) is a rather preposterous story, based on the pseudo-scientific notion that the body of a woman emotionally challenged by her mother-in-law can under psychological stress waft around the scent of orange blossoms.[5] *Il Marchese di Roccaverdina* (The Marquis of Roccaverdina, 1901) is usually singled out as Capuana's masterpiece. It probably is, but as a story of crime, remorse, and punishment the book pales before the novels by Dostoevsky that he could read in French and Italian translations.

The very same sense of proportion, on the other hand, is indispensable to understanding why Capuana is worth studying (the same goes for other writers named but not praised in this chapter), and important in the Italian context, even if it is doubtful whether anyone would now read his fiction had he not taken such a vigorous and controversial role in the literary debates of

---

4 One could also mention De Roberto's *L'imperio* (Power, posthumously published in 1929), which the author himself saw as a replacement for Verga's unwritten political novel.

5 Capuana probably derived it from Ernest Monin, *Un nouveau chapître de sémiologie. Essai sur les odeurs des corps humains* (Paris, 1885).

his time. There is no deterministic connection between the overall cultural and social profile of a country and the number of leading intellectuals it can produce. Indeed the history of Italy shows that many intellectuals took a leading role partly as a reaction against the backwardness of their society. Many bright lights thus shone in the least-favored and worst-governed parts of the peninsula, of which Sicily was one; and while we may in hindsight be cautious in assessing their worth, it would be wrong to deprecate their contributions to culture and society.

In this perspective Capuana's demonstrable critical inconsistencies must be set against his praiseworthy efforts over three decades to introduce a rather hidebound and uninformed readership to a variety of literary issues. When writing drama criticism in Florence for *La Nazione* in the mid-1860s, he read French writers; De Sanctis's essays on Darwinism, realism, and the relationship between science and art; and Angelo Camillo De Meis (1817–91), who had put forward in his strange novel *Dopo la laurea* (After Graduation, 1868) the notion, derived from Hegel, of the evolution of art forms leading to the progressive absorption of art into science. If art, as De Sanctis maintained, was the synthesis of content and form, the artist's personality could remain invisible. And if De Meis was right, the last stage in the evolution of narrative forms would be the "scientific" novel. Both propositions fitted beautifully the canon of impersonality and objectivity. But this formulation had serious flaws. The concept of form was ambiguous: it was both a constituent of the artistic synthesis and the shape that synthesis takes as text. This ambiguity allowed Capuana first to write stories that were "veristic" only because of their contents, and later to reject naturalism because its inherent determinism vitiated the autonomy of form and content. He tried to salvage artistic freedom by arguing that a work shaped by a scientific methodology could nevertheless claim its own kind of reality. However, if poetic reality is different from reality proper and it makes little difference if a character has actually existed so long as it is given credible life by the writer's imagination, there is no point in holding on to the naturalistic theory of the "human document." No wonder he ended by rejecting *verismo*: such an about-turn was also consistent with his political conservatism.

Neglected or negligible novelists?

What we said about Capuana applies also to other storytellers often classified as *veristi*. When not neglected and forgotten altogether, they are being read, if at all, mostly in Italy, not so much out of interest as out of duty, because they are part of the national literary tradition. Scholars of Matilde

Serao lament the fact that her works are no longer in print. Salvatore Farina, Verga's friend, was already "a forgotten novelist" three years after his death, in spite of the fact that some of his fiction had been translated into seven or eight European languages. Carlo Chelli was defined as "a forgotten *verista*" by the critic trying to revive his memory.[6] The British Library holds a store of Italian fiction from this period (many with the typical *verista* subtitles *romanzo sociale* or *romanzo storico-sociale*) by authors never mentioned in literary histories. Their plots are largely dominated by events within the personal dimension: adultery and extra-conjugal sex, failed relationships, family feuds, greed, bigotry, parochialism, the harm small-minded individuals cause to themselves and their immediate associates. What is missing is the wider social dimension of a country that was undergoing, after all, momentous economic and political changes. Such core themes as the repression of political and social dissent (which had more victims in the few years after unity than in the previous three wars of independence), the incipient colonial expansion in Eritrea and Somalia, the migration movement, the building of roads and railways throughout the peninsula, the Italian commercial expansion in northern Africa and the Near East, the very "atmosphere of banks and industrial enterprises" so often mentioned in *verista* prefaces, with the attendant financial and political scandals, to give a few examples, seem to be absent from Italian realist fiction.

It is furthermore difficult to pigeonhole the better-known writers. Federico De Roberto often appears as the third *verista* after Verga and Capuana. True, his first collection of short stories, *La sorte* (Fate, 1886), was rejected by Emilio Treves with the standard antiveristic condemnation, calling the book a description of "the ugly, the rotten and the sensual aspects of society." The title of the second collection, *Processi verbali* (Police Reports, 1890), harks back to Zola's definition of Balzac's *Cousine Bette* (*Cousin Bette*) as the police record of events which the novelist places before the readers. But in his preface to *Documenti umani* (Human Documents, 1888), in the form of a letter addressed to Treves, De Roberto seemed to move away from Zolianism, declaring that he wished the title to apply to stories with high ideals and not to stories filled with wretched and poverty-stricken protagonists, which is what "human documents" usually meant to the naturalists. His first novel, *Ermanno Raeli* (Ermanno Raeli, 1889), wavers between romanticism and psychologism, and is more similar to Verga's *beau monde* stories than to his masterpiece. His best novel, *I viceré*, gains a political dimension missing

---

[6] Roberto Bigazzi, "Un verista dimenticato: Gaetano Carlo Chelli," *La Rassegna della Letteratura Italiana* 68 (1964), pp. 111–29.

from Verga's work, but De Roberto's cold and dry impassiveness prevents him from achieving the tone of warm human sympathy with which Verga's narrator occasionally speaks of his characters.

Matilde Serao, who complained that she might have been recognized as the first Italian *verista* had she not "worn a skirt," has been aptly defined as an "intermittent naturalist, who occasionally used a 'realistic' style as Monsieur Jourdan used prose."[7] Unlike many *veristi* who claimed to expose in their novels the social evils of their time but failed because their artistic ability was not up to the task, Serao had plenty of descriptive ability; but it seemed to serve the cause more of book-selling sensationalism than of the wretched Neapolitan folk depicted in her stories. As the first woman journalist of nationwide reputation she might have been (and was often seen as) a role model; yet her strictures on the exploitation of women seem less motivated by her perception of the dignity of women's work than by her unspoken persuasion that women's place is the traditional family. None of the other female novelists showed a real understanding of gender issues. Of Serao's contemporaries, Neera (Anna Radius Zuccari, 1846–1918) was just as reactionary and antifeminist. Olga Ossani-Lodi (1857–1913), Gemma Ferruggia (1868–87), Ida Baccini (1850–1911), Luisa Amalia Paladini (1810? 1819?–1872), Cordelia (Virginia Treves Tedeschi, 1855–1916), Maria Torelli Viollier Torriani (Marchesa Colombi, 1846–1920), Emma (Emilia Ferretti-Viola, 1844–1929), Virginia Guicciardi Fiastri (1864–1929?), Clarice Tartufari (1868–1933), and Regina di Luanto (anagram of Guendalina Roti, 1853? 1862?–1914), of whom little is known and by whom nothing is now read or in print, do not rise above mediocre moralizing representations of the female condition. Ada Negri (1870–1945) stands out of this depressing panorama for her incipient feminism, her defiance of common middle-class morality and her lofty social and humanitarian ideals. These qualities earned her a Nobel Prize nomination and, at the same time, the antagonism of the establishment, which made sure the prize went in 1926 to the politically safer Grazia Deledda. Deledda deserves a mention not only for reasons of historical completeness but also because she was one of those interesting representatives of marginal areas whom Nobel selectors cannot afford to ignore if they wish the prize to have any meaning and dignity, and not to appear unfairly biased in favor of majority languages or trends. Her works are still in print as a due and proper homage to the first and only Italian woman writer so far to receive the Swedish Academy honor.

[7] Marie-Gracieuse Martin-Gistucci, *L'oeuvre romanesque de Matilde Serao* (Grenoble: Presses Universitaires de Grenoble, 1973), p. 148. Monsieur Jourdan is the character in Molière's *Le bourgeois gentilhomme* who spoke in prose without knowing it.

Further reading

Biasin, Gian-Paolo. *Literary Diseases: Theme and Metaphor in the Italian Novel.* Austin: University of Texas Press, 1975.

The Flavors of Modernity: Food and the Novel. Princeton: Princeton University Press, 1993.

Clerici, Luca. *Invito a conoscere il verismo.* Milan: Mursia, 1989.

Davies, Judith. *The Realism of Luigi Capuana: Theory and Practice in the Development of Late Nineteenth-Century Italian Narrative.* London: Modern Humanities Research Association, 1979.

Hemmings, Frederick William John, ed. *The Age of Realism.* Harmondsworth: Penguin, 1974.

Luperini, Romano. *Pessimismo e verismo in Giovanni Verga.* Padua: Liviana, 1982.

Madrignani, Carlo Alberto. *Capuana e il naturalismo.* Bari: Laterza, 1969.

Sipala, Paolo Mario. *Introduzione a De Roberto.* Bari: Laterza, 1988.

5

NICOLAS J. PERELLA

Popular fiction between Italian Unification and World War I

The two most popular works of Italian fiction written between Italian Unification (1860–70) and World War I were *Le avventure di Pinocchio: Storia di un burattino* (*The Adventures of Pinocchio: Story of a Puppet*, 1883) by Carlo Collodi, the pen name of Carlo Lorenzini (1826–90); and *Cuore* (*Heart, A Schoolboy's Journal*, 1886) by Edmondo De Amicis (1846–1908). The poles between which both books shuttle are the home (family) and school, although in the case of Collodi's ambivalently constructed protagonist (the boy/marionette) there is much straying. It cannot be surprising that these should be the institutions invested with the greatest authority and responsibility in creating a "new" citizenry for the new nation which until then had been a land made up of various regions, each of which had its own dialect and customs. The slogan of the time was "We have made Italy; now we must make Italians." The church of Rome was not prepared to participate in a state it felt had usurped much of its authority and land, but religious values were essential to character-building, the goal of the age. It is well to remember also that, except in some of Italy's northern regions and Tuscany, literacy was a rarity. And the values and virtues being proclaimed were in the cause of a productive, middle-class ethic. The "popular" fiction and culture in general referred to here were created, primarily at least, for and by Italy's bourgeoisie, not for and by peasants and the proletariat, although under the impulse of *verismo* of varying degrees it did not shy away from depicting the latter classes, sometimes in a way meant to point to supposed virtues that the petite bourgeoisie might embrace.

Before publication of his runaway best-seller *Cuore*, De Amicis was a fairly successful author of prose sketches of military life (*La vita militare* [*Military Life*, 1868]) and travel literature characterized by vivid journalistic reportage published between 1873 and 1879: *Spagna* (*Spain and the Spaniards*, 1873); *Olanda* (*Holland and its People*, 1874); *Costantinopoli* (*Constantinople*, 1878–9); and *Ricordi di Parigi* (*Studies of Paris*, 1879). De Amicis harbored within himself the sense that his truest vein was one in which feeling, the affective sensibility, needed to be expressed. "Heart" becomes the ineluctable principle by which he would be ruled, in spite of what the "head" dictated. Of himself he wrote that he was "always veering toward the heart, stealthily, when I should be ruled by my head." In *Il romanzo di un maestro* (*The Romance of a Schoolmaster*, 1890), a work he was writing while fashioning *Cuore*, "head" is mostly in command, but De Amicis is not averse to the use even here of scenes evoking pathos in what is essentially a pessimistic and acrimonious account of the failures of Italy's public school system. This bitter representation of his country's educational system is also at the core of a number of the author's subsequent writings, including a number of short stories. Hope and optimism, on the other hand, pervade his major book, *Cuore*.

Although *Cuore* has gone into eclipse in recent decades, for the first fifty years after its publication it enjoyed a success far greater than that of Collodi's little classic. While De Amicis's programmatically scholastic, character-building text seems but a book for children, its stunning international editorial success suggests that adult readers found in it a self-congratulatory representation of those middle-class values and ideals that transcend nationalistic antagonisms. Ostensibly, however, in a brief preface De Amicis aims his book at boys between nine and thirteen years old.

The book is constructed as the scholastic diary of one such boy, Enrico, kept over the nine months of an academic year in an elementary school in Turin, which was, with Milan, the new nation's most modern city. In addition to the schoolday's events, the diary also records the monthly edifying stories, one per month, from October to July, dictated by a schoolmaster who is a champion of interclass harmony. Curiously, but significantly, the book/diary includes observations and moral exhortations inserted surreptitiously from time to time by Enrico's parents! The dominant manner is in a pathetic-sentimental key, and all is in the service of the book's social ideology and values: study, work, respect for order and the reigning social hierarchy, dignity, honor, country, and family. Intended to illustrate the idea that heroism, love of country, sacrifice, and love of family know neither age nor socioeconomic differences, the schoolmaster's monthly tales take as their protagonists children from Italy's various regions and social classes, thereby attesting to the national society in its multifold and problematic whole. But the environment and the characters of *Cuore* are fundamentally from Turin. With the school (symbol of the nation) as setting, Enrico and his schoolmates are presented one by one somewhat in the guise of fixed types, i.e. stereotypes. One of them comes from the aristocracy; Enrico and two of the others are from well-off middle-class families, while the others belong to various levels of the proletariat and subproletariat; two of them know abject poverty and illness. Around the group of schoolboys moves a variety of adults: parents and schoolteachers (male and female), and various citizens of the town.

It is worth noting that the prevailing spirit in *Cuore* is not idyllic; rather, like *Pinocchio*, it depicts an encounter with contemporary reality that is dramatic and even traumatic, a feature that sets both books apart from most of the preceding tradition of Italian children's literature, where painful encounters with reality tended to be underplayed or avoided. Unfortunately, the appalling misery of so much of Italy's population is portrayed sentimentally by De Amicis. Poverty never appears as an unmitigable condition in his pages, where the middle-class gentry stand ready to assist the needy by way of charity and good works. The farthest De Amicis goes is to try to awaken in middle-class children an awareness of the unhappy conditions in which the poor live. To see how limited his vision is, one need only read the page in which Enrico's mother explains to him that starving beggars prefer to receive alms from children rather than from grown-ups because then they do not feel humiliated. Besides, she says, it is good to give the destitute something, because then they bless us, which is bound to stir in us a feeling of meltingly sweet gratitude.

Although not all the boys in *Cuore*'s classroom are "good good boys," only one, Franti, represents a serious threat and offense to their fierce virtue. Franti, who derides all that is good, noble, and pathetic, shoots paper arrows at the timid substitute teacher, bullies his smaller classmates, steals when he can, lies with a bold face, laughs at disabled soldiers or at the motionless form of a worker who has fallen from the fifth floor of a scaffold, and is even able, alas, to smirk at the schoolmaster's moving account of the funeral of King Vittorio Emanuele II, the first monarch of a unified Italy. As the type of the "bad bad boy" who will be the death, quite literally, of his mother, he is appropriately labeled *infame* (infamous) and *malvagio* (wicked), a foil to the chorus of "good good boys" and a reminder to them of the sort of wicked person best dealt with by being detested and removed from society.

Cuore, then, was eminently suited to its times. In it De Amicis propagandized the idea of school as having a great threefold mission – social, political, affective – and therefore as being the place, along with the home, where Italians were to be formed. His optimistic representation of school, complemented by the interwoven story of an equally idealized bourgeois family home, made for his book's huge success. Whatever dramas may occur in either setting, the reassuring presence of a benevolent schoolmaster or father, neither of whom has any doubts about what is right and both of whom are always ready with inspiring words, makes both institutions – school and home – secure and sheltered sanctuaries. Surely one of the most remarkable pages of nineteenth-century European oratory is the letter Enrico's father writes to him, encouraging him to overcome any resistance he might feel about going to school. De Amicis evokes awesome images of the masses of humanity in all stations of life from Italy to the farthest recesses of the world as single individuals and as armies marching to the same goal – the schoolhouse, hailed as the bulwark of civilization, the hope and the glory of the world. Enrico is "a little soldier of the immense army"; his weapons are his books, his squadron is his class, and his battlefield is the whole world.

Finally, it is noteworthy that save for an incidental reference to All Soul's Day (without mention of a transcendental destiny), God and the church are absent from the pages of *Cuore*. Its ideology and values are wholly secular and in accord with what the ruling classes of the age wished to instill in all of Italian society. God and the church have given way to patriotic and domestic symbols – the national flag and the figure of the mother. Interestingly enough, however, in depicting these secular icons, De Amicis sometimes reverts to the church's cultic and liturgical language which, being familiar to readers of the time, could be expected to have had great rhetorical appeal in its new context.

Carlo Collodi was a journalist, humorist, satirist, drama critic, polemicist, author of *bozzetti* (character sketches) and pedagogically oriented children's stories, translator of the great French fairy tales of Perrault and others, but above all creator of one of the most hugely successful classics of world literature: *Le avventure di Pinocchio: Storia di un burattino*. First published serially in the *Giornale per i Bambini* (1881–3), and then in 1883 in the first book edition, this marvelous tale is likely the most widely read work of Italian literature known to non-Italians, more popular than even Dante's *Divine Comedy* or Machiavelli's *Prince*. In a radical reversal of the more common circumstance in which a book originally intended for adults becomes a children's favorite, recent decades have seen *Pinocchio*, ostensibly a children's book, appropriated by Italy's intelligentsia. Comparisons have been made between Collodi's puppet and heroes (and antiheroes) ranging from Ulysses, Aeneas, Christ, and Dante to Don Quixote, Candide, and Manzoni's Renzo. Interpretations have been offered by specialists in fields ranging from the sociopolitical, the psychoanalytical, and the mythopoetic to the philosophical, the theological, and the generally allegorical. The truth is that *Pinocchio* is a book for children and adults alike.

Whatever else one may see in it, *Pinocchio* is an exemplary family drama that follows the nineteenth-century pattern of children's stories in serving as a vehicle for social instruction and, it would seem, for character-building in the cause of a productive, middle-class ethic. This aim fits the social and political needs felt in a recently unified and independent Italy (1860/70). Not surprisingly, the greatest of all Italian family dramas, Verga's *I Malavoglia*, is written in a very different vein and has a tragic dimension, even though Verga's masterpiece appeared at about the same time (1881) and shares important thematic elements with Collodi's tale.

There is a rich psychological ambiguity in Collodi's attitude. Although, like De Amicis's popular scholastic-oriented book *Cuore*, *Pinocchio* advocates the post-Risorgimento ideals of honesty, family, and the work ethic, all under a paternalistic cloak, in Collodi's tale these values are not connected directly with fervent patriotism; nor does Collodi make any appeal, sentimental or otherwise, to a solidarity of the classes. And although he eventually brings his wayward, hyperkinetic boy-puppet (a wooden marionette) to heel, he does not spare adult society and its hypocrisy. Pinocchio's unruliness seems so ingrained that it serves as the basis for a dramatic (and traumatic) encounter with the real world – an uncompromisingly egotistical world in which kindness is the exception. The essential *motto*, which Collodi seeks to inculcate in his protagonist and little readers, through an ambiguously sadistic admixture of ironic indulgence and severe pedagogical moralism, is the unblushingly un-Christian piece of wisdom: God helps those who help themselves.

Despite the presence of a fairy godmother, *Pinocchio* does not recount a magical from-rags-to-riches tale. Rather, Collodi, even with an ironic and parodic implementation of fairy-tale and picaresque elements, beats just that sort of foolish notion out of the boy-puppet. In this respect, *Pinocchio* as a whole is an anti-Cinderella story, just as its first fifteen chapters (concluding with the puppet's apparent death by hanging), at the end of which, in the original serial publication, the world *Finis* was appended, constitute a version of the cautionary tale of Little Red Riding Hood as told in Perrault's ironic but uncompromising version. The happy ending, in which the boy-puppet is metamorphosed into a real, that is, a "proper" boy, became mandatory once Collodi acceded to the demands of his little readers and his editor for more of Pinocchio. Only then, in fact, did the *Storia di un burattino* become *Le avventure di Pinocchio*, the original title being demoted to a subtitle. This change was both appropriate and timely once Collodi's tale more clearly took on the character of an initiatory adventure story which in incorporating the first "story" would lead the protagonist from perilous innocence (by way of a journey through adventures) to a return home and a final rebirth into adulthood.

As the "son" of a poor carpenter, Geppetto, Pinocchio was born into poverty, and it is not surprising that starvation anxieties and oral fantasies abound in *Pinocchio*. Food, or its absence, is so much the story's ruling image and theme that it is present even in the episodes involving the puppet's relationship with the fairy, who does not hesitate to use food as a pedagogic weapon in curtailing his rebellious ways. Nonetheless, the pedagogic restraints imposed on Pinocchio's spontaneous vitality and hedonistic instincts take other forms than just imposed hunger. Only somewhat less pervasive than the specter of hunger is the specter of death. Significantly, the same two specters haunt not only the world of fairy tales, but also Manzoni's *I promessi sposi* and Verga's *I Malavoglia*, where they inspire prose of tragic grandeur and pathos. For Collodi's child protagonist both specters have a bearing upon the acute separation anxieties (in connection with Geppetto and the blue-haired fairy – the tale's main father and mother figures) to which he is prey. The periodic evocation of death serves a positive function in calling Pinocchio and his little readers back to reality and order, but its persistent return, sometimes in a key of funerary or black humor, may suggest a preoccupation that far exceeds the patterning required by the tale's pedagogic purpose. In fact, however, its symbolic and narrative function is of the essence. Pinocchio dies twice: once by hanging, from which Collodi decided post factum to resuscitate him; and then by entombment in the belly of the marine monster, the Great Shark, from which he emerges with new life. The latter is one of the two greatest archetypal image patterns in the tale.

Although Collodi seems neither to sentimentalize nor idealize the child, a certain nostalgia is surely there, albeit masked; and almost surely his need to exorcise it accounts for much of the secret tension felt by adult readers, most of whom are bound to smile indulgently at Pinocchio, but not without some concern at his madcap flights and dangerously childish hopes. We are relieved to return to the author a knowing wink of complicity at his reassuring, if severe, curtailments of the puppet's misguided *élan vital*. Collodi's ambivalence is also our own, an ambivalence that derives from the regressive pull of the child in us, even as we enforce the role of responsible adults upon ourselves. Our idea of maturity and a workable social order necessitates the repression of the child, whose amoral vitality and primordiality represent a threat to that idea. Thus we classify children and puppets as ontologically and socially inferior or inchoate beings who do not possess the fullness of humanity. It is no wonder, then, that children's stories are often about growing up.

To have given his protagonist an equivocal dual nature is the most genial stroke of Collodi's inventiveness, for from this initial ambiguity, which literally equates a child with a puppet, there stems an endless chain of possible ironies, most of them quite consciously exploited. Even more important as an archetypal image or pattern than the redemptive imprisonment in the sea monster's belly is this image of the human being as a puppet created or shaped by a master puppeteer. Besides Geppetto, who created or shaped the puppet in order "to go around the world to earn his crust of bread," there is Fire-Eater, the master puppeteer of the sideshow of marionettes in whom Pinocchio recognizes his "brothers and sisters." The rebellion of the puppets (an ancient motif) is short-lived. But the true master puppeteer, of course, is the narrator himself. The Old Testament account of the creation of Adam may be cited here, but in that narrative, the puppeteer (God) allows the puppet (humanity) to have a will and a willfulness. The man-as-puppet archetype also appears in Plato's discussion of how best to educate youths so that they will become perfect citizens. Plato suggests that the puppet, man, is pulled in various directions by the strings of his passions, his likes and dislikes, whereas he should let himself be guided (pulled) by the golden cord of reason, "called by us the common law of the state" (*Laws* 1, 644).

Perhaps the most striking and lasting impression created by the prose of *Pinocchio* is the swiftness that characterizes the tale throughout, at least until the moment of the puppet's conversion. The puppet's paroxysmal resumés of his misadventures punctuate the narration, always following thematic pauses represented by his being checked in his reckless flights. The pauses themselves, however, enhance the sense of rapidity by bringing into relief the swift narrative that precedes and follows them. While a practical purpose is served by the rapid-fire resumés in a sporadically serialized story – to remind readers of important events after long intervals between installments – they counter the narrative pauses by giving a still greater sense of the rush of events.

The swiftness of the prose itself, in short, is an integral part of the story's principal motifs and images: the hyperkinetic marionette on the loose and on the road, forever tumbling into adventures. The long stretches of time during which Pinocchio is not on the road are given the barest notice, except for his stay in Funland – a stopping place on the road, allowing for an implicitly moralizing description of the life that leads to one's becoming an ass – and the description of his redemptive life with Geppetto (chapter 36), which offers a lesson in what it takes to become a boy-adult. But the road is at the heart of the adventures. Aside from the actual and frequently mentioned country roads (and main road or highway) and town streets as such, the settings in which the puppet often finds himself are metaphorical extensions of the road, milieux in which the quest or journey motif is developed, although each may also have a singular symbolic value in the context of the tale. Thus there are the country fields, the air, the forest (with its own path), and, in the last chapter, shore and sea. The "road" is everything outside the security of home and school, and it is because the puppet, between his initial rebellion and his final reconciliation with his father (the end of the road and the quest), moves for the most part outside the confines of such security that Collodi's tale is not merely the "story of a puppet" but the "adventures of Pinocchio."

A Collodi-like verve also characterizes the prose and the protagonist of the *Giornalino di Gian Burrasca* (The Day-Book of Gian Burrasca), a children's book that for the first half of the twentieth century rivaled in popularity *Cuore* and *Pinocchio*. Written by Vamba (the pen name of Luigi Bertelli [1858–1920]), it first appeared serially in 1907 and then as a volume in 1912. The child protagonist's name is metaphorically indicative: *burrasca* means *storm* in Italian. Forever running into trouble, and causing mischief, the impish ten-year-old, besides being a prankster, has the inconvenient habit of always telling the truth, much to the chagrin of the adults of the bourgeois world to which he belongs. Satire is practically inherent in such a context. Polite or complacent society's self-proclaimed ideals are shown to be too often at odds with its actual behavior. Exuberant and active, Gian Burrasca is by nature in rebellion against society's conventions, but the author has seen to it that at bottom he has a good heart.

The preeminence of "popular" children's literature in post-Unification Italy is attested not only by the writings of De Amicis and Collodi, but by a spate of books written for the young, even the very young. Two dedicated writers in the field who deserve to be mentioned here are Ida Baccini and Emma Perodi (1850–1918). Both women were actively involved in promoting the rise of periodicals given over to children's literature. For a time Baccini was a contributor to the *Giornale per i Bambini*, the journal for children in which Collodi's *Pinocchio* was serialized. Perodi, who was also an assiduous collaborator on the journal, became its director in 1883. It is the journal that defined the genre and set the course programmatically for many subsequent children's magazines. Both women understood that true communication with children could best be made by way of a language rich in images that speak to their imagination. Baccini's first book, *Le memorie di un pulcino* (The Memories of a Chick, 1875), provided just such a language and won its author a great success. Perodi's name remains alive for *Le novelle della nonna* (Grandmother's Tales), folktales that she collected and reelaborated in a lively and expressive style. In her hands the pedagogic tale acquires a surrealistic dimension.

In an age when tales of adventures enjoyed a great vogue, Emilio Salgari was by far the most successful producer of them. It was once thought that he drew upon his own widely traveled life as the source of his narratives, but in fact he pillaged encyclopedias, books of geography, and the available travel literature of his day for many of the descriptive passages (adroitly embroidered by him) that form the exotically turgid background of swiftly paced, action-packed narration. Mostly sedentary (though psychologically troubled), he was wildly adventurous in his creation of swashbuckling, titanic heroes of blood, thunder, and doom. Hardly a model of good grammar and prose style, Salgari's fantastical inventiveness in the matter of plots, intricacies of intrigue, and hyperbolic expressionism were such as to transport a vast devoted following of adolescents and escape-minded adults over the most perilous seas to the wildest settings: jungles, remote island countries, sundry extravagantly conceived places from the Far East to the Far West – realms of cruelty, blood, death, decay, terror, violence, sadism, and awesome mysteries, peopled by heroes and villains in a struggle between good and evil. Yet even the champions of good causes (such as liberty) could be sublimely monstrous, testing their primitive passions and energies against the tempestuous might of nature's adversarial side or beasts of the wild. But these very heroes, for all their bloodthirstiness and explosiveness, sometimes reveal in themselves a vein of melancholy and a sense of destiny that can in the end overmaster them. Paradigmatic of such heroes is the most famous of them, Sandokan, the protagonist of a whole cycle of novels, who makes an early appearance in Salgari's tales:

> He was the most terrible and most strong-willed of the pirates of Malaysia. More than once he had been seen drinking human blood and, horror of horrors, sucking up the brains of his dying victims. He was a man who loved the fiercest battles, and who hurled himself wildly into the midst of the fray where the slaughter was greatest. Like a new Attila, he left in his wake smoking ruins and fields of corpses.

The foregoing passage appeared in the first edition of *La tigre della Malesia* (The Tiger of Malaysia), which appeared serially between October 1883 and March 1884. However, when the revised version of the tale was published in 1901 as a volume under the title *Le tigri di Mompracen* (The Tigers of Mompracen), the passage was deleted. Even so, there was gore enough for readers to wallow in. In the end, Sandokan, smitten with love for a damsel who belongs to a race against whom he had sworn eternal hate, abandons his role of an avenging pirate and gives her a safe harbor, but not without murmuring through his sobs: "The 'Tiger' is dead forever." In another of Salgari's most popular novels, *Il corsaro nero* (The Black Corsair, 1899), the eponymous hero abandons to the sea the very woman he loves, daughter of his mortal enemy, in order to fulfill a fatal oath of revenge. The novel's last words are: "Look there, the Black Corsair is weeping." Of particular interest are the novels and short stories in which Salgari creates a mostly horrific vision of Africa as the "dark continent" – an Africa and Africans of a vividly extravagant imagination. These narratives were written, for the most part, in the last decade or so of the nineteenth century when the newly established Italian nation-state was making its first efforts to assert itself on that continent as a modern political force.

Francesco Mastriani, as Neapolitan a figure as one could desire, was judged by Benedetto Croce to be "the most significant 'serial' novelist Italy has produced." As with Salgari and, later, Carolina Invernizio (1858–1916), his more than one hundred novels first appeared serially. But not all of them would pass muster as examples of even the most generously accommodating definition of the genre "novel." At any rate, making allowance for some overlapping, one can distinguish two distinct periods of his work. The first, pre-Unification, was characterized by a Romantic-sentimental vein, best represented by the novel *La cieca di Sorrento* (The Blind Maid of Sorrento, 1852), a highly popular tale of considerable intrigue in its time, with emphasis on evoking a pathos abetted by macabre and pathological elements. The second phase is marked by a socialist-humanitarian vision in which the author occasionally interrupts the plot in order to indulge in long digressive disquisitions on various economic, social, philosophical, and moral questions. This tendency is best exemplified by I *misteri di Napoli* (The Mysteries of Naples, 1875), a work much influenced by Eugène Sue's enormously popular *Les mystères de Paris* (*The Mysteries of Paris*, 1842–3). Among the most interesting features of Mastriani's vast and chaotic almost naturalistic canvas of low life and high life in the Naples he knew so well is his plurilinguistic style which, while remaining simple and vigorous, yokes together learned or academic terms and popular or slang (dialectal) expressions.

In *Il ventre di Napoli* (In Naples' Belly, 1884) Matilde Serao proved to be a worthy successor to Mastriani as an evocator of the slums of Naples, a breeding ground of crime, misery, dire poverty, and daunting social ills. This remarkable work of high journalism appeared first as a series of articles in 1882–3. Its descriptive passages are characterized by the veristic trend of the age, but its denunciatory dimension bespeaks the author's impassioned participation. Yet even this rhetorically convincing work is occasionally spoiled by an intrusive dose of paternalistic sentimentality. Of her narrative works the short story "La virtù di Checchina" ("Checchina's Virtue," 1884) stands out for its sobriety of tone, lightened by a bemused irony, in relating with much visual detail, and no preaching, a story of seduction and would-be adultery that is thwarted by the beautiful but unhappily married middle-class protagonist's own unfamiliarity with the rules of the game, by the anguish she suffers in realizing her lack of self-confidence, and by a series of undramatic incidents that seem to conspire against her desire.

In *Il paese di Cuccagna* (*The Land of Cockayne*, 1891), Serao paints a vast canvas of all levels of Neapolitan society, from the humble proletariat to the aristocracy, all of whom are seen, or revealed, in the light of a common mania for the lottery. Tales and characters revolve around this game of chance, emblematic of the mad hope that sustains them. Much of Serao's writing belongs to the category of serial novels in which *verismo* or naturalism is abandoned for a trite pseudo-romanticism where objectivity yields to the desire to exalt the greatness in misery of female protagonists. Nonetheless, Serao stands at the head of a rich bevy of women writers who make a conspicuous entrance into the ranks of Italian writers in post-Unification Italy. This phenomenon can be seen as the first wave or concerted effort at establishing a niche in Italian literature for women writing specifically from a woman's point of view.

To a great degree the literary output of Italian women writers of the time was focused on the conflict between the sexes, with the woman seeking to adopt a strategy of rebellion, more or less openly, with regard to the male. But the results of the conflict are not always clear-cut. Thus in much of Serao's fiction the overriding themes are the relationship, indeed the antagonism, between male and female, followed by, and at times interconnected with, the question of social injustice. In this context, however, Serao sees woman as a creature who, for all the education and talent she may acquire, remains by nature committed to the life of passion, of sentiments; she is thereby fated to subservience to man, seen as the representative of intellect and logic, and above all as the great seducer. Try as a woman might, her efforts at breaking away from this role are destined to fail. Interestingly, a similar ambiguity characterizes Serao's treatment of social inequality and injustice. Despite her often remarkable descriptions and powerful denunciations of society's ills and of the wretchedness the proletariat is condemned to, her voice does not cry out for the need for change. Here too, as in the case of woman's auxiliary role in society, it is as though an incontrovertible law would have things as they are.

A painful awareness of the submissive role of woman in society at the cost of suppressing her own desires and potential creativity also marks the novels and short stories of Neera, an exact contemporary of Serao. Neera is especially apt in her analyses of the social and physiological conditioning of woman; her female protagonists writhe in physical pain but end by accepting their domestic role. Marriage is seen as the institutionalization of the surrender of the desire for emancipation; curiously, however, the choice of maternity (felt as a mystical experience) is considered as the only liberating possibility. Her best-known novels, including *Teresa* (Teresa, 1886), *Lydia* (Lydia, 1887), *L'indomani* (The Next Day, 1890), and *Anima sola* (*The Soul of an Artist*, 1894), analyze female protagonists doomed to struggle against a society dominated by masculine values. Other women novelists were popular in this era. Contessa Lara (Evelina Cattermole, 1849–96) produced works in which heroines belong to the category of *femmes fatales* living their D'Annunzio-like luxurious love life in the face of bourgeois propriety. Marchesa Colombi (the pen name of Maria Antonietta Torriani), was influenced by *verismo* and wrote popular "realistic" novels that evidence sensitivity and insight regarding the plight of woman as slave to family and work. Emma (pen name of Emilia Ferretti-Viola), explored the world of prostitution and relates the case of a "lost" woman from the victim's point of view in her novel *Una fra tante* (A Woman Among Many, 1878). Annie Vivanti (1868–1942), heedless of any restraints or moral scruples, writes in the novel *Marion* (Marion, 1891) of her own aggressive vitality, while her novel *The Devourers*, which appeared first in English in 1910 and in Italian (*I divoratori*) the following year, has as its twofold theme the dramatic succession of generations in which the new devours the old, and the depiction of the woman artist as a victim of the stronger and "devouring" maternal instinct. Anna Franchi (1866–1954) draws on her own painful experience in treating the theme of divorce in *Avanti il divorzio!* (Forward Divorce!, 1902). Ida Baccini, mentioned earlier for her work in the field of children's literature, was a "traditionalist" on the question of woman's place in society, and her efforts in adult literature resulted in a few novels that suffer from too patent a pedagogic intent, although the last of them, *Scintille nell'ombra* (Sparks in the Shade, 1910), deserves mention for its treatment of the contrast between the traditional and the modern types of woman.

With Amalia Guglielminetti (1881–1941) and Sibilla Aleramo (1876–1960) in the early years of the twentieth century, the emancipatory voice of feminism becomes unambiguously clear. In her versified autobiographical novel *Le seduzioni* (Seductions, 1909), Guglielminetti flaunted herself as a rapacious vamp, a role she lived amid much scandal and which counted as much as, if not more than, anything she wrote in the battle for woman's right to be free from male tyranny. Aleramo's autobiographical novel *Una donna* (*A Woman*, 1906) traces her life on her way to acquiring a full awareness of herself as a unique "individual," from her early adulation of her father to a gradual and ultimately definitive disillusionment.

Among the cascade of pulp novels intended primarily for women of the middle class, the serial thriller has a near relation in the popular serialized love stories known in Italian as *romanzi rosa*. Though the *romanzi rosa* kept interest alive by way of ingredients such as intrigue, heart-stopping scenes, misunderstandings and suspense, they are generally distinguishable from the full-throttle thriller by being considerably less melodramatic and more slowly paced. Tears, on the other hand, flow freely. Obstacles to the love of the central couple are inevitably overcome, and the author takes leave of the lovers at the moment of their supreme happiness – a marriage by which passion is made licit, with no hint of an unhappy aftermath. Sensationalism is the order of the day in the 130 or so novels (most of them first serialized) by Carolina Invernizio. This most popular of the purveyors of pulp is a past-mistress at controlling the ebb and flow of the lurid happenings that fill her stories. Unmatched in the invention of plots, ploys, and reversals, she sees to it that every crisis or highest point of tension is finally resolved to the nervous reader's surprise and/or relief. At the core of her work there is usually the family, whose values (honor in particular) are threatened or violated by some action such as, say, adultery, which sets off the struggle between good and evil. In her Manichean world, the repertory of emotions and events ground out by her extravagant thrillers make for a castle of horrors. In the perpetual seesaw of tension and release, we are treated to killings, rapes, vendettas, betrayals, persecuted and pursued maidens defending their honor, poisonings, adulteries, tears and kisses, fulminating passions, jealousy, shrieks, violence in general, generous and gallant thieves, prostitutes (redeemed and unredeemed), *femmes fatales*, and Satanic heroes, and more of the like. The title of one of her thrillers, *Amori maledetti* (Damned Loves, 1892), could serve as a splendid general title for many of her novels.

The relationship between the popular serial novels that were being churned out in ever increasing numbers (many, if not most of which, were translations from French originals), and their highbrow counterpart, the "literary" novel, is not always easy to determine. A certain amount of overlapping between the two was inevitable. Novels such as Verga's *Tigre reale* and Igino Ugo Tarchetti's *Fosca* (*Passion*, 1869) have thematic and atmospheric elements that are shared by the popular serial or "appendix" novels. Nonetheless, distinctions in lexical and tonal qualities are readily apparent. At any rate, the "literary" novelists tended to scorn this production of "paraliterature," as it has come to be called in recent literary criticism. Seen from the perspective of the proletariat, however, highbrow literature, with its learned or refined linguistic manner, failed to carry out an educative responsibility vis-à-vis the "people." Thus in the sprawling and amorphous serial novel with a socialist perspective entitled *La folla* (The Crowd, 1879) by Paolo Valera (1850–1926), the young proletarian protagonist feels frustrated in his efforts to read as much as possible as fast as possible so as to make up for a childhood and an adolescence without books:

> Hard-to-read books made him melancholy because they caused him to realize how far he was from the intelligence of youths from well-to-do families. He wished that writers would always remember that the world includes people who know less than they do and therefore have a greater need to learn and to temper their violent impulses by the example of others.

On the other hand, one such writer of the more sophisticated sort, Emilio De Marchi (1851–1901), made a deliberate effort at reconciling characteristics of the popular serial novels with those of the elitist type. De Marchi's avowed aim was to prove that an Italian author could provide Italy's common people with a serial novel that would be uninfluenced by French examples (notorious for their supposed "obscenities") and thereby more in keeping with common sense and a saner view of reality. In making this attempt (*esperimento*, as the author calls it), De Marchi upholds the virtues of the common people against their detractors who proclaim them (the people), as readers, to be like voracious beasts feeding exclusively on incongruities, filth, and naked flesh. Not so, says De Marchi, writing in the glow of the success of his "experiment," the novel *Il cappello del prete* (The Curate's Hat), which appeared first serially in June 1877 and as a volume in 1888. The novel is a nicely wrought "mystery" structured in the fashion of the appendix novel but written without the crudeness of style and language that too often characterized that genre. Rather, it is written in a readily accessible, yet dignified manner, and with just enough psychological probing to add some depth to the story.

Further reading

Amosu, Tundonu. *The Land of Adventure: The Representation of Africa in Emilio Salgari*. Lagos: Istituto Italiano di Cultura, 1988.

Collodi, Carlo. *The Adventures of Pinocchio*. Bilingual edition with original illustrations, translated with an introduction and notes by Nicolas J. Perella. Berkeley: University of California Press, 1986/91.

De Amicis, Edmondo. *Heart: A School Boy's Journal*. Trans. Isabel Hapgood. New York: Crowell, 1922.

Kroha, Lucienne. "Matilde Serao's Fantasia: An Author in Search of a Character." In Zygmunt Barański and S. Vidall, eds., *Women and Italy: Essays on Gender, Culture and History*. London: Macmillan, 1991, pp. 245–62.

Neera. *The Soul of an Artist*. Trans. E. L. Marison. San Francisco: Elder, 1905.

Panizza, Letizia and Sharon Wood, eds. *A History of Women's Writing in Italy*. Cambridge: Cambridge University Press, 2000.

Russell, Rinanda, ed. *Italian Women Writers: A Bio-Bibliographical Sourcebook*. Westport, CT: Greenwood Press, 1994.

Salsini, Laura A. *Gendered Genres: Female Experiences and Narrative Patterns in the Works of Matilde Serao*. Cranbury, NJ: Fairleigh Dickinson University Press, 1999.

Serao, Matilde. *The Essential Matilde Serao*. Ed. Anthony Gisolfi. New York: Las Americas, 1968.

Wood, Sharon. *Italian Women's Writing 1860–1994*. London: Athlone Press, 1995.

6

The foundations of Italian modernism: Pirandello, Svevo, Gadda

Geography played a crucial role in defining the Italian experience of "modernity." Italy's official modernist movement, futurism, was the offspring of the northern urban centers of Milan, Turin, and Genoa, cities in which the conflict between modernization and cultural tradition was the most severe, while the Italian modernists discussed here all approached the complex question of modern subjectivity from standpoints conditioned to a significant degree by their own regional origins. The culture of Pirandello's preindustrialized Sicily, remotely distant from the modern industrial province of Svevo's Trieste, accentuated the playwright's terror of life falling apart in a world of paradox and contradiction, a fear that Svevo had under control, and Gadda, armed with the weapons of a scientific culture, sought to overcome in parody and satire. However, in Italy, as elsewhere in Europe, the "modernity" these writers faced each in his own unique way was one with the industrialization of production, the acceleration of the tempo of life due to developments in science and technology, and the emergence of new forms of class struggle. The ambiguity, anguish, and spiritual fluctuation, deriving from the breakdown of old hierarchies and the expansion of the capitalist market, were the general life-symptoms of a collective Western humanity, which the literary art of these authors at once incorporated and attempted to treat.

Luigi Pirandello (1867–1936)

Pirandello dramatizes the disjunction between essence and life at the heart of the modern novel. His recollection of happier days, however, has a distinctly ironic ring to it. For him, such a comforting time is real only because we imagine it so.[1] Modern philosophy and science have destroyed the beautiful fable

---

[1] "Era un giorno la terra l'ombelico d'una sconfinata creazione. Tutto il cielo, il sole, gli astri s'aggiravan continuamente intorno a lei quasi per offrirle uno spettacolo e far lume dì e notte. Poteva ogni onesto morale con le mani intrecciate sul ventre godersi beatamente quest'immenso spettacolo e lodarne in cuor suo il Signore Iddio, che aveva creato per lui

of an integrated civilization and the world has been reduced to a common toy top spinning aimlessly in a void, its mortal inhabitants lost in an unintelligible and limitless space, disoriented and agitated by a now tumultuous life. The loss of an illusion of plenitude – the fusion of the world and the self, in Lukács' terms – is for Pirandello the point of entry into modernity. Some concrete historical situation, such as the rise of technology and the expansion of the market to include and determine cultural production, has dissolved all the pleasing illusions of life and has destabilized the economic base of artistic careers: hence the sensation of living on the threshold of an abyss created by science and reason; opposition to the modern world of abstract rationalism where secular interests dominate and political parties advance self-serving objectives; the destructive effect of progress and democracy.

Pirandello's importance for the modern stage consists in having incorporated into dramatic form the disintegration and estrangement at the core of modern existence. He did so not by simply representing thematically, as others had done before him, the disjunction between the self and the other, but by using the structure of the play itself to convey a separation of worlds that could never be united. The estrangement effect of theatrical artifice provided him with the means to carry out his revolution in drama. But before Pirandello had fully understood that the theater was the medium most congenial to his modernist vision of alienation, he had used the novel to probe the precarious status of the self. He maintained that traditional narrative realism, in particular its naturalist variants, was based on the false premise that reality was something out there to be copied; implicit in such a position was the belief that the writer and his characters shared a common humanity which formed the basis for identification. In opposition to this point of view, Pirandello maintained that reality was a complex of differential elements (perceptions, images, actions, and objects) that formed a problematical world. Knowledge of the world was uncertain and unstable because the status of the self was dubious and variable, thus making identification with the Other not only impossible, but also something to be feared.

The precarious condition of the individual in society was also a central theme of much realistic and naturalistic fiction. Particularly in the works of Verga, the deterministic logic inherent in events and in the conception of

---

tante cose belle." (Once upon a time the world was the nodal point of limitless creation. The entire sky, the sun, the stars rotated continually around it almost as if to offer a spectacle and to give light to day and night. Every honest mortal, with hands entwined on his belly, could enjoy this immense spectacle and give praise in his own heart to the Lord God who had created so many beautiful things.) Luigi Pirandello, *Saggi, Poesie, Scritti varii*, ed. Manlio Lo Vecchio-Musti (Milan: Mondadori, 1965), p. 895.

character was essential to the representation of historical and social necessity. It produced the drama of individual subjects trapped in a one-dimensional, quasi-mechanistic world, out of which no exit could be found. Pirandello inherits from the literature of his time such a drama; he draws from it the raw materials of his narrative art. These are for him realistic assumptions on which he inscribes a symbolic text. All of his stories, his novels in particular, manipulate commonplace situations and highlight improbable events and eccentric personalities for the purpose of creating anxiety and apprehension about modern life, while at the same time providing a means of escape. The rule of deterministic logic and material necessity, if not defeated, can be superseded, if the eye of the writer, in probing the dense fabric of human life and emotion, finds the incongruous situation on which he can build his art. Pirandello's novels, like his plays, all reflect back on the artistic process and, in so doing, emphasize the power of the imagination to create, rather than represent, reality.

With *L'esclusa* (*The Outcast*, 1893) Pirandello puts the raw materials of naturalism to use in constructing a narrative governed much less by causal necessity than by paradox. On the surface, *L'esclusa* appears to abide by the general poetics of *verismo*, as the novel's plot depicts the protagonist's fatal subjection to her environment. It presents situations and events that would appear to describe the suffocated lives of individuals in a world governed by necessity. Marta Ayala, a schoolteacher, is wrongly accused of adultery and is cast out of her marriage. Although innocent at the time of her exile, she is forced to conform to the role society has assigned to her and ends up taking as her lover the man she first resisted. Her eventual pregnancy would appear to exemplify the rule that, once defamed, a woman has no hope of salvation. But the story concludes with an ironic turn of events: Marta is reconciled with her husband and readmitted into polite society after she commits that very adultery for which she was originally castigated.

In *L'esclusa*, Pirandello does not reject the substance of a naturalist art that centered on the predicaments of individuals, nor does he dispute the naturalists' belief in the mysterious nature of human passion. Rather, by equating contradiction and paradox with authentic reality, he in effect denies the possibility of representing interpersonal relations as a system determined by social circumstance. Instead, human existence is governed not by a complex of physical and emotional relationships, but rather by unpredictable situations and occurrences. Pirandello's transition from *verismo* to modernism hinges on this outlook: the significant relationship between individuals so dear to classic realism and its naturalist variants is reduced to a surface narrative through which the reader is made to focus on the isolation of diverse existential possibilities.

But while *L'esclusa* breaks the rules of naturalism, it keeps the reader locked within a realistic situation. *Il fu Mattia Pascal* (*The Late Mattia Pascal*, 1904), Pirandello's second novel, enacts a radical break with the objective world of naturalist prose. It does so both thematically, by presenting that world as something from which the protagonist escapes, thus underlining his break with social authority, and formally by putting in the place of a social hypothesis a principle of epistemological doubt: perhaps the only thing about which Mattia Pascal is certain is his name. Hence the consciousness that pervades the narrative and the protagonist are one and the same. In telling his story, Mattia assumes the point of view of the humorist who, finding himself within a network of incongruent circumstances, comments of his *being there*. In order to triumph over an initially degraded reality (part 1 of the novel, which takes place in Mattia's home town), Mattia presents himself as invulnerable. His invulnerability is powered by the constant elation of the self, embedded in the brilliant display of paradox that constitutes the essence of his story. Mattia Pascal, on the brink of going mad because of an oppressive marriage and the almost simultaneous deaths of his youngest daughter and mother, secretly leaves town in search of diversion. While he is away, he learns that he is believed to be dead and, taking advantage of the error, attempts to make a new life for himself under a new identity. Then, after a number of significant experiences, realizing that his new life is just as oppressive as the one he left, he feigns suicide and, having restored his original identity, returns home to find that his wife is remarried to an old friend. The protagonist asks for no compensation whatsoever, but only to be left in peace to reflect on his own paradoxical existence as the late Mattia Pascal.

With *Il fu Mattia Pascal*, Pirandello becomes a genuine, undisguised modernist writer. In contrast to *L'esclusa*, which based its plot on a realistic, however exaggerated, hypothesis, the novel finds its justification in the self-irony and contradictions that animate its own creative capacities. Its form marks a radical turn from literary naturalism and philosophic realism, as it prioritizes artistic freedom, symbolized in the protagonist's artful self-creation, and, therefore, the mystical and wholly intellectual character of literary practice. The novel refers to nothing other than the mental processes by which it was created, its sole purpose being to produce pleasure by dismantling, through philosophical humor, preconceived schemes, and hierarchies, a practice that results, as Freud might say, in the displacement of psychic energy from a painful effect. The humorous pleasure we derive from Mattia's final words ("I am the late Mattia Pascal") produces an aesthetic harmony found amid the dissonance of human experience.

In many respects, the novels *I vecchi e i giovani* (1913) and *Suo marito* (*Her Husband*, 1911) represent an involution with respect to the modernist rhetoric and style of *Il fu Mattia Pascal*. The intention of *I vecchi e i giovani* is, in fact, to document the political and social problems that beset Italy in the wake of Unification, while the overarching theme of *Suo marito* relates to the question of the authenticity of art in a society that produces for commercial gain. Both works focus on historically documentable problems and both appear to have a social ax to grind. Yet although Pirandello reverts to a more traditional form in these novels (third-person narrative and chronological plot development), he does not fail to express his modernist perspective. For however present history may be in *I vecchi e i giovani*, it does not constitute a unifying factor that contains either the movement of Providence, as in Manzoni's *I promessi sposi*, or the power of common sense or contradiction we find behind the historical events recounted in Nievo's *Le confessioni di un italiano* and De Roberto's *I viceré*. That is to say, history no longer connotes the space in which mechanisms of power or reason operate and influence human life, but rather it becomes an existential space in which the individual breaks away from the determining forces that spell his destiny to be one and the same with life itself. In *Suo marito*, no matter how much the reader is forced to dwell on the theme of art's commodification, he cannot fail to see the paradoxes on which the novel is structured and which serve to accentuate the alienation of its characters. The female protagonist, Sylvia, a playwright, almost dies in giving birth to a child at the very moment her play is labeled a great success; the second paradox has her art prosper while her sick child deteriorates, his death coinciding with the brilliant solution Sylvia finds for her new play. Art has overcome nature and, while Sylvia despairs in her awareness of the horrific, destructive ferocity of nature, Giustino, her husband and agent, delights in the power of art that has a life of its own totally independent from its creator.

From the standpoint of form, *I quaderni di Serafino Gubbio operatore* (*The Notebooks of Serafino Gubbio: [Shoot!]*, 1916) marks with respect to *Suo marito* a definite change in narrative perspective. Here Pirandello adopts the concept of alienation, not only as a theme, but also as a structural principle. The novel becomes a diary, composed by a passive cameraman, a hand that turns the crank, nicknamed "Si gira" ("Shoot") to denote his mechanical function. The more proficiency Serafino Gubbio gains as a cameraman and the more overwhelming the alienating world of objects appears, the more impoverished he becomes and the less capable he is of taking possession of the reality around him. The central idea of Serafino's Notebooks is that in the modern world the mechanism has become the principal means of controlling production and, as such, it is an obstacle to human creativity.

Pirandello's last novel, *Uno, nessuno e centomila* (*One, No One, and a Hundred Thousand*, 1926) is the work of fiction that best presents the problem of human identity as developed in his plays. Vitangelo Moscarda, whose story begins when his wife casually observes that his nose appears somewhat tilted, recounts the novel in the first person. This apparently banal, innocent, and playful observation throws Moscarda headlong into a complex existential predicament: what is "oneself," if that self lives continuously at the mercy of others. Moscarda's story revolves around the position of the subject as the object of analysis and the ongoing process of verifying the radically divergent relationship between the narrative "I" and the "you" whom Moscarda continually addresses. Moscarda's existential dilemma cannot be resolved, but only transcended in the condition of pure subjectivity attained at the novel's end, when, having taken refuge in a mental asylum, he loses his specific identity in becoming one with nature, thus losing the self that had been endangered by the scrutiny of others, paradoxically avoiding non-being by ceasing to be.

Italo Svevo (pseudonym of Ettore Schmitz, 1861–1928)

At least in one respect Italo Svevo shares common ground with Pirandello: in his belief in reality as a field of possibilities. His modernist imagination, however, does not lead him to reject the social world and take refuge in nature, art, or madness. What appears to be his characters' defenselessness in the face of modern life is really their productive freedom, a capacity that, through daydreaming, allows them to defend themselves against threats to the self and to manage the discomforts of existence. Whereas for Pirandello life and the self are irreconcilable opposites, for Svevo they are one and the same thing. The focus of literature is shifted from self-creation as escape to self-analysis as therapy. All those paralyzing rules, institutions, and moral responsibilities that obstruct the free flow of living for Pirandello's characters, in Svevo are brought under the authority of a mind which subjects them to the neurotic movement of its desire.

Svevo's first novel *Una vita* (1892) has the effect of clearing the stage for his future modernist antiheroes. It tells the story of a young intellectual who cannot escape the pain of living in a society without ideals. Driven by the wish to fulfill his intellectual dreams, Alfonso Nitti moves from the country to the city of Trieste, where he takes employment as a bank clerk. His learning and intelligence gain him entry into the bank manager's home. There he meets his boss's daughter, Annetta, who sees in him a refuge from the material world of her father, and with whom he has an affair. But

Alfonso cannot face the social responsibilities of marriage, quits his job, renouncing his fiancée, and returns to the country in search of his roots. The letter he writes explaining his motivation is interpreted by the family as an attempt at blackmail. Annetta's brother invites him to a duel and Alfonso, seeing no way out of his hopeless predicament, commits suicide. Thus Svevo puts an end to the nineteenth-century, humanist intellectual so dear to Fogazzaro, the early Verga and D'Annunzio, who opposes with his learning and idealism the material culture of a world based on economic interests, while at the same time being attracted to the power that world possesses.

Una vita is written wholly in the naturalist vein, as it emphasizes the force of education and social milieu in determining the protagonist's negative fate. Svevo's second novel *Senilità* (*As a Man Grows Older*, 1898) has a very different story to tell. Its main character Emilio is just as incompetent at living as was Alfonso, but his ineptitude no longer spells opposition to the grey, monotonous existence of the urban bourgeoisie. He is a writer, as was his predecessor, but writing is a pleasurable hobby rather than a vehicle for displaying his moral and intellectual superiority. Emilio Brentani lives a stable, protected, but uneventful life as an insurance broker. His "senility" is an infection of the will that ensures a safe life; it is a malady he nourishes because it immunizes him against taking risks. But an object of desire in the form of Angiolina, a working-class woman who embodies all the energy and health he lacks, provides Emilio with a chance of escaping the monotony and taking on a new vitality. All he has to do is to call into question the basis of his "normal" life, which he refuses to do. Instead, he prefers to compromise, safeguarding himself against the force of passion by thinking he can be in love and remain aloof at the same time; that he can possess Angiolina while not being possessed by her; by really believing he can have an affair without running the risk of damage to his family (a sister whom he cares for) and his career. *Senilità* is the story of Emilio's self-deception and how he makes it work; it is also the story of a genuine passion that is always at odds with the forms of rationalization summoned to keep it under control. Emilio, therefore, is never really able to love, or to enjoy life; he will always vacillate and his motivations will always be marked by ambiguity. He will lose both the women who have ever meant anything to him (Angiolina and his sister Amalia, who dies from an overdose of ether), but, since peace and security are not at stake, he finds a way of defending himself against those losses. As his instinct for self-preservation safeguarded him against disruptive desire when he was young, it will come to his aid as he grows old. Time heals the wound of loss and Emilio's story ends with his return to the quiet and secure normal life and with the intellectual pleasure of being able to give new, more noble meaning to Angiolina and, therefore, to his experience of love.

Twenty-five years separate *Senilità* from *La coscienza di Zeno* (1923), Svevo's best-known and most important novel. Written in the first person, it contains the memories that Zeno Cosini writes down as a prelude to psycho-analytical therapy. The episodes he selects from his life become the different chapters of his story: his attempts to quit smoking, his father's death, his marriage, his infidelity, and lastly his business partnership. With the exception of the preface, in which Zeno's doctor explains that he has taken revenge on his patient by publishing his memoirs, the last chapter containing Zeno's reflections on psychoanalysis, and the final page, where the author's voice emerges to reflect on the general sickness of mankind, *La coscienza di Zeno* is wholly an interior monologue controlled by ironic commentary. Zeno not only recalls his past, but also interprets it, revealing how it is constructed of a mixture of truths and lies. Such a procedure generates a text thoroughly modernist in structure, in that it orders its plot not chronologically in lin-ear time, but according to the themes indicated in the chapter headings; so that the reader can enter the story virtually at any point and grasp its significance.

Like Emilio, Zeno lives in a dull, bourgeois world in which he finds se-curity and which he admires for the importance it places on such values as duty, truth, and legality. But, in having Zeno speak in the first person, Svevo brings his character's neurotic mind to bear not only on himself but also on the institutions and ideals that, he knows, are fashioned to protect his identity. His neurosis, while a handicap that prevents him from realizing his desires, is also a powerful hermeneutic that enables him to understand the contradiction and equivocation at the root of bourgeois life. Zeno does this not by being defeated by society, nor by striking out against the Other through parody or satire, but by self-analysis. Bourgeois alienation is thus treated like a patient, examined in the light of rationality (rather than rea-son), displayed in all of its incongruities and contradictions. Hence, Zeno is able to accept and reject life at the same time, to feel at home in his world, while displaying its sickness. Of his own neurosis, in fact, he is cured at the very moment he accepts it, and in accepting it, he becomes part of the general malady that paralyzes his entire world. Life, he writes, in the final note of his diary, is a terminal illness for which there is no cure. The social order in the modern age of machines cannot be changed. The only event that might lead us back to health is some incredible disaster. Someone, Zeno suggests, will eventually invent a powerful explosive and will destroy the world with it, returning the earth back to its original state, free from parasites (such as man) and disease.

Carlo Emilio Gadda (1893–1973)

If only a cataclysmic event of such horrendous proportions is the answer to the sick, bourgeois world of consumption and private life, then, it is clear, there is no answer at all. Such a prophecy, however, ends up being only a footnote to what in effect are for Svevo the comforts of analysis. His crippled subject in the form of Zeno succeeds brilliantly in safeguarding his beleaguered self by keeping that self in full view, while immunizing it through the power of irony. For Carlo Emilio Gadda the self is dead and its deadness is the foundation on which literature now rests. For both Pirandello and Svevo, the crisis of the self created the need for a compensatory form that epistemology or analysis could generate as a means of transcending the reality of dissolution. Gadda, instead, seeks no compensation in representing the self through its re-creation. His primary concern as a writer is to extract the self from representation by making its existence as a narrative structure problematic. In his narratives, the self becomes thing-like, reduced to a grotesque surface reality. Thus Gadda opens up a wholly new perspective on narration in which the modernist irony that compensated for the breakdown of human identity in a mechanized world is in turn fractured by the otherness it sought to control. Gadda's means of breaking down that control is violent comedy, the "*grin* upon the Deathshead," in the words of Wyndham Lewis.[2] Gadda himself would put it somewhat more philosophically, but his meaning is the same: "Lo scherno solo dei disegni e delle parvenze era salvo, quasi maschera tragica sulla metope del teatro."[3] ("Only the derision of figures and appearances was safe, as a quasi-tragic mask on the metope of the theater.") The passage from Pirandello and Svevo to Gadda is the passage from a modernist irony founded on the metaphysics of "life" in its opposition to "form," as in Pirandello, and, in Svevo, on the inner experience of the self, to satire and parody. Gaddian satire, and the baroque style that marks its expression, derive from a need to attack all that in literature and life is counterfeit, artificial, and spurious, while stylistic parody, chiefly of the tropes of realism and naturalism, is a means of interrogating the institution of literature in an age when the loss of the self makes the individual style impossible. In Gadda, satire and parody combine with pastiche as weapons used to undermine art's pretensions to absolute truth, private language, and illusion of autonomy.

Gadda's first novel, *La cognizione del dolore* (*Acquainted with Grief*, 1963) has all the qualities of a modern, autobiographical epic. It comprises

---

[2] Wyndham Lewis, *The Complete Wild Body* (Santa Barbara, CA: Black Sparrow Press, 1982), p. 101.

[3] Carlo Emilio Gadda, *La cognizione del dolore*, in *Romanzi e racconti* (Milan: Mondadori, 1988–9), vol. I: p. 704.

a series of segments which were serialized in the Florentine review *Lette-ratura* from 1938 to 1941. The book in its original form was left unfinished, its concluding chapters included in subsequent editions. The story is set in the imaginary South American nation of Maradagal situated not far from its age-old enemy Parapagal, satirical representations of Italy and Austria respectively. In 1924, the war between them had ended, each proclaiming to be the victor. Near the city of Pastrufazio (Milan), in a modern villa, live the Pirobutirros, a family of ancient European stock, reduced now to an aged widow and her forty-year-old son, Gonzalo, a sanguine, neurotic figure, who lives in constant friction with the world around him. Both Gonzalo and his mother are autobiographical caricatures of Gadda and his mother, Adele Lehr, a retired schoolteacher of German origin.

The reader is informed early on in the narrative that Gonzalo's principal characteristic is his lack of sociability, which borders on the misanthropic. When we meet him for the first time, a chorus of minor characters that gravitate around his mother and the villa, whose voices are deflections of the narrator's point of view, has prepared his entry on to the scene. José believes that Gonzalo has all of the seven capital sins enclosed in his belly like seven snakes. Battistina, a domestic, says that he is always angry and that at certain moments he mistreats his mother, often threatening to kill her. His cruelty in the popular imagination knows no limits; as a child, it is claimed, he delighted in killing lizards and once repeatedly threw a cat out of a third-story window, until finally it died, for no other reason than to prove that cats, falling from whatever height, will land on all fours. And an extraordinary account of his gluttony has Gonzalo hunched over a lobster, his eyes gleaming with desire and his nostrils flaring, as he devours his prey.

The novel's action begins on a clear summer morning, when the villa is quiet. Gonzalo, who suffers from some imaginary illness, takes advantage of his mother's absence to call in the family doctor. But he has nothing new to report, and rehearses the symptoms of his neurosis that the good doctor is familiar with and again attempts in vain to understand. To Gonzalo everything seems absurd; his only desire is to be engulfed by the immense, limitless light and by the harmony he perceives in the endless chirping of the cicadas and the rustling of plants. The specific objects of his discomfort are all those people and things that threaten his solitude and the absolute possession of his mother, such as the continuous movement of the servants who, he believes, exploit his mother's generosity, the bells, which symbolize spiritual oppression, in that their sound waves drown out the melodious chant of the cicadas, or the wall surrounding the villa, which for him has no other purpose than that of requiring the annual payment of taxes. Gonzalo, we are told, treats his mother with hostility for her attachment to the outside world, and refuses to enlist the protection of an association of night watchmen. One night, when Gonzalo is away on one of his many trips, his mother is found on the verge of death, the victim of some horrendous violence. It is not clear who is responsible for the crime, but the reader is left to believe that it is the watchmen or Gonzalo himself.

The conceptual foundation of *La cognizione* derives largely from Freudian metapsychology. It is based on the primordial event of patricide and the sublimation of guilt in social institutions: "Il male oscuro di cui le storie e le leggi e le universe discipline delle gran cattedre persistono a dover ignorare la causa, i modi: e lo si porta dentro di sè per tutto il folgorato soscendere della vita." (It was the obscure sickness of which histories and laws and the universal disciplines of the great chairs persist in having to ignore the causes, the stages: and one bears it within oneself along all the resplendent descent of a lifetime.)[4] Gonzalo is fully aware of man's innate aggressiveness and feels remorse for the painful fate shared by all men. But he has decided not to surrender to the illusions of life and to the repression of his sense of guilt. The origin of Gonzalo's particular friction with the world lies in his relationship with his father whom he respected and loved, but against whom he rebelled on account of his natural love for his mother. With his father's death, the authority of the external world is substituted for the paternal image. All that constitutes authority or oppression or is a hindrance to his life as a recluse is the target of Gonzalo's contempt and endless tirades.

Hence, the novel's subject (both its controlling consciousness and its subject matter) is Gonzalo who lives a life of melancholic solitude. The narrative voice reveals Gonzalo to the reader on two registers: first, by capturing his interior (lyrical) soul and the ethical dilemma manifest in his need to chose between an existence of absolute negation, which would lead to self-negation (the suicide of an existential hero), or to succumb to the illusions of life; second, by having the voice of the Other (the community detested by Gonzalo) form Gonzalo's character through legendary accounts of his eccentricity and misanthropic behavior. This latter mode of representing the protagonist is both satirical and parodic, while the former pastiches the immortal figure of Hamlet who was also engaged in a fierce struggle against the world on behalf of a truth that caused pain.

However we choose to interpret Gonzalo's pain and his melancholic existence and whatever meaning we assign to his bizarre actions, the intellectual and moral substance of a figure that pervades the text in all its perverse and masochistic movement overcomes us. We see the uselessness of the world through his gaze, ponder the obscurity of his depressive states, and rejoice

4 Ibid., vol. I: p. 690.

in the manic drive that unleashes a linguistic omnipotence from the depths of his sadness. At the same time, we can never get a hold on Gonzalo's life because it is overdetermined by a narrator who not only comments on and judges his actions, but mocks and impersonates him as well, yet often identifies completely with him.

Yet although the pastiche of self in the final analysis rescues Gadda's protagonist from his own melancholy, it also draws attention to his difference from the brilliant surface of reality that the author's linguistic spectacle seems to emphasize. In fact, the macaronic and the lyrical go hand in hand to form a tangle of perspectives that can never be truly unraveled. As Gianfranco Contini, the critic most responsible for Gadda's acclaim during the 1950s and 1960s, has shown, in *La cognizione del dolore* images are cast in extenuating rhythms within a syntax so abstract that it defies every attempt at clarification through paraphrase or translation. Compulsive and fragmented, Gadda's lyric mode is the means through which his and his character's anxiety is conveyed, together with the sorrow, pain, and grief, the causes of which are kept silent.

Gadda's second and best-known novel *Quer pasticciaccio brutto de via Merulana* (*That Awful Mess in Via Merulana*) was also serialized in *Letteratura* (1946) before it was published in revised form as a book in 1957. The years that separate it from *La cognizione* witnessed the triumph and fall of fascism and Italy's entry into the war. The catastrophic events of those years contribute to changing Gadda's satirical perspective from one that focused on a life lived *in extremis* to humanity in general, and to Mussolini and fascism in particular. *Quer pasticciaccio* follows the path of a simple detective story. Two crimes are committed in the space of twenty-four hours in the same apartment building in via Merulana. The first is the robbery of several pieces of jewelry belonging to a certain Contessa Menegazzi; the second is the murder of Liliana Balducci, a beautiful and generous Roman lady. Don Ciccio Ingravallo is the detective assigned to the case. The investigation begins in Rome and spreads to the countryside, where eventually the jewels are recovered. However, little is found out about Liliana's killer, the only suspicion being that it might have been the boyfriend of one of the victim's former maidservants, who had broken into the Balducci apartment with the intention of robbing it.

It does not take the reader long to realize that Gadda's aim is much less the creation of a well-structured detective story than using the conventions of detective fiction to indict an entire society. The process of detection and interrogation will thus lead the reader into a world without boundaries where everything and everyone is to some degree suspect. The principle of suspicion generates a total sense of causal ramification. As the scheme of things is disentangled, the reader learns not to dismiss any detail and that everyone is somehow guilty of something, the guiltiest of all being the Fascist state, embodied in the sordidly grotesque figure of its criminal idol Mussolini, for whom Gadda reserves his greatest disdain and most powerful dose of satire.

But however similar *Quer pasticciaccio* may appear to detective fiction, there is at least one important feature that sets it apart: it refuses to simplify its working complexity to provide a solution to the main crime. When it seems we are about to unravel the mystery, and thus, following the traditional detective story, move into the realm of order, Gadda blocks the story's movement. Once the investigation has exposed the social and institutional orders in which the crimes take place, and once it has probed and foregrounded the human and material orders as well, like a machine that has run out of fuel, it comes to a halt, the movement of its parts arrested in conjecture. The reader is likely to ask what drives the narrative away from its stated focus off at innumerable tangents. What motivates Gadda's baroque spectacle, propelling the complex machine of detection? A simple answer, and perhaps the only one that can be offered with some degree of certainty, is a pervasive desire to "murder" his object and thus to escape from any closed or transcendent meaning that the identity of the criminal would provide. But also, by refusing to assign guilt, Gadda compels his reader to remain within the sphere of the desire behind the narrative action, a desire gratified in the investigation, and that centers on the transgressive sexual activity that takes place at the heart of the mystery within the Balducci household between the lovely Liliana and her so-called adopted nieces. Gadda, then, has performed a double transgression: while exposing the sexual transgression through forceful innuendo, he, in subverting the formal codes of the detective story, prevents transgression from becoming the norm, sidestepping altogether the need for closure and resolution, i.e. the restoration of order.

So the reader, frustrated by the obscurity of the investigation and the lack of resolution, is forced to abandon the objective of narration as it is conventionally presented and focus on the descriptive layers of reference that engulf it in a form of destructive purification. What characterizes Gadda's prose in *Quer pasticciaccio*, even more than in *La cognizione*, is its fierce onslaught on reality, which results in the enlargement of the objective world of description, evermore intensified and energized by the expressionistic use of dialect. Such a procedure has a deep effect on the use of narrative time, a time that is constantly folding out as it follows the object in its infinite articulations and entanglements. In contrast to *La cognizione*, in which the subject/protagonist defends his own position threatened by the popular masses that encroach on his physical and emotional properties, *Quer pasticciaccio* has no narrative subject who speaks directly for the narrator, setting his claims against the

Other. Instead the Other is conceived as some pervasive social totality, a degenerated collectivity that begs to be cleansed, its fascism punished, its follies exhibited. This policing of an entire society frustrates the reader intent on knowing the identity of the killer and the motivation for the crime. Gadda has led him into what, from the standpoint of traditional detective fiction, is a labyrinth with no exit, thus a story with no ending. The story conventions of the traditional novel that survived the onslaught of Pirandello and Svevo are incompatible with Gadda's vision of the world as chaos. But for Gadda there is a deep order to the chaos, a system whose elements comprise other systems characterized by different elements with systems of their own, and so on ad infinitum.

The result is infinite descriptions and digressions. Every point on the map of possibility can be a starting point, every object a web that radiates outward. The most notorious example of Gadda's inventory of the world, one cited by Italo Calvino in his essay on multiplicity, is the episode in which Brigadiere Pestalozzi discovers the stolen jewels. Every precious stone is unveiled in all its chemical qualities and geological history, its associations extending outward to the whole of creation. The reader in fact, after having roamed through the horrors of the world, is given the impression of having arrived at the heart of creation, where the mute splendor of the stones, Gadda tells us, reflects some hidden order of Providence. But even in this instance, when Gadda's lyrical and scientific drives become one, we cannot help but notice that again the world is being distorted before our very eyes, made the object of an uncontrollable satiric gaze. In stark contrast to Pirandello and Svevo, whose novels illustrate in different ways how art can revive a world deadened by modernization and how the reified subject can regain its lost humanity through the artful reconstruction or management of reality's negative aspects, Gadda's texts display what one critic, speaking in reference to "high modernism," has called the "deathly" side of art, namely, an art that "kills" in the sense that it makes visible an aspiration to an absolute life of the image at the very same time as, through parody and satire, it exhibits "the error of the imaginary." What this means in practical terms is that the commodity status of culture is a natural barrier between the artist and reality, so much so that the author's genuinely mimetic impulses find no object on which to focus that has not been contaminated by cultural representation. The object, then, is an illusionary entity and the author, not to fall victim to the illusion, uses the degraded image against itself, thus revealing the deathly aspect of its material reality.

In conclusion, Pirandello, Svevo, and Gadda represent three different stages and ways of portraying and interpreting reality. Pirandello's humor implies a dialectic view of middle-class morality and its conventions: what seems normal and accepted by everybody is actually an incoherent way of life, a recital of rules that mask the impossibility fully to live a life outside such rules. Svevo accepts Pirandello's view, but he ironically proposes human weakness and incoherence as the only possible solution to cope with life itself and to survive. Finally, Gadda penetrates in depth the contradictions of modern society, bringing to the surface the impossibility of finding anything that is not already compromised by our way of life. The only thing the writer can do, then, is to focus upon the evidence of reality, no matter how illusory such evidence may be.

Further reading

Bertone, Manuela and Robert S. Dombroski, eds. *Carlo Emilio Gadda: Contemporary Perspectives*. Toronto: University of Toronto Press, 1994.

Biasin, Gian-Paolo and Manuela Gieri, eds. *Luigi Pirandello*. Toronto: University of Toronto Press, 1999.

Dombroski, Robert S. *Properties of Writing: Ideological Discourse in Modern Italian Fiction*. Baltimore: Johns Hopkins University Press, 1994.

  Creative Entanglements: Gadda and the Baroque. Toronto: University of Toronto Press, 1999.

Furbank, Philip Nicholas, *Italo Svevo: The Man and the Writer*. Berkeley: University of California Press, 1966.

Gatt-Rutter, John. *Italo Svevo: A Double Life*. Oxford: Oxford University Press, 1988.

Harrison, Thomas. *Essayism: Conrad, Musil and Pirandello*. Baltimore: Johns Hopkins University Press, 1992.

Lucente, Gregory. *Beautiful Fables: Self-Consciousness in Italian Narrative from Manzoni to Calvino*. Baltimore: Johns Hopkins University Press, 1986.

Maloney, Brian. *Italo Svevo: A Critical Introduction*. Edinburgh: Edinburgh University Press, 1964.

Sbragia, Albert. *Carlo Emilio Gadda and the Modern Macaronic*. Gainesville: University of Florida Press, 1996.

Stocchi-Perucchio, Donatella. *Pirandello and the Vagaries of Knowledge: A Reading of "Il fu Mattia Pascal."* Stanford: Stanford University Press, 1991.

7

LUCIA RE

Neorealist narrative: experience and experiment

Origins, models, themes, language, and politics of neorealism

Neorealism as an object of study has turned out to be a puzzling problem of literary history. Elio Vittorini – an important neorealist novelist, editor of the interdisciplinary journal *Il Politecnico* (1945–7) that championed neorealism, and editor of "I Gettoni," a series devoted to young writers published by Einaudi from 1951 to 1958 – maintained that each neorealist writer had his or her own neorealism.[1] Pier Paolo Pasolini thought that what neorealists had in common was basically just a "taste" for the real. Some critics point to *Gli indifferenti* (*The Time of Indifference*, 1929) by Alberto Moravia, to *Luce fredda* (Cold Light, 1933) by Umberto Barbaro (1902–59), and to *Tre operai* (Three Workers, 1934) by Carlo Bernari (1909–92) as examples of early neorealist novels, but other critics cite Cesare Pavese's *Paesi tuoi* (*The Harvesters*, 1941) as the only proto-neorealist text before World War II. The term *neorealismo* was used occasionally in Italy in the 1930s to refer to new forms of realism (for example, the German *Neue Sachlichkeit*) then emerging in Europe in opposition to nonrealist movements such as expressionism, futurism, and symbolism. In Italy, modernist forms of realism flourished in the 1930s, ranging from the "magic realism" of Massimo Bontempelli (1878–1960) to the experimental fictions, tinged with surrealism, of Paola Masino (1908–89), to the existential novels of Moravia and Barbaro. Novels such as *Maria Zef* (Maria Zef, 1936) by Paola Drigo (1876–1938) testify to the enduring legacy of *verismo* and foreshadow the neorealist interest in the economic underdevelopment of many regions of Italy, particularly the South or the Mezzogiorno.

The emergence of the term *neorealismo* in the more specific sense that it assumed during the war, however, can be dated to 1942. Film editor Mario Serandrei (1907–66), upon receiving the first few takes of *Ossessione*

---

[1] Editorial in *Il Politecnico* 28 (April 1947), reprinted in *Diario in Pubblico* (Milan: Bompiani, 1970), pp. 305–6.

(*Obsession*, 1942) by Luchino Visconti (1906–76) reportedly wrote back to the director in amazement, declaring that he had no idea how to define the new kind of cinema the film represented except by the word "neorealist." With its stark, unsentimental portrayal of the struggles, sexuality, including homosexuality, and crimes of its protagonists, *Ossessione* contradicted all the Fascist notions of family, gender roles, and the healthy productivity of the Italian provinces. It was based on James Cain's thriller *The Postman Always Rings Twice* (1934), but its tone and texture are more reminiscent of Giovanni Verga, whose *verismo* (seen as an antidote to the mystifications of fascism) became an inspiration for the new realist aesthetics in film and fiction.[2] *Ossessione* (which had many problems with censorship) is considered the first neorealist film, followed by masterpieces such as *Roma, città aperta* (*Rome, Open City*, 1945) and *Paisà* (*Paisan*, 1946) by Roberto Rossellini (1906–77); *Ladri di biciclette* (*The Bicycle Thief*, 1948) and *Umberto D.* (*Umberto D.*, 1951) by Vittorio De Sica (1901–74); and Visconti's neorealist classic *La terra trema* (*The Earth Trembles*, 1948), a free adaptation of Verga's masterpiece, *I Malavoglia*. These films made neorealism an international phenomenon and influenced the aesthetics of film and narrative worldwide.

After 1943, the term *neorealismo* began to be applied to narrative. There was also an extensive production of neorealist poetry and painting. Although there was no neorealist manifesto and no well-defined neorealist constituency, many older and younger writers and filmmakers began, in the midst of the political turmoil brought by the war, the anti-Fascist Resistance, and the fall of fascism, to feel a new desire to narrate, document, and share their wartime experiences, while celebrating the liberation and exorcizing the Fascist past. The national front that (until its collapse in 1948) united Marxist and non-Marxist political parties in a spirit of solidarity contributed to an opening up of communication and encouraged writers and artists to participate in the reconstruction process. The call for a new realism and the desire to tell and hear "the truth" coincided with a growing sense that the Fascist regime was built on lies and that both film and literature under fascism were either flawed by mystification or crippled by the need to be silent or hermetically ambiguous to avoid possible persecution. This highly reductive and in some cases self-serving view of the arts under fascism, and of fascism itself as a period of "unreality," became an extraordinarily productive collective mythology that allowed the neorealists to feel empowered to create

---

[2] Visconti originally wanted to film an adaptation of Verga's short story about a bandit and his lover, "L'amante di Gramigna" ("Gramigna's Lover"), but the Fascist censors did not like the theme and blocked the project.

new and politically committed, truthful works for the first time in several decades.[3] Neorealism is the body of wartime and postwar works produced either in this spirit or as a direct consequence of it, and while few are the authors whose works remained strictly neorealist, neorealism constituted a seminal moment in the history of narrative, with its own range of distinctive themes and stylistic features.

Neorealist film and literature, despite the difference between the two media, have much in common stylistically and thematically. In neorealism, an unprecedented cross-fertilization took place between literature and film. Ideas, narrative strategies, and representational devices were constantly being adopted and adapted from the novel by film and vice versa. They shared literary models, especially *verismo* and American realist literature. Many neorealist novels were made into films.[4] Although *Ossessione* is an idiosyncratic masterpiece, it contains thematic and formal elements that were to become typical of neorealism. Antifascism, though it does not in and of itself qualify a work as neorealist, is a neorealist constant, as is the determined effort stylistically to produce the effect of confronting the reader with a provocative reality that requires taking a critical position. This tendency to be politically "committed" took many different forms but was nevertheless pervasive. The neorealist depiction of reality and the response that neorealism required were never dispassionate, resigned, indifferent, or fatalistic. *Ossessione* inaugurated the tendency of neorealism to create a provocative effect of reality. This was done in part through the startling use of real landscapes and locations to frame the characters' actions (as opposed to the studio sets characteristic of Fascist-era films), and by reducing intrusive or expressive montage to a minimum. Long takes made it look as if events were narrating themselves (a strategy amplified by Visconti in *La terra trema*). As pointed out by André Bazin, the most influential film critic of postwar Europe, this technique had the effect of "preserving the mystery" and the sense of the ambiguity of reality.[5] *Ossessione* excludes explicit moral or political commentary by presenting the story only through the eyes of the participants, yet it has a devastating impact on the viewer, implicitly dismantling

---

[3] As Ruth Ben-Ghiat has shown, in "Fascism, Writing, and Memory: The Realist Aesthetic in Italy, 1930–1950," *Journal of Modern History* 67 (September 1995), pp. 627–65, this often implied a convenient amnesia on the part of artists and authors, such as Rossellini and Moravia, who produced high-quality realist works during the Fascist era.

[4] In 1945, Visconti planned and actually signed a contract to do an adaptation of Steinbeck's *Grapes of Wrath*; at about the same time, he also planned to turn Vittorini's *Uomini e no* into a film.

[5] For Bazin's important definition of neorealism's aesthetics, see "An Aesthetic of Reality: Neorealism," in *What is Cinema?*, vol. II, ed. Hugh Gray (Berkeley: University of California Press, 1971), pp. 16–40.

Fascist ideology. Aiming for a similar effect, many neorealist novelists take a quasi-cinematic approach and strive to make us see the events of the real as if we were actually watching them "unedited" through the unflinching eye of a camera, or as if we were present, looking with our own eyes and listening with our own ears from the same perspective as the protagonists. The first page of *Il sentiero dei nidi di ragno* (*The Path to the Nest of Spiders*, 1947) by Italo Calvino takes this cinematic approach, and the novel renders the ambiguity of the real (a series of episodes of the anti-Fascist Resistance involving a partisan brigade made up of misfits and renegades) as if we were seeing it and hearing it through the eyes and ears of Pin, a pre-adolescent street urchin. Both Visconti and Calvino have derelict characters from the lowest strata of society as their protagonists; this thematic choice can be traced back to *verismo*, and it becomes another constant of neorealist narrative. However, unlike Verga, whose portrayal of a wretched humanity disclosed no possibility for change, the neorealists implicitly indicted the political and social situation that made the real tragic and unbearable for the subaltern groups. In opposition to the Fascist idealization of the working poor, the neorealists polemically chose to focus on realities of exploitation, abuse, greed, and violence. They also sought to avoid the moralism of nineteenth-century realism exemplified by Manzoni's *I promessi sposi*, though neorealist novels sometimes replaced the pieties of Catholic paternalism with those of socialist realism.

Ossessione and *Il sentiero*, like most neorealist narratives, have an episodic structure: they retain a loose, segmented plot but, for the sake of realism, they avoid the tight interconnectedness of the nineteenth-century novel. There was heated debate among neorealists about the ethics and politics of plot. The most radical theorist and practitioner of neorealism in this regard was Cesare Zavattini (1902–91), best known as the co-author of the screenplays for De Sica's *Sciuscià* (*Shoeshine*, 1946), *Ladri di biciclette*, and *Umberto D.* He argued that plot had to be replaced with a purely documentary portrayal of the randomness and sluggishness of events in real time and space and of real people, whom he suggested the filmmaker should patiently follow, waiting for things to happen. Yet neorealist novels and films (including De Sica's) retained plot (however loose or episodic) as a formal device signifying two of its basic ideological tenets: first, the idea that human events and actions can be grasped together as having a shape, rhythm, and direction; second, the notion that human events and actions are consequential, and therefore can and do make a difference historically and politically. This constructive, purposive, and positive political dimension of plot is precisely what is lacking in most Fascist-era novels such as Moravia's *Gli indifferenti* and Bernari's *Tre operai*, whose plots configure patterns of meaninglessness, endless repetition, impasse, indifference, and angst. In requiring the reader to take an active critical position, the typical neorealist plot, even if often tragic, also differs from the plots of most *verista* novels. The subjects and style of *verismo* are sometimes very close to those of neorealism, but Darwinian or fatalistic ideologies that are extraneous to neorealism inform *verista* novels. Plot also assumes a particular political relevance for the neorealists in contrast to the beautiful prose fragment (*prosa d'arte*) that was the privileged high-literary mode between the wars (along with the densely metaphorical lyric poetry of the hermetic poets). Plot, as the narrative representation of human action and its significance, implicitly constitutes a call for action. It is the device that best underlines the new neorealist concern with history and with the collectivity, as opposed to the lyric and the individual's emotions seen in isolation, as well as a rebirth in the belief of the consequentiality of human events.

In the best neorealist novels, the dramatic quality of events speaks for itself. The political message emerges from the way the events are narrated; it is implicit rather than explicit. Not all neorealist texts have the unsentimental tone of Visconti and Calvino, however. Neorealist *engagement* sometimes appears excessively rhetorical. Cesare Pavese's neorealist novel, *Il compagno* (*The Comrade*, 1947), despite its vivid portrayal of prewar working-class Turin, is burdened with a protagonist and narrator – Pablo, a guitar-playing, uneducated, rootless, and restless young man – whose process of "political education" in light of the nascent anti-Fascist resistance appears excessively programmed and predictable. It resonates (especially in the second half, set in Rome, where Pablo's political awakening takes place) with the political imperatives of the leftist parties at the time regarding the need to "reeducate" the people after the liberation and to provide positive models through the arts. Nevertheless, the first half of the novel, especially the scenes set on the River Po and in the hills around Turin, and the account of the lazy and random days spent by Pablo casually pursuing the beautiful but fickle and venal Linda, have a syncopated rhythm that is highly evocative. Even though this particular novel is excessively Manichean, Pavese was a master of style, and all the younger neorealists learned from him. Calvino absorbed the lesson of Pavese's style but avoided his mistakes. Calvino's felicitous choice of a politically oblivious and naive focalizer for his first novel was, as he noted in the preface to *Il sentiero* that he added to an edition of 1964, made in conscious opposition to the newborn rhetoric of the Resistance and the reconstruction that was already becoming dogma in 1947, calling for "positive heroes" and for politically correct storytelling. The best neorealism in the novel is – like Calvino's novel or the classic neorealist films – deliberately antirhetorical.

De Sica and other neorealist filmmakers often used real people and locations instead of professional actors and studio sets. The visual emphasis on a recognizable, nonidealized landscape was one of the hallmarks of cinematic neorealism. Visconti employed professionals for the principal roles in *Ossessione*, but the landscape and the people in the country near Ferrara and in the Ancona location sequences were unmistakably real. Neorealist Resistance novels also emphasize regional and local landscapes. *L'Agnese va a morire* (Agnese Goes to Her Death, 1949) by Renata Viganò (1900–76) is set in the Comacchio marshes of the Po valley. Calvino's *Il sentiero dei nidi di ragno* takes place in San Remo and the Ligurian hills. And *Il partigiano Johnny* (Johnny the Partisan, 1968) by Beppe Fenoglio (1922–63) is set in the Langhe region of Piedmont. These works not only reference real and recognizable landscapes, but articulate human action within them in such a compelling way that those landscapes become, for those who happen to travel through them, animated by and inextricably associated with the people and the incidents of those novels. The best Italian neorealist narratives (both novels and films) unforgettably incorporate and rewrite the Italian landscape for us. A similar effect is achieved through the narrative inscription and referencing of recognizable city landscapes, such as Milan in Elio Vittorini's *Uomini e no* (Men and Not Men, 1945), for example, or Turin in Pavese's *Il compagno*. Like the Rome and Naples in films by Rossellini or De Sica, such novels rewrite the city maps of major Italian cities.

Neorealism also rewrote the way spoken Italian "sounds." In contrast to Fascist film, which homogenized language to promote the myth of a unified nation, directors such as Rossellini and De Sica employed nonprofessional actors and often asked them to improvise in their own words and with their regionally inflected voices, basing what they said on their personal experiences. In the same vein, neorealist fiction was widely based at least in part on real people's experiences (often the author's own) and tended to foreground its authenticity by seemingly reproducing real conversations – replete with the repetitions, redundancies, hesitations, silences, contradictions, and ambiguities of actual speech. *Uomini e no* contains several examples of this kind of conversation or dialogue. Vittorini, like Pavese, was a master of style and especially influenced the writing of neorealist dialogue. His autobiographically based novel *Conversazione in Sicilia* (*In Sicily*), generally considered his masterpiece, while far from neorealism in most respects – it could be called a "hermetic" novel because of its use of symbolism and reticence – experimented with the use of repetition, reiteration, silent pauses, and a ritualistic cadence in the rendition of dialogue, creating an effect that was both musical and uncannily natural. This strategy was modeled in part on the realist American literature that Vittorini and Pavese admired and helped to publicize in the 1930s and 1940s through their translations (especially of Ernest Hemingway, William Faulkner, and John Steinbeck, but also, in Pavese's case, Theodore Dreiser and Sherwood Anderson), contributing with their own novels to make it one of the most influential literary models for neorealism. As Calvino and others indicated on several occasions, the American model absorbed through Pavese and Vittorini was both politically and stylistically a means to explore and attempt to express the Italian reality – with its plurality of accents and regional voices – outside the artificially unifying parameters of Fascist nationalism. The colloquial, informal "spoken" quality and monotonous cadence of neorealist prose that Vittorini and Pavese helped to create could be highly effective and beautiful (as, for example, in some of Beppe Fenoglio's work), but it could also quickly become a shabby mannerism, as was the case for many of the experiential novels quickly written in what some have called the "neorealist deluge" of the late 1940s.

Both neorealist films and novels experimented with the use of dialect (most radically in Visconti's *La terra trema*, shot entirely in Sicilian and subtitled) or regional Italian; it was another technique that suggested a "direct-take," objective, and unadulterated approach to the real. The desire to communicate to as wide an audience as possible, however, precluded the use of dialect alone. Authors of neorealist narratives that focused on a particular city or region, such as *Spaccanapoli* (The Spaccanapoli Quarter, 1947) by Domenico Rea (1921–94), *Le terre del sacramento* (*The Estate in Abruzzo*, 1950) by Francesco Jovine (1902–50), and *Ragazzi di vita* (*The Ragazzi*, 1955) by Pier Paolo Pasolini devised, as Verga, Deledda, and other *veristi* had done before them, various literary strategies to incorporate dialect and regional elements and expressions from popular culture into their language, creating an effect of authenticity without compromising clarity. Pavese's *Paesi tuoi* was a brilliant precursor of the neorealist experimental use of dialect and regional language, and became an inspiration for the postwar writers. His own *Il compagno* successfully adapted the syntactic structures, rhythms, and tonalities of spoken Piedmontese into literary language. The transcription verbatim of colorful snatches of dialect was, on the other hand, the preferred (and easier) solution in some neorealist fiction and film. How treacherous the rendering of lower-class points of view could be even for a skilled writer can be seen in Moravia's attempt to write as if through the mind and voice of a young Roman prostitute in *La romana* (*The Woman of Rome*, 1947), his only quasi-neorealist novel. Moravia avoids dialect and regional inflections, but the effect is one of grotesque neorealist masquerade, and the novel fails thematically by reinscribing stereotypical notions of female sexuality and "naturalness" that can be traced back to Zola and Rousseau.

As pointed out by Pasolini, only by taking an experimental position towards both linguistic material (including dialect) and subject matter would a truly innovative approach to writing the real become possible.[6] In fact, neorealism was most compelling precisely when it was critical and when it took risks. Such is the case of Pasolini's early work as a novelist (*Ragazzi di vita* and *Una vita violenta* [*A Violent Life*, 1959] and filmmaker: his neorealist film *Accattone* (*Accattone*, 1961) is based upon *Una vita violenta*. In a sense, while it cannot be called simply neorealist, all of Pasolini's work – his essays, his poetry and his "cinema of poetry" (to use his own definition) – bear the traces of his critical appropriation and reinvention of neorealism. Pasolini gave heroic dimensions to neorealist commitment. Nor should it be forgotten that in his plea to deal openly with the realities of sexuality, Pasolini was voicing an essential concern of neorealism, however distasteful it might have been to some critics. Until his sudden and tragic death, Pasolini kept reexperimenting with essentially neorealist topoi such as the perversions of fascism and the meaning of resistance.

Calvino's early short stories about the armed Resistance and *Il sentiero dei nidi di ragno* were also experimental, as was all the best neorealist fiction and film. Although Calvino's last neorealist work is *La giornata di uno scrutatore* (*The Watcher*, 1963) the later Calvino – as late as *Palomar* (*Mr. Palomar*, 1983) – still retains traits of his neorealist debut. Mr. Palomar's naive and intense way of scrutinizing the real resembles Pin's. Many writers, like Calvino and Pasolini, found their voices for the first time – or found new and different voices – during the neorealist narrative explosion. It was precisely in its avant-garde form that neorealism was most fruitful, not only in terms of works written during the neorealist era proper but also because, for many of its protagonists and participants, neorealist experimentation was an immensely productive platform, a way to get started and go on researching other forms of thinking and writing about the real. Indeed it took the absolute obsession with the real, with facts and with actual people characteristic of the neorealist era, to precipitate among many of the best writers and intellectuals (including Calvino and Pasolini) a sense of the epistemological value of the fantastic and of the mythic or purely speculative and utopian dimensions of literary discourse as a means to render problematic realism's assumption and the reality, the narratability, and the "facticity" of facts and

---

[6] See Pier Paolo Pasolini, "La libertà stilistica," *Officina* 1 (1956); reprinted in *Passione e ideologia* (Milan: Garzanti, 1960).

events. Whatever may have been its shortcomings, the neorealist boom was an extraordinarily energizing phenomenon, and it gave new life to the Italian novel as well as Italian film.

The career of Anna Maria Ortese (1914–98) is significant in this respect. Her book documenting everyday life in Naples, *Il mare non bagna Napoli* (*The Bay is not Naples*, 1953), although constructed with self-conscious organic form and filled with recurrent themes and motifs, has the hybrid, composite quality that characterizes some of the best neorealist experimentalism. Not unlike the internationally popular novel *Cristo si è fermato a Eboli* (*Christ Stopped at Eboli*, 1945) by Carlo Levi (1902–75), Ortese's novel combines fiction and lyric transfiguration with the modes of documentary description, reportage, and the essay. However diverse, Ortese's entire oeuvre, including the startlingly fantastic *L'iguana* (*The Iguana*, 1965), whose premises are unmistakably rooted in neorealism, is marked by the same stylistic and humanitarian tensions and the urge to test and try different modes of structuring "the real" that emerged with *Il mare non bagna Napoli*.

Vittorini and Pavese were among the writers deeply affected by neorealism, even though both wrote only one truly neorealist novel (respectively, *Uomini e no* and *Il compagno*). Pavese's masterpieces – *La casa in collina* (*The House on the Hill*, 1948) and *La luna e i falò* (*The Moon and the Bonfires*, 1950) – while they cannot be ascribed to a hypothetical canon of the neorealist novel, cannot be understood without relating them to Pavese's attempt to come to terms with the imperatives of neorealism. *La casa in collina* combines a compelling account of the effects of war on the people of Turin with a retrospective personal narrative told by Corrado, a character whose existential self-questioning and incapacity to act make him a close relative of some of Pirandello's and Svevo's protagonists. The strength of the novel derives precisely from the tension between the neorealist topos of the purposiveness and necessity of human action, symbolized by the Resistance and the tragic story of Corrado's partisan friends (including his lover, Cate), and Corrado's sensibility, his anguished self-consciousness and self-reflectiveness that lead him to question everything, including his own self-questioning. Ultimately, however, Corrado's sense of shame and regret point to an existential perspective as the novel's underlying ethos: the individual's need to choose and to act even in the face of apparent meaninglessness and futility. *La luna e i falò* is a synthesis of Pavese's personal and original vision of neorealism with his archetypal and symbolic poetics of memory, of myth, and of the psyche (a poetics which was already well in place before the war). The referential, matter-of-fact stylistic register and the colloquial discourse filled with constructs and expressions adapted from Piedmontese are used to connote the topographical and linguistic reality of the setting and to tell the story of the return home of the first-person narrator and protagonist, Anguilla, after a long time away in America. A lyric register with the lexical and rhythmic complexity of the most exquisite prewar *prosa d'arte* is used on the other hand to narrate the circuitous paths of memory and desire in Anguilla's mind, and his feelings of unconquerable alienation and estrangement. In looking for his past, Anguilla tragically learns the story of sexual transgression and ritual violence behind a local episode of the anti-Fascist Resistance, which turns out to have been uncannily similar to an ancient fertility ritual in the use of bonfires to purge transgression of the community's rules. Mythic repetition and archetypal sameness seem to overtake any sense of historical progress and the possibility of liberation. Although Pavese was in many ways one of the fathers of neorealism, then, his best work was substantially shaped by a poetics that both predates neorealism and renders it problematic.

The same can be said for Vittorini's largely misunderstood *Il Sempione strizza l'occhio al Frejus* (*The Twilight of the Elephant*, 1947) and *Le donne di Messina* (*Women of Messina*, 1949). Rather than an impasse of neorealism, these experimental works embody Vittorini's stubborn pursuit of an allegorical and ethical realism whose premises were already evident in the beautiful *Conversazione in Sicilia*. *Le donne di Messina*, a novel that Vittorini retouched considerably for the 1964 edition (he was never fully satisfied with his own work), has often been dismissed as "utopian" (as if utopianism in itself were negative). The novel is centered on an imaginary community, a group of derelict, unemployed, rootless people, including women from Messina, Milan, and elsewhere, who decide to put an end to their restless peregrinations across the peninsula and settle among the ruins of a small town destroyed by the war. They clear the rubble, sow the fields, and, like Robinson Crusoe after his shipwreck, start building again, apparently forgetting their political differences and prewar conflicts. The seeds of violence and the shadows of the past, however, haunt the community, and the utopia threatens to turn into a dystopia. Vittorini's cautionary tale was meant to allegorize the need to transcend social and political differences, and to forget and forgive for reconstruction's sake. One of the most interesting techniques of the novel is the use of "interviews" to allow the villagers one by one to tell their stories and the tale of how they arrived there. The mythic structure of the journey is a constant element of most of Vittorini's work, and the early pages of the novel, with the image of displaced Italians trying to go home or forced to flee from home towards the end of the war, offer one of the most striking examples of Vittorini's particular blend of neorealist immediacy and allegorical myth.

Modes of neorealist narrative

The real catalysts for the boom of the neorealist novel between 1945 and 1947, which was the peak year,[7] were the war and the passions of the anti-Fascist Resistance and the civil war, during which – as Calvino tells in his 1964 preface – a new oral narrative tradition was born. The novels – often, as in Calvino's case, first novels – of the immediate postwar period were indebted to that new oral tradition and often written under pressure: the urge to tell and bear witness. Suddenly everybody felt entitled to write, not only about their experience of the war but also about their "rediscovery" of Italy. The war brought an unprecedented mingling of the social classes from all regions of Italy. Proletarian and peasant voices emerged to tell their own stories or to have their stories retold. Novels such as *Pane duro* (Hard Bread, 1946) by Silvio Micheli (1911–90), which received the Viareggio Prize; *Rancore* (Resentment, 1946) by Stefano Terra (1915–86); and *L'uomo di Camporosso* (The Man from Camporosso, 1948) by Guido Seborga (1909–90) typify this first outpouring of rather rough neorealist novels. Neorealism as a whole is inseparable from this specific social, cultural, and political situation. Franco Fortini (1917–94), who co-edited *Il Politecnico*, remarked in 1957 that the war had revealed the incredible diversity and cultural potential of the Italian provinces, and the energy emanating from the social classes that had been silenced during fascism. Neorealism was thus to a large extent not only a (sometimes risky) experiment with language and narrative structures, but also a passionate attempt to discover more about those realities. Refinements of style seemed irrelevant or even politically suspect to many, who associated literariness with elitist academicism and the Fascist past. Even great stylists such as Pavese and Vittorini sought experimentally to create an effect of stylelessness and conversational immediacy. The level of formal and aesthetic achievement of neorealist narrative was therefore tremendously varied. Critics (especially in Italy) have judged neorealist novels very harshly for the most part, either because they did not measure up to the critics' own highly politicized expectations regarding realism, or because (on the

---

[7] Besides *Il sentiero*, *Spaccanapoli*, and *Il compagno*, the following exemplary neorealist novels appeared in 1947: *Cronache di poveri amanti* (*A Tale of Poor Lovers*) by Vasco Pratolini; *Il cielo è rosso* (*The Sky is Red*) by Giuseppe Berto (1914–78); *Dentro mi è nato l'uomo* (Man Was Born Inside of Me) by Angelo Del Boca (1925–); Carlo Bernari's *Prologo alle tenebre* (Prologue to the Darkness); and *La parte difficile* (The Difficult Part) by Oreste Del Buono (1923–).

opposite front) they were seen as excessively political, vulgar, and lacking in literary refinement and elegance.[8] Yet, even in its uneven and exceedingly broad spectrum of literary achievements, neorealism remains a fascinating phenomenon, a constellation of texts in which narrative, war, political passions, and the multifaceted cultural realities and plights of different Italian regions and cities are inextricably interwoven.

Vasco Pratolini's *Cronache di poveri amanti* is in many ways one of the most representative books of neorealism as well as one of the most celebrated. Although Pratolini had planned this book almost a decade earlier, it was only in 1946, under the impact of the liberation and the reconstruction spirit, that he felt able to write it. While his previous novels were mostly lyric, elegiac, and personal and belong to the modes of hermeticism and *prosa d'arte, Cronache* marked a break with his prewar aesthetics and the turn to the public narrative dimension of the "chronicle." In telling the vicissitudes of the inhabitants of a working-class Florence neighborhood during the first decade of the Fascist era, Pratolini wove a tapestry of interconnected stories that became a collective, multivoiced history. The neighborhood emerged as a community where tales of love, violence, courage, and cowardice unfolded as in a microcosm that reflected the larger world, including its political realities. The cast of characters is neatly divided into two camps – the good (the Communists, first of all the young male character, Maciste) and the bad (the Fascists, headed by the sinister, evil La Signora). Although there are gradations of good and evil, the novel is profoundly Manichean, in a way that resembles the captivating and simple logic of popular narrative modes like those of traditional oral storytellers and the traveling puppet theaters of a bygone day. Manicheanism seemed justified in that historical moment; the assumption that fascism was simply evil was reassuring, though it could not and eventually did not stand the test of historical and critical scrutiny. Pratolini's narrator (who is not, strictly speaking, one of the characters but only the teller of their stories), speaks to the characters, solicits their storytelling, encourages them, and comments on what they do as if he were indeed one of them; he is on an equal level with them rather than in a position of control and ironic superiority. This narrative strategy promotes the sense of reality that Pratolini had in mind; he wanted to produce the effect of having "transcribed" events as faithfully as possible, as in a chronicle. Hence also the "spoken" stylistic register of the novel: not only is there a prevalence

---

[8] See, for example, the negative assessment given by Enrico Falqui in *Prosatori e narratori del Novecento italiano* (Turin: Einaudi, 1950). Other important postwar critics, including Carlo Bo, Emilio Cecchi, Eugenio Montale, and Giorgio Bassani – all protagonists of postwar Italian culture whose intellectual roots may be traced back to the prewar period – were all equally negative.

of dialogue, but even the more properly narrative sections are written in a syntactically simplified, "poor," and colloquial Italian filled with Florentine terms.

Ritratto di Anna Drei (Portrait of Anna Drei, 1947) by Milena Milani (1917–) did not receive the acclaim of Pratolini's novel, but provides an interesting contrast and an example of how different neorealist themes of love and gender conflict could look when seen from a female perspective. The novel has many typically neorealist traits. It is made up mostly of dialogue; it uses an extremely linear, paratactic syntax, and, although a work of fiction, it has the structure and tone of a "real-life" story, set in Rome in the immediate postwar period and told in the first person by a female narrator. It includes extracts from Anna Drei's diary, presented as evidence of the reality of this character, whose story the narrator recounts along with her own. The interpolated diary is a literary journal of sorts and is written in the lyric prose style associated with prewar high culture. Milani implicitly suggests that this style is lifeless, and the diary turns out to be in fact a prelude to Anna's death in the violent conclusion of the novel. Specific places in Rome are constantly mentioned; through most of the novel the characters walk endlessly through the bleak and beautiful streets of the city in winter, much as in De Sica's *Ladri di biciclette*, though the atmosphere of this novel rather foreshadows the cinema of early Antonioni, such as *Nettezza urbana* (*Sanitation Department*, 1948) or *Cronaca di un amore* (*Chronicle of a Love Affair*, 1950). The rhythm of the narrative is defined by walking and by the other principal activity of the characters: waiting (another neorealist motif). Although the novel does not explicitly speak its anti-Fascism, it is about one of the themes that the Fascists considered most politically subversive and worthy of censorship: female homosexuality. Milani deals with her narrator's homosexual desire and the intolerant violence of male-dominated patriarchy in an understated and subtle way devoid of moralism. As in Visconti's *Ossessione*, Milani's sexual politics in the novel is subversive, not only of Fascist patriarchy, but also and especially of the pieties and gender stereotypes ingrained in Italian culture (including most male-authored neorealism). Although there are no specific references to the war, Milani's characters are misfits whose lives have been uprooted and thrown open by the war and whose attempts to "reconstruct" their identities and to give a meaning to their lives in the liberated city are undermined by fear, confusion, and postwar tedium (rather than euphoria).

The Resistance and the war were catalysts for a number of other neorealist writers who, on the other hand, chose to write specifically about them. Before the novel, a direct, antiliterary, matter-of-fact and yet (for the exceptional nature of the tragic or heroic events narrated) fabulous and epic way of narrating emerged in the short chronicles and accounts published in the partisan broadsheets and other wartime publications. These narratives, based on oral sources, had a crucial influence on neorealist Resistance literature, including *Uomini e no*, *Il sentiero dei nidi di ragno*, *L'Agnese va a morire* and Fenoglio's unfinished *Il partigiano Johnny* (published posthumously in 1968). Although each of these novels incorporates in different ways some stylistic traits of the partisan narrative style and tells of different chapters and aspects of the anti-Fascist warfare in the cities and the mountains of northern Italy, they are hardly homogeneous. The first three, for example, share some structural elements: a simple, episodic narrative line that unfolds as if we were witnessing the events directly; a single main protagonist seen in action whose knowledge of events is limited and who, in the interaction with a concisely sketched-out set of characters, struggles to understand and make sense of violent events; and a dramatic but not melodramatic conclusion (the tone is subdued and controlled; understatement rather than emphasis prevail). Dialogue is used more extensively than narration, summary, and even description. Parataxis is the preferred syntactic form in all three, as in most neorealist prose. Otherwise, however, the three novels are radically different.

Vittorini's protagonist, Enne 2, is a partisan and an intellectual. The third-person narration of his tragic story, divided into numbered segments or "scenes," and the author's first-person commentary (printed in italics) are given in alternate sections. The commentary includes the author's imaginary dialogues with his characters and adds to the text a metaliterary, self-reflexive and ironic quality that is quite unusual among neorealist novels, giving it an almost Pirandellian tone. The more strictly narrative section often uses filmic techniques, such as slow motion and the sort of "waiting" used at the time by neorealist filmmakers. Characters seem to wait endlessly for things to happen and events to take place. A love story between Enne 2 and a married woman, Berta, who keeps deferring her decision to leave her husband, is woven into the narrative. Enne 2 dies fighting the Fascists in a deliberate act of self-sacrifice. The text is layered with allusions to Faulkner, Hemingway, and Sartre. There is no attempt to integrate the two levels of the novel: the author's commentary interprets the events of the narrative in terms of a universal Manichean logic (good and evil, men and not men, partisans and Nazi-Fascists) that was typical of Vittorini's tendency towards allegory as early as *Conversazione*. Vittorini's allegorism was a huge disappointment to Marxist critics, who saw it as a betrayal of history, when in fact it was Vittorini's attempt to become a modern Dante. *Uomini e no* became among the most imitated of all neorealist texts.

Calvino, who admired and learned from Vittorini no less than Pavese, nevertheless had doubts about their self-conscious attempts, as intellectuals, to come to terms with the social and political realities that emerged with the fall of fascism. Polemically, and in order to carve out his own creative space, he decided (unlike Pavese) to avoid completely first-person narration and the problems inherent in pretending to speak with a lower-class voice without sounding grotesque or condescending. He opted for third-person narrative and (unlike Vittorini) he chose a naive rather than intellectual protagonist and focalizer. Although an ironic intellectual commentary is supplied in the ninth chapter through the character of Kim (a partisan leader who in his own mind questions the meaning of partisan warfare and perceives the contradictions inherent in each fighter's motives), the main body of the narrative is focused through Pin's enchanted eyes. Calvino incorporated in his novel the structure of the adventure story and the fairy tale, used estranging expressionist and surrealist elements, and demystified the rhetoric of the Resistance and of the positive hero, ending the novel in a completely ambivalent way that could be interpreted either as tragic or as fantastic wish-fulfillment.

Like Calvino, Viganò chose to distance her autobiographical experience. She wrote in the third person and opted for an uneducated and naive focalizer and protagonist, based on a real person met by the author: a peasant widow in her fifties who worked as a courier for the Resistance fighters. *L'Agnese va a morire* combines the paratactic syntax, short sentences and plain, colloquial language typical of neorealism (but entirely devoid of dialect) with a particularly effective, concise use of descriptive notations that allows the reader to visualize the landscape of the valley, the river and the marshes with their seasonal rhythms and peasant life, suddenly devastated by explosions of violence. We are consistently given the ruminations of Agnese's mind and even her dreams, as well as brief reality notations about the humble foods she prepares, the objects she handles. Her heavy, motherly, asexual body and her seemingly endless strength are associated with nature and nurture: now that she no longer has a husband Agnese becomes the "mother," cook, and nurse of a group of partisans. As she witnesses the vicissitudes of the struggle, she progressively comes to understand the meaning of the Resistance and to take an active role in it, showing extraordinary courage and determination and even killing a man before being killed herself. Agnese's selflessness and her life-giving sacrifice become an allegory of the partisans' struggle: her winter death grants the spring rebirth that comes with the liberation. The novel's mythic and allegorical strength is also its weakness: the novel is devoid of irony or self-reflexiveness, and it endows Agnese's character with mythic dimensions by exploiting gender stereotypes. *L'Agnese va a morire* is the only neorealist work by a woman that acquired canonical status. Indeed, if one looks at most critical accounts, neorealism seems to have been almost exclusively a male phenomenon. Yet there was no scarcity of neorealist women's writing, including writing about the war and the Resistance, although not much critical attention has been devoted to it yet.[9]

In publishing *Il partigiano Johnny* in 1968, Lorenzo Mondo fused two substantially different manuscript versions of the novel about the Resistance on which Fenoglio worked for almost two decades. There is still a lot of debate about the legitimacy and value of Mondo's operation, but the various extant versions of Fenoglio's novel (the first draft dating probably from the late 1940s) constitute one of the most intriguing neorealist works and the only neorealist novel to have a truly epic breadth. Fenoglio, who was writing about his own experience, not only charts for us a memorable landscape (the Langhe hills of Piedmont), animating it with the movements and fighting of the partisans, but successfully endows his partisans with the grandeur of epic heroes. Fenoglio gives his autobiographical protagonist and his heroes a deep sense of inner solitude as they live in the shadow of impending death – but a heroic and "good" death that is symbolically opposed to the "bad" death reserved for their Fascist opponents. Yet he miraculously avoids all rhetorical emphasis. His narrative rhythm and his imagery are deeply influenced by the language of cinema; not only neorealist film but also American adventure classics such as *Beau Geste* (1939), a Gary Cooper classic directed by William Wellman about a doomed regiment of the French Foreign Legion fighting a desert war against the Arabs. Fenoglio's language is uniquely experimental. He used his passion for Shakespeare, Marlowe, and the English language (shared by his protagonist Johnny) to coin surprisingly poetic and brilliant neologisms and syntactic structures, and he was able to create a sublime, epic style of his own, in contrast to the low style characteristic of so much neorealist prose. Fenoglio's tireless rewriting belied the myth of neorealist directness and spontaneity, yet the intensity of his prose has much to do with his desire to recount his experience of the Resistance, the central theme of all his novels with the exception of *La malora* (Ruin, 1952), a powerful portrait of the dismal life of peasants in the Langhe, published in Vittorini's "I Gettoni" series.

Perhaps the most striking of all neorealist modes, however, is precisely the body of documentary memoirs written by nonprofessional writers seemingly

---

[9] Many short stories were published in *L'Unità* and in Alba De Céspedes' journal *Mercurio* in the 1940s but have not been reprinted since. Women's novels that deal with the war and the Resistance from a female perspective include *Tutti i nostri ieri* (*All Our Yesterdays*, 1953) by Natalia Ginzburg (1916–91); *Prima e dopo* (*Between Then and Now*, 1955) by Alba De Céspedes (1911–97); and *Tetto murato* by Lalla Romano. Women's memoirs include *Diario partigiano* (Partisan Diary, 1956) by Ada Gobetti; and *I giorni veri* (True Days, 1963) by Giovanna Zangrandi.

devoid of any literary training or intention, whose only goal was to bear witness. Works in this autobiographical form of neorealist literature include: *Guerriglia nei castelli romani* (Warfare in the Castelli, 1945) by Pino Levi Cavaglione; *Banditi* (Bandits, 1946) by Pietro Chiodi (a direct source for Fenoglio, who was Chiodi's student); *Il mio granello di sabbia* (My Grain of Sand, 1946) by Luciano Bolis; *Mathausen, città ermetica* (Mathausen, Hermetic City, 1946) by Aldo Bizzarri; *Il campo 29* (Camp 29, 1949) by Sergio Antonielli; *Il sergente nella neve* (The Sergeant in the Snow, 1953) by Mario Rigoni Stern (1921–); and *Croce sulla schiena* (Cross on the Back, 1953) by Ida D'Este. They recount real-life experiences of war, prison camps, guerrilla warfare, and – most tragically – concentration and extermination camps, thus forming a body of "literature of extreme situations" that is probably one of the most lasting legacies of neorealism and that still awaits its due recognition. Primo Levi's masterpiece, *Se questo è un uomo* (*Survival at Auschwitz*, 1947), a documentary narrative account of the author's internment at Auschwitz, is deservedly now among the canonical books in the new and developing field of Holocaust historical and literary studies, but it should also be related to this tendency within neorealism.

One of the most controversial and earliest texts of the neorealist era was the autobiographical *Cristo si è fermato a Eboli* by Carlo Levi. Although this enormously popular book has nothing to do with the war per se, and tells of the author's experience as an exile confined by the Fascists in a small village in Lucania in the south of Italy, it was finally written (after a long gestation period) during the war, when the defeat of fascism seemed imminent. Levi's declaration of antifascism and the tone of indignation in his exposé of the primitive living conditions of the southern peasants made it seem both timely and necessary. Levi's book typified some of the key impulses behind neorealism: it was an autobiographical and documentary narrative, it was anti-Fascist, and it disclosed a subaltern regional reality that fascism had both exploited and covered up. It also relied heavily on a repertoire of oral narratives – stories that the author had heard first-hand during his confinement. Although not a novel per se, the book was novelistic, or rather, an experimental, composite aggregate of the novel, the anthropological and political essay, travel narrative, and autobiography. Levi framed the oral narratives of the peasants within a perspective that today appears rather colonial but that at the time seemed revealing and enlightened in its own way. Levi's literary models were also typically neorealist; they included Verga, Deledda, and Vittorini's *Conversazione in Sicilia*. Levi was a libertarian and saw what in his eyes was the primitive, archetypal, and animalistic world of Lucania as belonging to a different, immemorial, and ahistorical civilization whose autonomy should be protected. This was not a politically popular position in a period that valorized the subaltern classes and their role as historical agents, but the book became a milestone of neorealist literature.

Levi provided a northerner's view of the "southern question," and contributed to making this one of the most hotly debated issues of the postwar period, as Italy was rediscovering its regional diversity. The publication of the first volumes of Antonio Gramsci's works, beginning with the *Lettere dal carcere* (*Letters from Prison*) in 1947, followed by selections of the *Quaderni del carcere* also helped to place the southern question at the center of discussion, along with the issue of the political responsibility of intellectuals and artists. The appearance in 1949 of the first Italian edition of *Fontamara* (*Fontamara*), a novel based on oral narratives about the Fascist oppression of the peasants of an Abruzzi village published in exile in 1930 to international acclaim by Ignazio Silone (1900–78), also contributed to highlighting the southern question, although Silone's subsequent *Una manciata di more* (*A Handful of Blackberries*, 1952), a polemically anticommunist and moralistic novel also set among the Abruzzi peasants, had few if any literary merits and was very coldly received. Gramsci denounced the exploitative and paternalistic nature of northern and bourgeois economic and intellectual hegemony, and faulted Italian literature and the novel in particular for not having developed a "national and popular" tradition through which the realities, values, and needs of the subaltern classes could be both expressed and given shape, contributing to form an anti-Fascist political and historical consciousness. Gramsci's critique (as it could be gathered from the fragmentary body of his notes) became enormously influential and contributed to fueling the factional and censorious spirit that characterized a lot of Marxist literary criticism in Italy for several decades after the war. Practically every writer was accused of being populist, "decadent," and "too bourgeois," and of not being organically tied to the working classes.[10] On the other hand, Gramsci's work encouraged the programmatic production of a number of "national-popular" novels in the neorealist period, most of which are today more interesting as sociological documents than as imaginative works of art. One of the few examples of a deliberately Gramscian novel that achieved some degree of literary value is the celebrated *Le terre del sacramento* by Francesco Jovine. Set among the peasants of Jovine's native Molise (a province in the southern part of the peninsula) in the early years of fascism, the novel tells of an episode of the peasants' rebellion against the Fascist landlords and has a tragic hero, the young student Luca Marano, skillfully constructed to epitomize both the anxieties and hopes of an "organic intellectual" (to use

---

[10] The single most influential example of this critical discontent is Alberto Asor Rosa's *Scrittori e popolo* (Rome: Samonà and Savelli, 1972).

Gramsci's term) and the subalterns' yearning for revolt, action, and emancipation. Luca's tragic sacrifice is presented as an event that precipitates the peasants' awareness and their determination to continue to hope and fight. Jovine's language has the typical linearity and flatness of neorealist prose, and although it incorporates popular sayings and dialect, it does so almost exclusively in the dialogues, creating a "direct-take" or transcription effect, as in the peasant women's ritual lament for Luca's death.

Some of the most persuasive neorealist texts about the "rediscovered" reality of the different regions of Italy, especially the South, however, were not novels at all but rather collections of short stories and sketches, such as Rea's *Spaccanapoli*, a book that created a sensation and revealed a powerful new writer. Rea was not trying to create positive heroes or historically profound and politically arousing plots: in a language whose expressive use of dialect seemed miraculously natural, he portrayed the multiple and tragicomic vicissitudes of the destitute inhabitants of Naples during the war and their attempts to survive and fight poverty and malnourishment. Among the many writers who contributed to making Naples one of the main subjects and centers for neorealism were Carlo Bernari, with books like *Speranzalla* (*Speranzalla*, 1949) and *Vesuvio e pane* (Vesuvius and Bread, 1952); Giuseppe Marotta (1902–63) with *L'oro di Napoli* (The Gold of Naples, 1947); and Anna Maria Ortese.

Women, often all but ignored in critical discussions of neorealism, wrote some of the most compelling novels about the marginal regional and human realities of Italy and its people. Examples include the masterful *Maria* (*Mary*, 1953) by Lalla Romano; and *La vigna di uve nere* (The Vineyard of Black Grapes, 1953) by Livia De Stefani (1913–91). These two novels are radically different. *Maria* is structured like a chronicle based on the real life and family tales of a peasant woman from a mountainous region between northern Piedmont and France who was the author's maid and her child's nurse for many years. The narrative spans the years from the 1930s to the war and the immediate postwar years, and historical events are seen from below, through the destructive effects they have on Maria's village, family and community. Their dignity as characters whose stories are worth recording and remembering is the implicit premise of the book. The autobiographical narrator lovingly retells the web of family stories narrated to her by Maria during their time together in a laconic, understated prose, with extremely short paragraphs and very brief dialogues. Romano's novel is one of the stylistic pinnacles of neorealism and a vivid testimony of the persistence in modern times of the spiritual role of the storyteller.

La vigna di uve nere is set at the opposite end of Italy, in a remote corner of Sicily in the 1920s and 1930s, and unlike *Maria* it is a tightly plotted novel closer in tone and spirit to the savage atmosphere of *Ossessione* and of Paola Drigo's *Maria Zef* than to Romano's delicate fabric of storytelling. The reality explored and exposed by De Stefani is the mind of a *mafioso* in his small-town and rural social and political context, and the process through which he establishes himself and asserts his power of life and death over his wife and children, as well as the community. Although the novel is a devastating indictment of patriarchal violence and its specific forms and consequences in Sicily during the Fascist era, it is completely unsentimental and devoid of moralism. It is written in a spare colloquial style with a predominance of dialogue that subtly echoes the Sicilian regional cadences and turns of phrase, but without the least shade of the picturesque. In contrast to Pavese's novels, where violence against women and children is presented in light of the archetypal necessity of ritual repetition, De Stefani's novel foregrounds the tragic consequences of violence instead. And unlike Sciascia's better-known novels about Sicily and the mafia, De Stefani eschews any Pirandellian ambiguity, opting instead for the distinctive matter-of-factness of neorealism.

The perils inherent in the attempt to construct a deliberately Gramscian novel are evident in Vasco Pratolini's controversial *Metello* (1955), hailed by some as the peak achievement of postwar realism, while others saw in it the symptoms of neorealism's exhaustion. New social and political conditions (modernization and the disappearance of peasant culture, the economic miracle, the Christian Democratic political hegemony, the crisis of the Soviet political model, and the beginning of the cold war) increasingly seemed to make neorealism obsolete by the late 1950s, while the neo-avant-garde emerged at the forefront of literary experimentation. But in reality things were not as simple as that. Neorealism continued to bear fruit well into the 1960s and beyond. Some of the best works of neorealism, for example Fenoglio's, were the result of painstaking reflection and rewriting, and appeared only when the neorealist moment seemed already over. The most extraordinary neorealist work, an eloquent *summa* and critical rethinking of its themes and stylistic and ideological innovations in both fiction and film, is Elsa Morante's *La storia*, published in 1974 to enormous popular success and considerable critical controversy. At the time Morante's novel seemed an anachronism, but more recently it has begun to be seen as a source of inspiration among a new generation of young writers for the return – in the postmodern age – of the desire and strength to narrate and to think critically about the real.[11]

---

[11] See Filippo La Porta, *La nuova narrativa italiana* (Turin: Bollati Boringhieri, 1999), p. 30 and passim.

Further reading

Bondanella, Peter. *Italian Cinema: From Neorealism to the Present.* 3rd rev. edn. New York: Continuum, 2001.

Ben-Ghiat, Ruth. "Fascism, Writing, and Memory: The Realist Aesthetic in Italy, 1930–1950." *Journal of Modern History* 67 (September 1995), pp. 627–65.

Bo, Carlo, ed. *Inchiesta sul Neorealismo.* Turin: ERI, 1951.

Calvino, Italo. "Preface to *The Path to the Spiders' Nest.*" Trans. Archibald Colquhoun, rev. edn by Martin McLaughlin. London: Jonathan Cape, 1998.

Corti, Maria. "Neorealismo." In *Il viaggio testuale.* Turin: Einaudi, 1978.

Falcetto, Bruno. *Storia della narrativa neorealista.* Milan: Mursia, 1992.

Heiney, Donald. *America in Modern Italian Literature.* New Brunswick, NJ: Rutgers University Press, 1964.

Marcus, Millicent. *Italian Cinema in the Light of Neorealism.* Princeton: Princeton University Press, 1986.

Overbey, David, ed. *A Reader on Neorealism.* Hamden, CT: Archon Books, 1978.

Procaccini, Alfonso. *Francesco Jovine: The Quest for Realism.* New York: Peter Lang, 1986.

Re, Lucia. *Calvino and the Age of Neorealism: Fables of Estrangement.* Stanford: Stanford University Press, 1990.

8

JOANN CANNON

Memory and testimony in Primo Levi and Giorgio Bassani

In the works of Primo Levi and Giorgio Bassani, Italy has made a lasting contribution to Holocaust literature. This is a mode of writing that has few of the characteristic features of a literary genre. A term that came into use in the 1960s, Holocaust literature includes a wide and varied range of texts, from the diaries of the victims of the Holocaust, to the memoirs of the survivors, to the fiction of writers who have taken the Holocaust as the subject of their works. The characteristic feature of Holocaust literature is the commitment to preserve the memory of the offense and the memory of the victims. Those who survived the atrocity and took up their pens to bear witness are generally recognized as the great Holocaust writers. These include Elie Wiesel, Paul Celan, Tadeusz Borowski, and Primo Levi. Of all these Holocaust writers, the Italian Jewish writer Primo Levi occupies a special place. Imprisoned in Auschwitz for eighteen months, from the summer of 1943 until the end of the war, Levi was one of the very few Italian survivors of the concentration camp. His first book, written only two months after his return from the concentration camp – *Se questo è un uomo* – is widely recognized as one of the most lucid and dispassionate accounts of the *lager*, the German term for the death camps. His last book published forty years later shortly before the author's apparent suicide – *I sommersi e i salvati* (*The Drowned and the Saved*, 1986) – returns to the same theme. While Levi's work provides chilling testimony to the offense, Bassani's *Il giardino dei Finzi-Contini* (*The Garden of the Finzi-Continis*, 1962) commemorates the victims of the Holocaust.

In many ways the works of Levi and Bassani are in sharp contrast. Primo Levi's account of the dehumanization of the Nazi concentration camp in *Se questo è un uomo* and *I sommersi e i salvati* is the portrait of a dystopia. Bassani's loving portrait of Ferrara's Jewish community in his novel presents an account of a quasi-utopian existence shattered by the insidious encroachment of racial intolerance. Bassani's book serves as a vivid backdrop on which the drama of the deportation and destruction of the Italian Jews unfolds. The role of memory is a crucial element in the works of both writers.

If one of the functions of Holocaust literature is to record the enormity of human loss, then Bassani's *Il giardino dei Finzi-Contini* is indeed a masterpiece of this genre. Bassani's fictionalized account of the Jews of Ferrara provides the chronology of the major events leading to the deportation of the Jews of Italy in 1943. The book opens in 1957, a moment when many Italians and Europeans were beginning to reconsider and reevaluate the enormity of what they had lived through and how many lives had been lost. Bassani's narrative is filtered through a framing story, a Sunday outing to visit the Etruscan tombs with family friends and their young daughter, whose precocious question, as to why older tombs are less gloomy than newer ones leads the author to think back to the Finzi-Contini family and those so recently lost. By filtering the story of the Finzi-Continis through this framing story, the author invites the reader not only to remember and to reflect upon the events of the recent past, but also to examine our relationship to those events: to measure our suffering as we contemplate the loss. The novel's framing story both lays bare the commemorative function of Bassani's text and implicates the reader in the act of commemoration.

Elie Wiesel once stated that "writing is a *matzeva*, an invisible tombstone, erected to the memory of the dead unburied."[1] It is thus fitting that the first chapter of Bassani's novel opens with the description of the Finzi-Contini tomb. The tomb holds several generations of the family, beginning with Moses, the first Finzi-Contini to witness the abolition of the ghetto in 1863. The Finzi-Contini tomb is a symbol of the civil liberties guaranteed to the Jews of Ferrara for the first time in 1860 by the newly unified, secular state of Italy formed during the Risorgimento. The emancipation of the Jews marked the beginning of a long period of prosperity that lasted well into the Fascist period. The two principal families of the novel – the Finzi-Continis and the family of the narrator, Giorgio – are representative of the different choices made by Jewish Italians during the Fascist period. Giorgio's father typifies the assimilated, middle-class, "modern" Jew who in the mid-1930s was often a card-carrying member of the Fascist Party. Jewish adherence to fascism was a mark of the assimilation or integration of Italian Jews into middle-class Italian society.[2] Between 1928 and 1938, as Zuccotti has pointed out, 10 percent of the Italian Jewish population belonged to the Fascist Party, roughly the same membership percentage as among the non-Jewish population. Many Jews were loyal Fascists and held important positions in the Fascist government. In contrast to Giorgio's middle-class Jewish family is the

---

[1] *Legends of Our Time*, trans. Steven Donadio (New York: Holt, Rinehart and Winston, 1968), p. 10.

[2] See Susan Zuccotti, *The Italians and the Holocaust* (New York: Basic Books, 1987), pp. 23–5.

aristocratic Finzi-Contini family. Wealthier and less assimilated, they voluntarily segregate themselves from Ferrara behind their garden walls. The patriarch, Professor Ermanno Finzi-Contini, politely but resolutely refuses membership in the Fascist Party. Yet Ermanno Finzi-Contini is also typical of the Italian Jewish population of his day. He proudly shares with young Giorgio his prized possession, the precious letters written to his mother by Carducci, the founding poet of the Italian nation-state. In his profound patriotism Ermanno Finzi-Contini resembles Italian Jews of his generation across the political spectrum.

As the narrator commemorates his childhood in Ferrara, he asks himself the meaning of the word "Jew." His query underscores the extent of the integration of Italy's Jews in mainstream Italian society. Both Bassani and Levi confirm this fact throughout their works. In *Il sistema periodico* (*The Periodic Table*, 1975), Primo Levi captures the extent of his family's assimilation with an amusing and telling anecdote. His Jewish father so loved *prosciutto* that he was well known to all the pork butchers of the neighborhood. For the vast majority of Italian Jews, to be Jewish in Italy in the 1920s did not mean observing dietary restrictions but rather feeling a mild sense of guilt when these were broken. Like the majority of Jews of his generation, Levi only came to understand and embrace his Jewish heritage as a result of his persecution by the Fascists.

The narrator of *Il giardino dei Finzi-Contini* understands in retrospect that to be Jewish in Italy, despite the high degree of integration of Jewish Italians, is indeed significant. It means that, unlike the non-Jews, the Jewish characters Micòl and Alberto, and Giorgio the narrator, share what Bassani calls "a certain special complicity." They understand the rabbi's Hebrew litany, the subtle differences between the German and Sephardic synagogues, the rituals that dictate the separation of the men and the women in the temple. This somewhat exotic world of the Ferrarese Jews is lovingly and nostalgically recreated in part 1 of the novel. The use of the imperfect tense to describe scenes such as the exchange of glances between Micòl and Giorgio as Micòl stands under the prayer shawl recreates a scene of ritual stability, of what was wont to occur with reassuring regularity. Only one "event" occurs in part 1. After failing his math exam Giorgio wanders disconsolately outside the walls of the Finzi-Contini villa, where Micòl, perched atop the garden wall, beckons to him. As at all crucial junctures of the novel, the reader is reminded that the story of the Finzi-Continis is being filtered through the narrator's memory of a remote, yet still vividly remembered past. Over thirty years have passed since this meeting occurred. But the distance in time is evoked only to be overcome by the vividness of the recollection. When the narrator closes his eyes, Micòl Finzi-Contini is still there. Micòl alternately comforts and ridicules Giorgio for his scholastic failure and then invites him to enter the garden. But, by the time he parks his bike and pauses in anticipation and trepidation, Micòl, summoned by her coachman, disappears behind the garden wall with one regretful backward glance.

In part 2 of the novel, ten years have passed and the racial laws are beginning to be enforced in Ferrara. Giorgio finally manages to gain entrance into the Finzi-Contini family garden as the racial laws strip the Italian Jewish population of the right to public education, employment in many sectors of the economy, and property ownership. Indeed, it is ironically because of the enforcement of the Fascist racial laws that the Finzi-Continis open the doors of their estate to the young Jewish college students who have been expelled from the tennis club. The story of Giorgio's unrequited love for Micòl plays out against the backdrop of the increasing persecution of the Jews of Ferrara. While Giorgio seeks refuge in Micòl's garden, he does not delude himself about the significance of such events as his expulsion from the municipal library or his father's expulsion from the Fascist Party. Giorgio's father, by contrast, continues to hope that the racial laws are a mere nuisance, a half-hearted compliance with Hitler's antisemitic policies that he erroneously believes to represent no real threat in the more tolerant climate of Italy. The narrator's father is typical of what one scholar has called "the prisoners of hope" – the many Italian Jews who failed to appreciate the growing threat to them from Mussolini's increasingly antisemitic tendencies.[3]

The unused carriage in the Finzi-Contini carriage house in which Micòl and Giorgio shelter from the storm functions as a point of intersection between the story of Giorgio and Micòl and the history of the Italian Jewish community. The unused carriage symbolizes the loss of function of the Jews in Italy, a country to which the industrious and highly educated Jews had heretofore contributed so much. Micòl Finzi-Contini mocks the ancient coachman for the care he lavishes on the family carriage and asks derisively if it is worth such effort. The same question might be applied to Micòl's various plans for the future. Micòl alternately announces decisive plans – to get a driver's license, to finish her thesis – and then lapses into lethargic contemplation of her lack of a future. Micòl's increasing realization of the futility of planning for the future mirrors the overall hopelessness of the Italian Jewish community with the advent of the racial laws.

As the subplot of Giorgio's unrequited first love concludes, the author dedicates a mere two pages to an apparently matter-of-fact account of the

[3] See H. Stuart Hughes, *Prisoners of Hope: The Silver Age of the Italian Jews, 1924–1974* (Cambridge: Harvard University Press, 1983) for a portrait of the Italian Jewish community from 1924 until the postwar period.

family's fate, already presaged in the opening pages of the novel. Alberto, who died in 1942, was the only one buried in the Finzi-Contini tomb. The others were taken by the Fascists and deported to Germany where they fell victim to the Holocaust. The narrator, Giorgio, who, like the author himself, escaped the fate of so many of Italy's Jews, leaves that story to others, like Primo Levi, to tell. His book, which begins and ends with the mass deportation of the Jews in the fall of 1943, serves, in Weisel's words, as a literary tombstone to the memory of the unburied dead and stands as testimony to ensure that the victims of the Holocaust will not be entirely forgotten. Bassani's book is both a commemoration and a reminder of the enormity of Italy's loss. By embedding the story of the Finzi-Continis within the framing story of the "present" moment in which the story was written, the author reinforces the importance of the act of remembering.

In Italy and in the rest of Europe, interest in the Holocaust greatly increased within a decade of the end of the hostilities in 1945. In the aftermath of the reconstruction of Europe, many Europeans began to recognize the importance of keeping alive the memory of the offense. *Il giardino dei Finzi-Contini* appeared precisely during this period and signaled an era of renewed interest in the Holocaust. Levi's first book, by contrast, appeared with great difficulty and little fanfare in the immediate postwar period. The manuscript was rejected by several publishing houses, including Einaudi, and was finally published at Levi's own expense by a small publishing house (Silva) in 1947.[4] It was not until 1956 that Einaudi finally recognized the importance of Levi's work and published *Se questo è un uomo*. It has been in print ever since. Levi's first book was the earliest major survivor memoir. Other works which have become part of the canon of Holocaust literature, from Wiesel's *Night* (1958) to Borowski's *This Way for the Gas, Ladies and Gentlemen* (1967), appeared only after the passage of considerable time. Levi's account was produced, remarkably, in four short months immediately following his repatriation. The urgency behind the writing is eloquently explained within the book itself. The obligation to remember and to record in the most painstaking detail the experience of Auschwitz was recognized by Levi not after his return from the camp but at the very moment of the offense. Indeed, this obligation seems to have sustained the author throughout his ordeal.

Both the addresser and the addressee, the narrator and the reader, are partners in the act of remembering as envisioned by Levi. From the first

---

[4] For a detailed discussion of the reception of Levi's work, see JoAnn Cannon, "Canon-Formation and Reception in Contemporary Italy: The Case of Primo Levi," *Italica* 69 (1992), pp. 30–44.

pages of the book, *Se questo è un uomo* draws the reader into the work. The poem that serves as an epigraph to the book opens with an invocation to the reader:

> You who live safe
> In your warm houses,
> You who find, returning in the evening,
> Hot food and friendly faces.

The narrator's appeals to the reader, while infrequent, constitute one of the most effective and compelling aspects of *Se questo è un uomo*. Levi recreates the scene on the eve of the deportation of the Jews from the detention center at Fossoli to what was, at the time, their unknown destination. The actions of the mothers are uncannily familiar: "Nor did they forget the diapers, the toys, the cushions, and the hundred other small things which mothers remember and which children always need. Would you not do the same? If you and your child were going to be killed tomorrow, would you not give him to eat today?"[5] By this simple rhetorical question Levi invites the reader to identify with the victims of the Holocaust as they enter the inhuman, absurd, and incomprehensible world of the *lager*.

By the time the reader "reaches" Auschwitz with Levi, it is clear that the only possible analogy with this dystopia is Hell itself.[6] In the first chapter the sentry who guards the prisoners in the convoy and courteously asks for their money and watches, since (as he puts it), they will no longer need them, is described by the narrator as "our Charon," an obvious reference to the infernal boatman described by both Virgil and Dante. Levi's second chapter confirms the precise identification of the concentration camp as Hell, while he introduces the reader to the peculiar "logic" of his grotesque and inhumane other world. Levi notes the absurd precision of the daily roll call, the senseless and innumerable prohibitions. The prisoners are ordered to remove their shoes, which are then mixed up and swept away, to be replaced by wooden clogs. Prisoners quickly learn that everything is forbidden and forbidden for no reason: "Hier ist kein warum [There is no why here]."[7] Chance plays an important role in every aspect of the prisoners' lives, from the moment of their arrival in the *lager*. The selections, theoretically used to sort out the fit from the unfit, often become a farce. Survivors later learn that life and death decisions are made as much by chance as by conscious choice:

[5] Primo Levi, *Survival at Auschwitz*, trans. Stuart Woolf (New York: Macmillan, 1961), p. 10.
[6] Alvin H. Rosenfeld introduces this term to describe Holocaust literature in Alvin H. Rosenfeld and Irving Greenberg, eds., *Confronting the Holocaust: The Impact of Elie Weisel* (Bloomington: Indiana University Press, 1978), pp. 24–7.
[7] Levi, *Survival in Auschwitz*, p. 25.

at times, climbing down from the wrong side of a train meant immediate dispatch to the gas chamber.

Many of the features that have since been recognized as generic in Holocaust literature appear in sharp relief in *Se questo è un uomo*. The analogy this early work establishes between a Dantesque Hell and the concentration camps is a recurring theme in all Holocaust writing in every national literature, and Primo Levi was the first Holocaust writer to draw upon it and to sustain it throughout his memoir. Levi's perception of Hell is undeniably filtered through Dante. Both *Se questo è un uomo* and *I sommersi e i salvati* are substantially informed by the physical structure as well as the moral universe outlined in Dante's *Inferno*.[8] Another characteristic feature of all Holocaust writing is the sense of the insufficiency of language to capture the atrocity, absurdity, and dehumanization of the *lager*. A number of critics have argued that writing about the Holocaust is impossible and that doing so is possibly immoral, given language's inherent inability to capture such a horrible event in linguistic terms.[9] At issue is the immorality of a literature that would in some way aestheticize or exalt the Holocaust and the inadequacy of any language to speak the unspeakable. Primo Levi falls into the category of those writers who recognize the inadequacy of the means at their disposal but who also recognize the greater danger and immorality of remaining silent. As Levi notes in *I sommersi e i salvati*:

> Except for cases of pathological incapacity, one can and must communicate, and thereby contribute in a useful and easy way to the peace of others and oneself, because silence, the absence of signals, is itself a signal, but an ambiguous one, and ambiguity generates anxiety and suspicion. To say that it is impossible to communicate is false; one always can.[10]

While all writers of Holocaust literature have ultimately resisted the impulse to remain silent, none have expressed the obligation to communicate as forcefully as Primo Levi. Yet the inadequacy of the means at his disposal is never underestimated.

The insufficiency of language strikes Levi not only as he takes up his pen to write his Holocaust memoir. Already by the end of his first day in the *lager* he is aware of that inadequacy. Nonetheless, Levi proceeds to attempt

---

[8] See Lynn Gunzberg, "Down Among the Dead Men: Levi and Dante in Hell," *Modern Language Studies* 26.1 (1986), pp. 10–28; or Risa Sodi, *A Dante of Our Time: Primo Levi and Auschwitz* (New York: Peter Lang, Inc., 1990).

[9] See Rosenfeld and Greenberg, *Confronting the Holocaust*, pp. 23–5, for a summary of the debate about the possibility of Holocaust art and a discussion of the tension between silence and speech in Holocaust writers.

[10] Levi, *The Drowned and the Saved*, trans. Raymond Rosenthal (New York: Summit Books, 1988), p. 89.

the impossible, to use the only, albeit inadequate, means at his disposal to describe to the reader the demolition of man. In *Se questo è un uomo*, the author repeatedly appeals to the reader to imagine what is so vividly engraved in his memory: "Imagine now a man who is deprived of everyone he loves, and at the same time of his house, his habits, his clothes, in short, of everything he possesses. He will be a hollow man, reduced to suffering and needs, forgetful of dignity and restraint."[11] Such appeals to the reader punctuate the book with regular reminders of our obligation to pay heed to Levi's testimony. Levi's commitment to preserving the memory of the offense is reflected in every page of *Se questo è un uomo*. Levi first identifies this obligation to remember in a fellow prisoner, the dignified and disciplined Steinlauf, who lectures Levi on the importance of refusing to succumb to the Nazi machine that aims to reduce the prisoners to beasts. Levi is not entirely convinced at the time by Steinlauf's reasoning. But he is endowed with a memory that will allow him to bear witness with a meticulousness and clarity unequalled in Holocaust literature.

While the prisoner Levi is committed to preserving the memory of the offense, he cannot allow himself to court memories of home. The author contends that memory of home rarely surfaces in the prisoners' waking hours. When it does, it is an unwelcome intrusion, making the present more difficult to bear. The Italian prisoners quickly give up the practice of meeting every Sunday evening to reminisce. Like his fellow prisoners, Levi had to let go of his memories of his family and his former life in Turin. Forgetfulness is a means of survival. Never, however, are the memories of home completely obliterated. Throughout *Se questo è un uomo* Levi calls attention to the accuracy and vividness of his recollections. Describing the cruel motto *Arbeit Macht Frei* ("Work Makes Free") above the entrance to the *lager*, Levi remarks that the memory of this grotesque statement still haunts his dreams. Time and again Levi testifies to the extraordinary power of such memories. He never entertains for a moment the notion that memories are fleeting or that conjuring up images and figures from his past is a difficult mental operation. It is a cause of grief to him when he cannot reproduce the exact words Steinlauf spoke to him, but his insistence on the reliability of his recollections becomes a powerful narrative device. It is as if, by a simple act of will, Levi stares through the mists of time like a seer in order to fulfill his obligation to Steinlauf's admonition to survive, to tell the story, and to bear witness to his readers.

Levi's greatest fear is not that his memory will fail nor even that he will not survive to tell his tale. His greatest fear is that, should he somehow

[11] Levi, *Survival in Auschwitz*, p. 23.

survive, he will tell his story but the narrative will fall on deaf ears. This fear, says the author, is the source of the greatest pain he suffered in Auschwitz – what he calls "pain in its pure state." After being obsessed with this fear in his frequent dreams in the camp, Levi learns with amazement that others also experience the same fearful nightmare. The thought that the crimes in the *lager* might be ignored, rather than forgotten, represents a collective fear of the inmates. This fear haunted Primo Levi throughout his life and undoubtedly drove him to write his final work, *I sommersi e i salvati*.

At the heart of *Se questo è un uomo* is the relationship between memory and testimony, as well as that between testimony and judgment. The need not only to preserve the memory of the offense, but also to testify against the offenders – not only to bear witness but also to judge – comes into sharp focus in the chapter entitled "Chemistry Exam." Here Levi tells of the moment when his absurdly reliable memory allows him to pass a chemistry exam administered by a Doctor Pannwitz with flying colors. It is this quirk of fate that eventually releases Levi from some of the worst rigors of camp life and allows him to survive the final, brutal winter in the relative shelter of the Buna Monowitz chemistry lab. From the moment Pannwitz raises his eyes from his desk and looks at prisoner #174517, Levi comes to the realization that the doctor's look was not the kind that is exchanged between two men but, rather, the kind of glance that is exchanged between two different species through the glass of an aquarium. Levi further realizes that if he could understand how another human being, such as the doctor, could look at another man as if he were another species, he would have unlocked the mystery of why Nazi Germany had, in effect, gone insane. That look and that realization impressed themselves on Levi at the time and did not leave him from that day until the writing of his memoir. And, for that look, Levi says simply but emphatically at the end of the chapter "I judge him." The author does not say "I loath him, I fear him, I want to avenge this injustice." He says, clearly and convincingly, "I judge him."

Levi is often characterized as a writer who preferred understanding to judgment. But Levi's accurate, controlled, rational testimony inevitably implies judgment. The story of the chemist Muller in *Il sistema periodico* parallels the story of Pannwitz in *Se questo è un uomo*. While working as a chemist in a paint factory years after the war, Levi has occasion to correspond with the German supplier of a shipment of resin. The author discovers that his correspondent is the same Doctor Muller who had inspected the lab outside Auschwitz where Levi was a slave laborer. As Levi and Muller exchange letters, it becomes obvious that Muller sought something akin to absolution from Levi. Instead, Levi sends him a copy of *Se questo è un uomo* and asks whether Muller accepts the judgments, implicit and explicit, in his account.

Muller resists Levi's implicit judgments and thus becomes a perfect example of what Levi calls the "German silent majority."

Levi believes that an ability to judge is a human characteristic that distinguishes man from beast. The author portrays that ability as having been temporarily extinguished in himself and his fellow sufferers in the *lager*. Levi and the other prisoners are called to witness the execution of a resister who had the strength and courage to blow up a crematorium at Birkenau – in short, to act. As the man cries out to his comrades that he is the last man to resist, Levi dejectedly concludes that the Germans had finally succeeded in killing the strong among the prisoners and that they had nothing to fear from them – not even a look of judgment. For Levi, the destruction of even the faculty of judgment among the victims would represent the final stage in the ultimate triumph of Nazi Germany's plan to demolish humanity, the near success of which Levi's works portray vividly.

Yet Levi's work stands as proof that the look of judgment was not extinguished in the camps. Levi invites his reader to share this act of judgment, used sparingly but with tremendous moral power in *Se questo è un uomo*. This invitation is extended in the poem that serves as an epigraph to the novel. Levi commends his words to us so that we may know what to do with his testimony. The author arms the reader with the memory of the offense so that we shall be capable of exercising the role of judge.

The act of judgment is even more powerful in Levi's final book, *I sommersi e i salvati*, published four decades after *Se questo è un uomo*. Essentially both books tell the same story. In the preface to *I sommersi e i salvati*, Levi reminds us that the initial response to the story of Nazi extermination camps was denial. The Nazis, who had taunted the prisoners with the depressing thought that their accounts of how they had suffered in the camps would not be believed by posterity, had foreseen this response. The fear that this might well be true was the source of the prisoners' recurrent nightmare – that they would tell their story to a loved one who did not believe or would refuse to listen. As Levi details the various denials of the Holocaust that have emerged in the forty years after the appearance of the first accounts of the atrocities down to the writing of *I sommersi e i salvati*, the reader comes to understand why Levi's retelling of the story of the Holocaust took on such a renewed sense of urgency in his life. By the end of his life, Levi believed that it was more important than ever for the author to bear witness to what he had seen and experienced.

As Levi points out in the preface to *I sommersi e i salvati*, historical events acquire their "chiaroscuro" and can be seen in perspective only some decades after they have concluded. One element of Levi's story that has changed from the account found in his first book to the narrative contained in his final work is that the dark side of the original story becomes darker still in *I sommersi e i salvati*. This is particularly apparent in the author's discussion of the "gray zone," an expression employed by Levi to refer to the place where oppressor and oppressed seem to merge. At a distance of forty years, the phenomenon of this "gray zone" has come into sharper focus for the author. Levi contends that some accounts of the *lager* have been influenced by a Manichean worldview, a simple dichotomy of good versus evil. For Levi, the reality of the camps was much more complex, and he discusses the ways in which some prisoners collaborated to a greater or lesser degree with their oppressors, as well as their motives for such collaboration. While the author shuns the role of psychologist, he carefully details the factors that led some to collaborate. He concedes that the complicated structure of the "gray zone" is intricate enough to confuse the human need for judgment. He concludes his discussion of the prisoners who by their collaboration occupied the "gray zone" with a forceful admonition to the reader: no one is authorized to judge the experiences of those who survived the Holocaust and even less of those who died in the camps. But while he forbids the reader to judge the oppressed, Levi has no difficulty judging the oppressor. The author's eloquent and searing testimony invites the reader to join Levi in the act of judgment.

Further reading

Bassani, Giorgio. *A Prospect of Ferrara*. Trans. Isabel Quigly. London: Faber and Faber, 1962.

Ezrahi, Sidra. *By Words Alone: The Holocaust in Literature*. Chicago: University of Chicago Press, 1980.

Langer, Lawrence L. *The Holocaust and the Literary Imagination*. New Haven: Yale University Press, 1975.

Levi, Primo. *The Reawakening*. Trans. Stuart Woolf. Boston: Little, Brown and Co., 1965.

The Periodic Table. Trans. Raymond Rosenthal. New York: Schocken Books, 1984.

If Not Now, When? Trans. William Weaver. New York: Summit Books, 1985.

The Monkey's Wrench. Trans. William Weaver. New York: Summit Books, 1986.

Patruno, Nicholas. *Understanding Primo Levi*. Columbia: University of South Carolina Press, 1995.

Schneider, Marilyn. *Vengeance of the Victim: History and Symbol in Giorgio Bassani's Fiction*. Minneapolis: University of Minnesota Press, 1986.

Stille, Alexander. *Benevolence and Betrayal: Five Italian Families Under Fascism*. New York: Penguin, 1993.

Tarrow, Susan, ed. *Reason and Light: Essays on Primo Levi*. Cornell Studies in International Affairs/Western Societies Papers XXV. Ithaca: Cornell University, 1990.

9

MANUELA BERTONE*

The Italian novel in search of identity: history versus reality – Lampedusa and Pasolini

The writings and biographies of Giuseppe Tomasi di Lampedusa and Pier Paolo Pasolini seem so different as to prevent any useful comparison. Yet the novels for which these two authors are best known – Pasolini's *Ragazzi di vita* and *Una vita violenta*; and Lampedusa's *Il Gattopardo* – have in common an identical cultural environment. In fact, while they gestated in the minds of their authors in entirely different ways, these novels were all received and reviewed by the same critical establishment and, within the span of a few brief years, launched into the same publishing marketplace. One can even say that Lampedusa's *Il Gattopardo* and Pasolini's *Una vita violenta* crossed paths, and after an almost contemporaneous first printing (the former in November of 1958, and the latter in May of 1959), the two works shared the stage at the 1959 Strega Prize ceremony, the prestigious award for the best narrative in Italy. The prize was awarded to Lampedusa's novel, while Pasolini's book took third place. Pasolini's two novels and Lampedusa's posthumous novel (the only one the Sicilian nobleman ever completed, which was approved for publication after his death) are also comparable in terms of the happy fate bestowed upon them by the larger reading public. They enjoyed immediate popular success, and not only in Italy: the first edition of *Ragazzi di vita* (May 1955) sold out within a month, *Una vita violenta* was immediately translated into eleven foreign languages, and *Il Gattopardo* became the first Italian international best-seller in the postwar period. It was translated into virtually every language and reached an eighteenth edition in Italy in the span of only six months, selling more than one hundred thousand copies. The sales figures in Italy alone make of Lampedusa's masterpiece the first true best-seller in the history of the Italian novel. Even today, after almost half a century, the novels of Lampedusa and Pasolini continue to enjoy a lively readership both in and outside Italy, and, along with Primo Levi, Sciascia, Eco, and Calvino, Pasolini and Lampedusa are without a doubt the Italian

* Translated by Viktor Berberi.

writers of the second half of the twentieth century who are most read and studied abroad.[1]

If the response of their publics was one of unconditional warmth and enthusiasm, the same cannot be said of the critics. At least two of these unexpected, atypical novels, *Il Gattopardo* and *Ragazzi di vita*, provoked, as we shall see, intense reactions. A vast chorus of consensus rose up around *Il Gattopardo*, accompanied, however, by the negative assessments (harshly criticizing, if not panning the novel) of critics who a few years earlier had with equal violence attacked and liquidated *Ragazzi di vita*. The wave of deep aversion directed at Pasolini's first novel as well as at Lampedusa's only novel was manifested by leftist intellectuals: that is, by the most vital force driving critical discourse, and one that dictated and disseminated lines of conduct in the arts, at least those areas of them most useful to the ends of propagandistic exploitation. It is not surprising that the left felt insidiously threatened by Prince Lampedusa's aristocratic (though not ideological) writing, by the novel it was so quick to evaluate according to the yardstick of the historical novel. Lampedusa's novel is in fact difficult to classify according to the usual labels, and imposes a "severely redimensioned version of the early Risorgimento in its most classically epical chapter."[2] What might surprise us instead is the left's hostility with regard to Pasolini, a progressive intellectual whose aesthetic thought, however paradoxical and contradictory, had until then increasingly demonstrated itself to be highly concerned with civic matters and whose artistic work was openly and passionately stimulated by a continuous revisitation, although tormented and subjective, of Marxist thought. As a Marxist intellectual, Pasolini would in fact be profoundly struck by the fate his comrades accorded his first novel to the extent that his second novel,

---

[1] Details about the reception of the first novels by Lampedusa and Pasolini underline the fact that their popularity reached far beyond the narrow bounds of academic or literary circles to reach mass audiences, both within Italy and abroad. In 1963 alone, no less than five editions of *Il Gattopardo* were published in Great Britain. In 1998, the fiftieth anniversary of the publication of *Il Gattopardo*, the Teatro Stabile of Turin staged a public reading of the entire novel. Two years earlier, for the one hundredth anniversary of Lampedusa's birth, the city of Palermo sponsored three talks on his novel. The public in Turin and Palermo literally stormed these two events in an atmosphere that might lead one to conclude that readers of the novel had passed beyond being the author's "public" and had become his "fans," as avid to learn about him as other Italians were to attend soccer matches or rock concerts. In Pasolini's case, there have been dozens of revivals and public celebrations of his works, and his international notoriety owes something to the fact that he was both writer and film director, not mention poet and critic. In North America, the first volume inaugurating the "Major Italian Writers" series published by the University of Toronto Press is dedicated not to Dante or to Pirandello but to Pasolini, underlining Pasolini's role as an extremely popular writer among academics.

[2] Giuseppe Paolo Samonà, *Il Gattopardo, i racconti, Lampedusa* (Florence: La Nuova Italia, 1974), p. 7 (translator's translation).

Una vita violenta, "will respond to the criteria of an ideological confinement of poetic inspiration,"[3] and would be *tailored* by him precisely to answer, by adhering to the party's requests, the criticisms that exploded against his bolder, nonconforming *Ragazzi di vita*. Unlike Lampedusa, whose death removed him from the literary scene even before his official debut, Pasolini was an important presence between 1955 and 1959, not only as a novelist, but also as an active participant in critical and intellectual debates, engaging individuals both inside and outside the Communist Party. In fact, both of what might be called his "Roman novels" were also replies and reactions to such individuals and represented the interventions of a cultural protagonist already engaged for some time in a personal meditation on linguistic invention, on "learned" and popular poetry, on poetics, on history, and on reality and its possible representations. Whereas Lampedusa's novel was the mature fruit of a formidable literary background, although cultivated in isolation for decades, and may be said to represent an unexpected miracle that appeared on the literary scene like a bolt of lightning without aiming programmatically at any precise critical objective, Pasolini's two novels were, instead, the product of his expressed convictions and literary intentions and, consequently, must be taken to represent more deliberate assertions.

While both Lampedusa and Pasolini shared equally negative critical reviews and attacks from the intellectual establishment – often the same critics rejecting the works of both writers – while enjoying an unparalleled public success, such a public reception does not authorize the literary historian to treat the aesthetics of the two writers in the same fashion. The critical destinies of both writers (transformed into two outstanding examples of transgression by those who were subjected to a single alchemical formula – that of literary realism in the service of politics and ideology) indicate how ideological games dominated or even poisoned an entire phase of Italian culture at a moment when Italian neorealist fiction and its penchant for social realism seemed to have reached an intellectual impasse.

While by 1955 Pasolini already had a number of significant publications under his belt, Lampedusa lacked any real contact with the publishing world, and the late appearance of his only novel occurred after a laborious editorial process. Before finally being published in the so-called "complete" version in eight parts, *Il Gattopardo* was presented by Lampedusa himself, first to Mondadori, then to Einaudi. Only after his death, when the hope of having it published seemed to have vanished, did the manuscript of the novel end up in the hands of Giorgio Bassani, who, according to the account of Lampedusa's

---

[3] Alberto Asor Rosa, *Scrittori e popolo. Il populismo nella letteratura italiana contemporanea* (Turin: Einaudi, 1988), p. 59 (translator's translation).

widow, "immediately intuited its beauty and had it published by Feltrinelli, with startling success."[4] Another powerful writer-editor, Elio Vittorini, had with reservations rejected Lampedusa's submission to Mondadori, asking that the manuscript be reworked and modified. Later, Vittorini rejected the manuscript for the Einaudi "I Gettoni" series for ideological reasons, as well as for reasons of literary trends. For Vittorini, an intellectual who had embarked upon "a line of strongly anti-traditional linguistic and stylistic experimentation,"[5] and who was constantly in search of edifying and innovative texts, *Il Gattopardo* represented an uncomfortable novel on a historical topic that could be defined as traditional in that it recounted fifty years of Sicilian history beginning with Garibaldi's landing in Marsala in 1860. However, its major defect was that it transformed the glorious events of the Risorgimento and Italian Unification as recorded by the official historiography of the day through the private, interior story of its protagonist, Prince Fabrizio di Salina, into a tale of defeat and disillusionment. Thus, in Vittorini's view (and in the opinion of most Marxists) Lampedusa had erased the so-called objective forces of history to give place to an intimate, introspective storyline more suitable in a psychological novel, a style that was certainly unthinkable in the realist or neorealist sort of novel that Vittorini, along with the Marxist left of the times, would have praised. In short, this quite unexpected novel rose above the mass of much of the utopian literature of the period, as well as the well-worn paths of postwar neorealism. The novel available today exists in two different forms: one published by Feltrinelli in 1958, based on an early typewritten version; and another published by Mondadori in 1969, taken from the author's manuscript of 1957. The English translation was based on the first version, although some scholars have claimed that the second text published may actually be closer to the author's final intentions.

The technique of the realistic novel would have been a possible strategy for Lampedusa, if he had limited himself to a central historical theme revolving around the Salina family, set against the backdrop of the political catastrophe that struck the entire southern aristocracy with the fall of the Bourbon regime and the Unification of Italy, followed by the decades of normalization that followed that initial revolutionary event. But Lampedusa grafted onto the initial thematic center of his novel interests and aspirations that proved to be incompatible with such a traditional unified historical structure, as well as with the objectifying character of a naturalist narration.

---

[4] Alessandra di Lampedusa, interview with S. Bertoldi in *A futuro memoria* (Milan: Rizzoli, 1981), p. 59 (translator's translation).
[5] Giancarlo Ferretti, *L'editore Vittorini* (Turin: Einaudi, 1992), p. 271.

This occurred because both the historical scenario and the Sicilian setting serve Lampedusa only insofar as they shed light on the individual destiny of the aristocratic Prince Fabrizio (a fictional figure inspired by Lampedusa's grandfather, the astronomer-prince Giulio di Lampedusa), whose emotional reactions are recorded along with his story. In various letters written in the 1950s, Lampedusa himself confides to his friend Guido Lajolo that the background and setting of his work are portrayed in a tone that is "ironic, bitter, and not free of malice" (1955); everything, he notes, in the book "is only hinted at, and symbolized: there is nothing explicit, and it might seem that nothing happens" (1956). In writing *Il Gattopardo*, and in recounting the years of turmoil that struck Sicily in the wake of the fall of the Bourbons, Lampedusa places less stock in the lessons that might have been learned from the masters of Sicilian *verismo* in the nineteenth century (Giovanni Verga, Federico De Roberto) than in what he learned from his private encounters with the great reformers of the modern novel – James Joyce, Marcel Proust, Virginia Woolf – who stimulate him to contemplate at length the question of time in the novel and, consequently, to question the possibility of reconstructing and representing a historical process and a character's experience in realistic terms in an effective manner. The "time" that Lampedusa succeeds with extraordinary skill in fixing and in setting into motion in his pages is one that flows in immobility. In no way does he avoid the question of the unfeasibility of the objective representation of the cycles of history. Instead, he allows this question to assume a kind of *philosophical* significance in a narrative driven by fragmentary visions and by the amplification of the protagonist's interior time and, therefore, by the increasing insignificance of external events for the individual's existence where outward events serve above all to embody the sensation that everything is precipitating toward death. What Lampedusa stages is principally a vision of the world and not of a particular historical period: a vision of one who is fully aware of the instability of points of reference and of the relativity of perceptions over time. Lampedusa is equally aware of the need to rethink historical events with regard to the present day and to insert into the work a point of view other than that which might have characterized a Sicilian aristocrat between 1860 and 1910. His attitude toward the historical materials he wants to reconstruct resembles that of an archeologist contemplating a landscape of ruins and asking himself how to define and represent his own relationship with the remains of a past asking to be understood. It seems impossible for him to pretend, today, to be seeing an intact landscape. On the other hand, it is useless to describe that landscape as it was, forgetting that in the meantime it has been destroyed. In his novel, this knowledge is not translated into a nostalgic comparison between modern times and times past but, rather, it presents a staging of distinct perceptions with regard to the same historical reality. There is the perception of Prince Fabrizio Salina, a character belonging to the past who sees a landscape in the process of disintegration and decides to ignore its more troubling features. There is the perception of the novel's narrator, a figure belonging to the present who is unable to ignore the distance separating him from the prince and who, unlike the prince, cannot embrace the illusion of the erasure of the historical moment and turn to the consolation afforded by the contemplation of the stars. The narrator, in contrast, wishes to call upon all the resources of his knowledge in order to describe the stages of that process of disintegration that he sees as having taken place. The hypothesis of reading the protagonist as representative of Lampedusa's point of view with regard to the historical events cannot, therefore, be maintained as a critical approach to this novel. It is clear that Prince Salina shares with Prince Lampedusa not only certain aspects of his character but also a position as a skeptical and bitter observer of the facts, as a man faithful to his class and to the class culture that distinguishes him from the masses surrounding him. The condition of an erudite observer thoughtfully following from the margins a transformation in customs and thought may be said to characterize both the author and his protagonist. But while in Salina's world it is still possible for an aristocrat to consider culture to be a privilege tied to *social condition*, as opposed to the rising middle class, personified in the novel by Don Calogero Sedàra, who struggles after mere material wealth (Verga's celebrated *roba*), in Lampedusa's world, class no longer offers any guarantee, and aristocratic privilege has been either dismantled or survives in individuals as refinement and good taste. It would be naive to believe, as many inattentive readers of the novel have claimed, that Lampedusa espoused the by now proverbial formula of the cynical Tancredi, Prince Salina's nephew, who was ready to strike a pact with the new, rampant bourgeoisie through his marriage to Sedàra's daughter, Angelica. Fabrizio seems to share the cynical perspective of the novel: "if we want everything to remain as it is, it is necessary for everything to change." But, in the novel, such points of view are again and again criticized and cast into doubt by the narrator. Don Fabrizio deceives himself, represses the repellent residue of history, attempts to flee from reality, and wants to turn his back on the present, knowing he can no longer effectively insert himself into the dynamics of history. The narrator presents him in this way, as the prince succumbs to the new rulers without reacting, renouncing any form of engagement with, or projection into the future, and seeking his own individual redemption in solitude, introspection, and science. Prince Salina is far from being presented as a positive hero, as a just man or demiurge. The narrator who sets the events in motion, seeing them change in the span of time that separates him from

Don Fabrizio, has the capacity to evaluate the situation and to supply us with a more reliable perspective than Fabrizio's. Yet the narrator's perspective is called into question as well, especially in the section of the novel dedicated to Concetta, the mature survivor and favorite daughter of the prince, and her meditation on her precipitous refusal of Tancredi's hand when she might still have bettered her rival Angelica. At this point in the narrative, safe from the whims of history with the disappearance of his princely protagonist, the narrator faces the problem of the existence of truth:

> From the timeless depths of her being a black pain came welling up to spatter her all over at the revelation of the truth.
>
> *But was this the truth?* Nowhere has truth so short a life as in Sicily; the fact has scarcely happened five minutes before its genuine kernel has vanished, been camouflaged, embellished, disfigured, squashed, annihilated by imagination and self-interests . . . And poor Concetta was hoping to find the truth of feelings that had not been expressed but only glimpsed half a century before! *The truth no longer existed*. Precarious fact, though, had been replaced by irrefutable pain.[6]

Concentrated in Concetta's unresolved doubt is a conviction regarding the impossibility of a reliable reading of the past, even (or especially) in a novel describing historical events. The individual, whether it be the prince or his female counterpart, finds himself in an existential state of vulnerability and uncertainty that escapes the mechanism of the events of an ever-changing history. His bewildered, defeatist attitude is in fact reevaluated, through Concetta, at the mercy of the fleeting instant, in her vulnerability and naiveté, after she has seemed so haughty and obstinate in acting as the repository of unquestionable certainties. Individual defeat, which weighs much more heavily than the historical defeat of a ruined class (the aristocracy), appears on the horizon as life's only promise, giving humanity no certainty other than that of death. Lampedusa does not propose in the novel concrete hypotheses as solutions to the problem of existence, or in any case not historical or ideal solutions. If anything, he limits himself to suggesting an answer worthy of the aristocracy, one that consists in a withdrawal into an arcane, meditative dimension, such as Fabrizio's contemplation of astronomy. The help that comes from distancing thought or expression, such as irony, the shield and banner of refined detachment – of which Lampedusa, especially through Don Fabrizio, makes knowing use throughout the duration of the novel – is one solution, if only a partial one. The novel seems to be dotted with impulses and flourishes that introduce an "Other," destructuring vision, further cracking its historiographical surface and converging

[6] Giuseppe Tomasi di Lampedusa, *The Leopard* (London: Pantheon, 1960), p. 314.

to overturn the assumptions of the historical novel. But the entirely modern awareness of the extinction of traditional narrative measures, of the grounding of the very concept of truth, does not undermine the novel's fundamental fluidity, as Lampedusa is unwilling to insinuate into the narrative in the form of text the "fracture" he has recognized in reality, the cosmic uncertainty that has generated his representation of things. Nevertheless, Lampedusa's novel is certainly disharmonious, organized as it is in vignettes of varying importance and length (the author chooses in fact to divide the work into "parts," rather than chapters); and this *defect* in its construction also contributes to its being situated far outside the conventions of the historical novel.

Critics are unanimous with regard to the limitations of the plot's organization and the structural imbalances that detract from an otherwise lucid and controlled work (one whose knowing use of language is "native, new, splendid," free of "forced expressionist elements"[7]). They are unanimous as well in seeing in the novel a destructuring of the historical novel's narrative processes, an exaltation of the internal adventure of a protagonist coming to terms with history unsuccessfully, and a psychological dimension in the work that contrasts with a simple historical recreation of the events of the Italian Risorgimento. They also agree in seeing *Il Gattopardo* as an ironic and detached, disheartened and pessimistic reading of history. Critics are divided, however, when it comes to evaluating such a reading imbued with negative certainties. For the many authoritative readers who express a clear approval of Lampedusa's narrative vision, lucidity and rationality – not indifference and detachment – inform Lampedusa's narrative meditation. The novel, then, is certainly worthy of being received as a knowing, painful exercise that suggests – according to some – a fruitful reflection on the events it takes as its subject. Strong reservations regarding the significance of the novel's content are held both by the intelligentsia of the left and by intellectuals not completely dominated by party ideology, who point to the novel's indolence and indifference, its nostalgia and apathy, as bolstering the aristocratic, reactionary vision that Lampedusa wants to construct. Those lined up along positions in defense of the historical novel hasten to deny that there is in Lampedusa's book any reliable perception of the political reality of the experience of the Risorgimento. Some critics declared that the novel ignored the ideas, sentiments, and passions that were produced by the period and that Lampedusa's rather restricted view of the Risorgimento made it impossible for him ever to represent its reality.

---

[7] Giuseppe De Robertis, "*Il Gattopardo*," in *Altro Novecento* (Florence: Le Monnier, 1962), p. 328 (translator's translation).

For the contemporary reader, it may be difficult to imagine that even in 1959, decades after the publication of the great European modernist novels by Proust, Joyce, and Svevo, critics and intellectuals could have been incapable of imagining the depiction in a novel of anything other than the reality of a historical period according to a traditional nineteenth-century narrative framework. *Il Gattopardo* represented a new test for the Italian left, already suffering from the impact of another literary debate only several months earlier provoked by the translation, publication, and international fame of Boris Pasternak's *Doctor Zhivago*. Pasternak received the Nobel Prize in 1959, and his dramatic representation of the story of an individual against the historical-political backdrop of the Soviet state apparatus had provoked intense critical debate in Italy. In 1959, Italian Communists largely accepted the aesthetic and ideological reflections on realism proposed by the great critic Georgy Lukács. Lukács basically condemned and rejected contemporary art, including that of the avant-garde, seeing in it an expression of bourgeois decadence, while he championed the grand tradition of the nineteenth-century historical novel as the ideal model for the representation of reality. According to Lukács, in the realist work the writer rises above his own ideology in illustrating social reality and reflecting on the historical process in its progressive tension toward the new. Italian Communist intellectuals read both *Il Gattopardo* and *Doctor Zhivago* as containing startling and dangerous traces of decadent formalism, whereas they did not detect any trace of a dynamic tending toward moral ends in either work. To summarize the intellectual poverty of such an ideological approach, which prevented them from seeing beyond a restricted horizon, following Lukács to the letter, the French Communist writer Louis Aragon reclaimed *Il Gattopardo* for the left by reading the work as a lucidly bitter, critical, but realistic account of the Risorgimento, while Lukács himself in his old age found *Il Gattopardo* to be the most successful historical novel of recent times.

A few years before the polemics over history and the novel aroused by the stunning success of Lampedusa and Pasternak, Pier Paolo Pasolini had entertained the idea, shocking to leftist intellectuals, that realism in the novel could be achieved without socialist realism. *Ragazzi di vita* constituted the first and most striking Italian attempt at innovation with regard to the neorealist movement in the novel. This original novel recounts the various adventures of Riccetto and his companions, a group of adolescents in chaotic postwar Rome. Born and raised in the capital's subproletariat districts and accustomed to the violence typical of the city's extreme outskirts, these boys live by their wits without ever breaking out of their desperate poverty. At times, they do stray from the territory of the *borgate* (the poor suburbs of Rome) and venture into the city of Rome along the banks of the Tiber or head for the beach at Ostia. The eight chapters comprising the book do not form a unified whole (another parallel to Lampedusa's masterpiece): the episodes do not always focus upon the same protagonist and follow each other as contiguous scenes, while the novel lacks a true plot tying them all together. As the novel's title itself reveals, the protagonists are the children of the urban subproletariat, of that unruly, irregular life that had never before been depicted in an Italian novel. As the title of Pasolini's second novel implied, such a life was essentially filled with violence. The reader observes Pasolini's protagonists as they undergo various trials, but they never achieve the status of fully rounded characters, and the novel contains no individual who might supply the eight chapters with a plausible, unifying framework. Such a lack of structure or tightly woven plot, as well as the absence of well-defined characters, make of Pasolini's novel an anomalous, unconvincing work on structural grounds, even though the fragmentary form of the text reflects the liminal condition of its characters, who stand "on the edge between the world of instincts and the awakening of a basic conscience that makes the development of a plot impossible."[8] Pasolini's linguistic choices render the text's physiognomy even more problematic. He opts for a curious solution never before pushed to its limits, grafting the Roman dialect onto the trunk of the standard Italian literary language with shades borrowed from the slangy variant belonging to the delinquents of the *borgate*. Naturally, Pasolini's refined literary Italian influences the novel's dialogue, while in the descriptive sections his standard Italian alternates with the mixed language of the narrator, contaminated by expressions proper to the world under analysis. Typically, the narrator mingles the jargon of the characters' spoken language and the narrator's polished literary language containing occasional shades of dialect borrowed from the environment he describes.

In order to mitigate the contrast between "high" and "low" languages, Pasolini makes insistent use of free indirect discourse, which allows him to render the character's expressiveness although this is filtered through the voice of the narrator. But his mimetic artifice and the narrator's strategy of adhering consistently to the perspective of the "Other," do not avoid the substantial linguistic rift that dominates the story. As a result, the reader is struck "on one hand by the decadence and literariness of the narrator, and on the other by the adolescent mentality and expressive monotony of the sub-proletariat of the *borgata*, with their characteristic exaggeration and overstatement."[9]

[8] Marco Antonio Bazzocchi, *Pier Paolo Pasolini* (Milan: Bruno Mondadori, 1998), p. 160.
[9] Cesare Segre, "Punti di vista, polifonia ed espressionismo nel romanzo italiano," in *Intrecci di voci: la polifonia nella letteratura del Novecento* (Turin: Einaudi, 1991), p. 39.

The formal energy and the vitality of *Ragazzi di vita* owe a great deal to its marriage of a unique ideological stance with what must be described as a kind of mystic vision. At one and the same time, Pasolini represents a reality based upon class at the margins of society and also exalts the complete purity of the mob that inhabits this world, and he manages to do this in such a way that this representation also contains his own personal love, his own compassion toward these adolescents, as well as his visceral and even irrational hatred for the bourgeoisie. Thus what the distinguished critic Gianfranco Contini called an "an unabashed declaration of love" also serves as an explicit declaration of war against positive values, against those engaged in the building of a different society, and against a populist narrative of hope and class redemption.

The critical counteroffensive to *Ragazzi di vita* was swift in coming. The novel was immediately attacked by supporters of the cultural policies of the Italian Communist Party (the PCI), who attempted to demolish its ideological and its linguistic or structural framework. Marxist critics, particularly those associated with the PCI's official newspaper, *L'Unità*, as well as the Marxist editors of the review *Il Contemporaneo*, accused Pasolini of a false "naturalism," of a tendentious use of the most unseemly and deviant shades of Roman dialect, even approaching the jargon of the criminal underworld – stylistic accusations that led logically to other charges of amorality, morbidity, and a disreputable content. In short, Pasolini breaks the ideological axis of realism, removing himself from the party's healthy, populist pedagogy and from its posture of respectability, perspectives irreconcilable with the unsocialized brutality of the underworld found in the Roman *borgate*. In a new cultural journal called *Officina* that he helped to found in 1955, Pasolini reacted to the relentless assaults of the Communists. In April 1956, just after the twentieth congress of the Soviet Communist Party and shortly before the Hungarian Revolution against Communist rule there, Pasolini attacked the clumsy and mechanical use made of ideology by his antagonists, calling his attackers not only naive and virtually illiterate but also bureaucratic. Far from retreating, Pasolini's leftist critics showed no sign of changing their opinion of *Ragazzi di vita*, even as the novel itself was confiscated for obscenity and disappeared from bookstores. In July 1956, Pasolini and his publisher Garzanti were tried for public obscenity. Supported by obviously conservative witnesses such as the critic Carlo Bo (1911–) and the poet Giuseppe Ungaretti (1888–1970), who affirmed the moral and religious values of the novel, both men were acquitted. After the events in Budapest in October 1956, Pasolini directed a polemic in verse against the Communist leaders and received additional attacks from *Il Contemporaneo* in turn. The debate ended with attention shifting to Pasolini's new collection of civic poetry, *Le ceneri di Gramsci*

(*The Ashes of Gramsci*, 1957), as leftists reacted positively to this new work without, however, changing their negative assessment of *Ragazzi di vita*.

A true rehabilitation of Pasolini the novelist by the left in Italy begins only in 1959 with the publication of his second novel, *Una vita violenta*. In this work, Pasolini realigns himself once more with the Italian Communist Party's cultural politics and obtains the blessing of those critics who only a few years before had demolished *Ragazzi di vita*. Without renouncing his beloved world of the *borgate*, Pasolini designs the novel's plot and the adventures of its protagonist, Tommaso Puzzilli, in order to produce a novel with socialist ideology. Unlike his predecessors, Pasolini's character experiences a true process of transformation, beginning in a condition of desperate marginalization but concluding in complete ideological maturity. Initially a hoodlum associated with neo-Fascists involved in ordinary criminality, Tommaso undergoes the crucial experience of falling in love, which leads to his engagement to Irene, a prelude to the gradual socialization that will take place when his family moves from the slums to an apartment in the projects. Not indifferent to his new life of relative ease, Tommaso is willing to adapt: he goes to work, thinks about marriage, and flirts with the idea of registering with the Christian Democrats. Struck by a lung infection, he is taken to a sanatorium, where close contact with patients leads to his new political conscience and culminates in his joining the PCI. Having helped slum residents during a flood, he becomes sick again and dies, sealing – if not through heroism, at least through generosity and unselfishness – his full integration into an acceptable trajectory for a Marxist hero.

Satisfied that Tommaso's narrative was consonant with their ideological aims, the intellectuals of *Il Contemporaneo* praised the novel, while such praise provoked unease in critics who did not share their Marxist perspective. Pasolini managed to eliminate some of his first novel's most serious defects by accentuating characteristics specific to individual speakers in his use of the Roman dialect, by avoiding the systematic clash of high and low literary languages, by concentrating his attention on the protagonist's personality, and by establishing a less frenetic and broken narrative pace that helps hold the novel together. Nevertheless, Pasolini applied a rigid scheme too literally and unquestioningly, almost out of a duty to the ideology that he espoused. Today, with the clarity of hindsight, the reader cannot but agree with Walter Siti's judgment that Pasolini's second novel reflects the catastrophic failure of the novelist's ideological project.[10]

[10] Walter Siti, "Descrivere, narrare, esporsi," in Pier Paolo Pasolini, *Romanzi e racconti* (Milan: Mondadori, 1998), vol. I: p. cxxiii.

Pasolini intended to conclude his Roman novels with a third work, but the trilogy was never to be completed, probably because new and more satisfying creative stimuli (the cinema, poetry, the travel-story journal) distracted him from the narrative form of the novel which ultimately may well have been his least favorable literary genre. As Siti observes, "Pasolini's use of the novel might seem to be tied to an ideological stance and a yearning for success... rather than to any intimate need."[11] On the other hand, Pasolini himself, interviewed shortly after the publication of *Una vita violenta*, stated: "In the end, I am not a novelist; I wrote those two novels because I felt I had a world behind me."[12] Pasolini was no doubt moved by the life of the *borgate* and excited by the project of restoring the oral tradition of its primitive inhabitants by intellectualizing it. It is therefore not surprising that critical interest in Pasolini's two novels remains limited. Not even the posthumous publication of *Petrolio* (*Petroleum*, 1992), which originated in his period of Roman experimentation and contains a shifting narration difficult to classify according to the conventions of traditional literary genres, has stirred increased interest in the first two novels. Yet, beginning with *Petrolio*, the discussion of Pasolini as a narrator has been reopened, and, paradoxically, it is around the figure of Pasolini, perhaps one of the least traditional novelists in Italy during the twentieth century, that the most intense and impassioned debate over the definition and uses of literary space has developed in Italy in recent decades.[13]

Il Gattopardo has enjoyed a critical reception that is quite different from the history of opinion on *Ragazzi di vita* and *Una vita violenta*. At regular intervals, and for various reasons, critical interest has continued to return to Lampedusa's novel. The release of Luchino Visconti's film adaptation of the novel in 1963 kept the critical debate over the novel alive, particularly as Visconti's version of Lampedusa's story was made from the perspective of a director who was both an aristocrat and a professed Marxist. The discovery made in 1968 of a manuscript version of the novel that was different from the one sent to Bassani resulted in the release of a second edition of the work in 1969. Furthermore, beginning in the 1970s, an impressive number of Lampedusa's writings on French and English literature emerged from the author's archives, and these important essays breathed new life into critical studies of the novel. New and previously unpublished writings included in the

---

[11] *Ibid.*, vol. I: p. cxli.   [12] Interview with A. Chiesa in *Paese sera* (5 July 1960).

[13] See Carla Benedetti's essay *Pasolini contro Calvino: per una letteratura impura* (Turin: Bollati Boringhieri, 1998). This important book is essential to a critical rereading of Italian literature in recent decades and stands at the center of renewed theoretical interest in Pasolini.

1995 edition of Lampedusa's complete works further broaden the horizon of reference for *Il Gattopardo* and ended any doubt that further study of the novelist and his masterpiece was required. In short, Lampedusa was spared the unfair destiny of the short-lived debate, of the episodic outburst, to which he seemed to have been relegated by his book's initial reception. Pasolini, as well, in spite of the many critical attacks on his novels, has now been canonized by the recent publication of his complete works in 1998. Far from being confined or mummified within a monumental research project, Pasolini's entire works are now finally collected in a form that emphasizes their vitality and takes into account the unending dialogue that characterized Pasolini's writings.

Despite the contradictions and paradoxes marking the circumstances of the birth and early reception of Lampedusa's nonconventional historical novel and Pasolini's transgressive novels about life in the Roman suburbs, these works have continued to play an important role in contemporary Italian culture. Their surprising emergence in the 1950s when all the cards of the postwar neorealist novel in Italy seemed to have been played, as well as their resistance to the passage of time assisted by a constant following among the Italian reading public, are signs that contradict those who complain about the death of literature. The continued success of Lampedusa and Pasolini with the reading public suggests that we should emphasize the resources of literature, its vitality, and its capacity to escape institutional decrees and verdicts, while continuing to recognize the uses and the obligations of the critical discourse that analyzes literature.

Further reading

Pier Paolo Pasolini

Barański, Zygmunt G. "Pier Paolo Pasolini: Culture, Croce, Gramsci." In Z. G. Barański and P. Lumley, eds. *Culture and Conflict in Postwar Italy. Essays on Mass and Popular Culture*. London: Macmillan, 1990, pp. 139–59.

Benedetti, Carla. *Pasolini contro Calvino: Per una letteratura impura*. Turin: Bollati Boringhieri, 1998.

Pasolini, Pier Paolo. *The Ragazzi*. Trans. Emile Capouya. New York: Grove, 1968.
  A Violent Life. Trans. William Weaver. New York: Pantheon, 1992.
  Romanzi e racconti. Ed. Walter Siti. Vol. I: (*1946–1961*). Milan: Mondadori, 1998.

Rumble, Patrick and Bart Testa, eds. *Pier Paolo Pasolini: Contemporary Perspectives*. Toronto: University of Toronto Press, 1994.

Schwartz, Barth David. *Pasolini Requiem*. New York: Pantheon, 1992.

Siciliano, Enzo. *Pasolini: A Biography*. Trans. John Shepley. New York: Random House, 1982.

Giuseppe Tomasi di Lampedusa

Bertone, Manuela. *Tomasi di Lampedusa*. Palermo: Palumbo, 1995.

Dombroski, Robert S. *Properties of Writing: Ideological Discourse in Modern Italian Fiction*. Baltimore: Johns Hopkins University Press, 1994.

Gilmore, David. *The Last Leopard: A Life of Giuseppe Tomasi di Lampedusa*. New York: Pantheon, 1998.

Lucente, Gregory. *Beautiful Fables: Self-Consciousness in Italian Narrative from Manzoni to Calvino*. Baltimore: Johns Hopkins University Press, 1986.

Orlando, Francesco. *L'intimità e la storia. Lettura del "Gattopardo."* Turin: Einaudi, 1998.

Tomasi di Lampedusa, Giuseppe. *Two Stories and a Memory*. Trans. Archibald Colquhoun. New York: Grosset, 1968.

The Leopard. Trans. Archibald Colquhoun. New York: Avon, 1975.

Opere. Ed. Gioacchino Lanza Tomasi. Milan: Mondadori, 1995.

10

SHARON WOOD

Feminist writing in the twentieth century

In 1902 Anna Franchi published *Avanti il divorzio!*, a largely autobiographical work that explored with frank directness the moral squalor engendered by the failure of Italian political leaders to pass divorce legislation. Franchi's radical and dramatic demand for an end to the sexual and economic oppression of women burst into a climate where few politicians dared challenge the legal status quo on the family, and where feminist demands focused more on the vote and improving women's working conditions than on a fundamental overhaul of social and family life. If Franchi's experience was a product of her times, her rebellion was ahead of her day. Almost thirty years later in *La mia vita* (My Life, 1940) she looks back on her youth and describes her life then as a curious mixture of the end of romanticism and the rise of new theories that seemed attractive to a younger generation of women. The "theories" she refers to obliquely are new political positions forming on the left associated with anarchism, socialism, and feminism that achieved comparatively little in terms of legislation but which had a substantial impact on social and cultural thought in Italy during the twentieth century.

Avanti il divorzio!, dedicated "to those who suffer," describes the vicissitudes of Anna, a bright and gifted child whose passion for music is held in check by her bourgeois family and who, like all the girls of her class, has nothing to occupy her lively adolescent mind but thoughts of love. Her new piano teacher, the violinist Ettore Streno, comes preceded by a bad reputation that can only fascinate a young mind brought up on romantic novels, and she marries him. Her sensual nature is soon repelled by his sexual brutality, while she returns from her honeymoon with the first symptoms of a venereal disease that is to plague her for years. Marriage gives her three children, two of whom are born sick with syphilis; Ettore bleeds the family dry financially to pay his debts, contracted through gambling and adultery, including forcing the sale of Anna's wedding jewelry and faking suicide in order to extract more money. Anna finds herself courted by another man,

Gisleno Della Casa, and while her husband's behavior is tacitly ignored, she becomes the subject of strict surveillance and local gossip, not to mention a beating from her husband for besmirching his name. Anna's experience focuses on women's economic and sexual servitude, widely condoned domestic violence, and the lack of legal status or protection for women, and her disease is the physiological correlative for a hypocritical society that relentlessly applies its double standards in exacting its punishment for female transgression.

Anna finds relief and comfort in art, nature, and writing. Here, as in so much later feminist writing of the twentieth century, literature offers consolation and redemption, the assertion of the self in the public sphere. It is also closely bound in with motherhood, a maternity transfigured and transposed. The appearance of Anna's first poem is described in terms of a painless, joyful childbirth, and, in a feature again to typify self-consciously feminist writing, the question of language is foregrounded. Anna becomes a writer, but in the process she loses her health, her money, and her children, not to mention her reputation. Her wayward husband – who can himself be prosecuted for adultery only if he conducts his affair within the marital home – sues her for adultery. Her lawyer's shockingly cynical observation, that her position would have been better had she contracted syphilis from her husband once more and then killed him, reveals at a stroke the enormity of the obstacles between women and any real emancipation or equality. In 1902 there could be no solution to Anna's dilemma, but at the close of the novel, called to defend herself in a second adultery trial, Anna gives an impassioned plea to a moved public and judge. In literature, if not in life, in the reader's mind, if not in the eyes of the law, Anna can be vindicated.

On the final pages of this extraordinarily honest novel, where under the light guise of fiction Franchi gives a far more complex and disturbing account of marriage than in her autobiography, Anna receives two letters that dramatize her position. A letter from her husband threatens prison, and suggests she kill herself; in the other, she reads a favorable review of her first book. Anna's description of her own work is a defense less of literary naturalism (called *verismo* in Italy) than a passionate claim that literature should speak to our female and human condition, and not separate itself from the reality of our lives. Anna's description of her work – not, then, simply behind the times as Capuana had said women's writing would always be – anticipates the work of neofeminist writers more than half a century later, who refused to be seduced by avant-garde techniques and adhered to realism as an aesthetic and ethical choice:

> The crazy conceits of the aesthetes, the symbolists, had always wearied her...
> frivolous, adorned, rouged creations which stood on their own two feet only
> by virtue of their elaborate decorativeness, and then only in a half-light.
> The dazzling light of the sun shows them up to be ridiculous and false...
> But the true, whatever its nature, is always beautiful, in sweetness or in
> horror: the humanly true, which has so many examples to give us, and so
> much to teach us   (*Avanti*, p. 314).

Franchi continued to explore the family as social structure and the relations
between the sexes in a prolific output that is also mute witness to her need
to write for her living, and she adhered to the faith in realism as outlined
in this early work. Books of art criticism, children's tales, and short stories
jostle with numerous novels. In 1946 (the same year in which women finally
gained the vote), she published the remarkable *Cose d'ieri dette alle donne
d'oggi* (Things from Yesterday Recounted to Women of Today). In this work,
Franchi sets out to place this achievement in the historical and political
context of a tradition of female courage and effort, whether of women like
Anna Kuliscioff, Anna Maria Mozzoni, and Paolina Schiff who fought for
the vote, the women who staked a claim for female emancipation during the
French Revolution, or, more recently, the countless women who had been
involved in the Resistance, the women who "would all become involved
fearlessly, whether at home, in the street, in prison, faced with the German
gun or the torture of the needles" (*Cose d'ieri*, p. 26). In spite of Franchi's
achievements – her novels, her public lectures on the need for divorce, her
constant lobbying for legislative change – she has remained a largely and
undeservedly forgotten figure in Italy and abroad.

In contrast, the much more famous *Una donna* (1906) by Sibilla Aleramo
covers a good deal of the same ground as the early work of Anna Franchi.
While Aleramo's text received mixed reviews from the critics, it was a popular
and international success, reprinted throughout the Fascist era and rediscovered by neofeminism in the 1960s with the shocking realization that, more
than half a century on, women's position in the family and in the eyes of
the law was still subordinate and subservient. Aleramo (pen-name for Rina
Faccio) went on to write further novels and several collections of poetry,
but *Una donna* remains her most influential achievement. Like Franchi's
text, *Una donna* is the *Bildungsroman* (a novel of formative education)
of an emerging female consciousness, tracing a woman's experience from
childhood and adolescence to the crushing of illusions under the brutality
of male possession, to the development of an awareness of the self apart
from the family and all imposed roles. Aleramo's protagonist comes from
a more freethinking, intellectual milieu, and as a child wishes to emulate
her beloved, strong, irreverent father. When the family is moved away from

metropolitan, cosmopolitan Milan to a small southern town where her increasingly irascible father is to run a local factory, the young girl's education comes to an abrupt halt. With no external opportunities for schooling, she works alongside her father, her mother at this stage being just a shadowy background figure. A young man at the factory reveals that her father is having an affair that is common knowledge; in her shock and distress, she is an easy victim for seduction.

The resulting marriage follows a similar pattern to that of Anna Franchi's character in its brutal subjection. There are, however, a number of marked differences. *Una donna* bears explicit witness to a chain of servitude handed down the generations, as she discovers herself following unwittingly in her mother's footsteps in her despair and thoughts of suicide. It is a common pain between mother and daughter that becomes a common bond, as the protagonist begins to rediscover her mother after her death, and to ally herself emotionally and intellectually with her. Motherhood is also given far higher status in this novel, another reason perhaps why it resonated so powerfully with feminists fifty years later, as they sought to redefine mother–daughter roles. The protagonist speaks compellingly and movingly of her love for her son; and it is of course this very motherly passion which gives the novel's climax its wrenching power, as she leaves him in order to rescue herself from the horrors of marriage, disease, infidelity, and a moral abyss. Also, Aleramo makes specific reference to the feminist movement as an empowering, nurturing force, while Franchi's Anna must muddle along as she can, and it is left to Franchi's later books to explore the nexus of women's rights and the political status quo, and the precarious relationship between feminism and socialism. *Avanti il divorzio!* is a novel whose climactic scene in the courtroom, while it gives a marginal victory, must yet end in defeat. While the character in *Una donna* can hardly be said to win, the resolution is clearer, the break with the past more definitive, the act more heroic, more tragically theatrical.

The novels of Aleramo and Franchi emerged from a post-Unification climate in which increasing education and a widening publishing industry, much of which was specifically directed at a new female readership, went hand in hand with emerging feminist and socialist movements. While government surveys explored the state of the new nation, many women writers explored the condition of marriage and the institution of the family, where ideological and legal pressures kept women subservient. Franchi and Aleramo demanded legal equality and social emancipation, but they also, unlike the previous generation of writers such as Neera (pen-name for Anna Zuccari) and Marchesa Colombi (1840–1920), began consciously to consider literature, and language itself, as gender-inflected. Aleramo went further, calling for what in more contemporary parlance would be called *écriture feminine*, indignant at the flood of mediocrity penned by the new wave of women writers, calling them only parodies of fashionable novels written by men: "How on earth could all those 'intellectuals' not understand that woman cannot justify her entry into the already overcrowded field of literature and art, unless with works which bear her own stamp and imprint?" (*Una donna*, p. 135). Aleramo realizes that language and style reflect a complex web of social and hierarchical relations, since the dominant intellectual and cultural discourse has inevitably been shaped by patriarchy. The language of culture is, then, a male language – one that is not her own and that cannot therefore express her inner self.

Maria Messina (1887–1944), brought back to the attention of the reading public by her fellow Sicilian Leonardo Sciascia, sets her stories amongst the petty bourgeoisie and minor intellectual classes of Sicily. *Casa paterna* (The Paternal Home, 1921) and *La casa nel vicolo* (The House in the Alley, 1921) are extraordinary tales of contemporary patriarchal Sicily and the difficulties faced by women in establishing an autonomous identity outside imposed familial roles. The slightly earlier work *Alla deriva* (Going Downhill, 1920) explicitly contrasts male and female intelligence against a wider background of war and military and cultural slavery. In a provincial town, a professor's two star students are the wealthy northerner Angelo Fiore and the relatively poor Sicilian, Marcello Scalia. Yet the women in the novel are seen to have a deeper, if unacknowledged, intelligence. The professor's career has been nurtured by his self-sacrificing sister, while his witty, cultured daughter, Simonetta, has managed to fool an art professor by passing off one of her own paintings as a work of the thirteenth century. Marcello writes the professor's reviews and is in love with his daughter, despite Fiore's condescending view that girls like Simonetta are superficial and their culture is false, like fake furniture. The marriage between Marcello and Simonetta founders, less because of brutality or ignorance than through a failure to recognize the woman's modernity (she would like to try flying), her intelligence, and her desire to act as companion and intellectual equal rather than be banished to the nursery. Messina avoids easy platitudes and simple answers. Her characters struggle with their partial visions, their own cultural and intellectual baggage. Marcello's traditional view of the male as a virile staunch provider, while not rendering him unsympathetic, destroys rather than sustains his marriage; Simonetta's death is simultaneously a melodramatic conclusion and a stark indication that once more women's relationship to modernity is perilous and precarious.

If Messina wrote largely within the tradition of the realist novel or novella, the prewar flowering of futurism also saw an intense intellectual and cultural debate about the role of women in Italian social and political life, with a significant number of women writing and publishing on women's issues. The irreverent *Come si seducono le donne: manuale dell'amore futurista* (How to Seduce Women: A Manual of Futurist Love, 1917) by Filippo Tommaso Marinetti (1876–1944), the founder of the avant-garde movement, called for free love without amorous complications and criticized women for their residual sentimentalism. Valentine de Saint Point countered his argument in *Manifesto della donna futurista* (The Manifesto of the Futurist Woman, 1929), in which the heroic woman is androgynous and only lesser beings are classified according to gender. Women wrote creatively as well as polemically. Enif Robert (1886–1976), Rosa Rosà (1884–1978, pen-name of Edyth von Haynau Arnaldi) and Marinetti's wife, Benedetta Cappa Marinetti (1897–1977), produced strikingly original and vibrant work. Robert followed de Saint Point's concept of absolute parity between the sexes, through a model of the strong, virile, intelligent woman. Rosà sought a more personal dimension, a third way between the domestic drudgery of reproduction and the childless state of emancipation, although she too would distinguish in terms of intelligence rather than sex. Her best novel, *Una donna con tre anime: romanzo futurista* (A Woman with Three Souls: Futurist Novel) appeared in 1918, although she had already published a number of articles in *L'Italia Futurista* with titles such as "La donna del posdomani" ("The Woman of the Day after Tomorrow") and "Le donne cambiano finalmente" ("Women Are Finally Changing"). The first of these underlines the importance of women's contribution to the war effort, or perhaps the contribution of the war effort to women, producing a transformation which surpasses the results the most feminist of feminists hoped to achieve, turning them from tearful dolls to sturdy, loving companions. Her futurist conception of woman is that of daughter rather than mother: the traditional self-sacrificing mother figure must disappear. The protagonist of Rosà's antiromantic, antirealist, utopian novel *Una donna con tre anime* is a petty-bourgeois housewife who undergoes startling transformations of personality, pointing to the creation of a new Eve and an androgynous ideal.

Rosà's circle at *L'Italia Futurista* was much influenced by ideas of esoteric magic, the occult, theosophy, and Einstein's theory of relativity, which would allow for the coexistence of different realities and different dimensions in time. The novel is structured around a scientific experiment gone wrong: chemicals have disappeared from Professor Ipsilon's laboratory, and there is much slapstick humor as he describes how this loss, together with a dramatic bolt of lightning, has led to disproportionate growth in his guinea pig. Meanwhile Giorgina Rossi, a "dusty," unremarkable, totally uninteresting nobody, is just coming home with the shopping when she experiences an "astonishing intensification of her whole vitality" and "a heady expansion of all her female sensibilities, a sudden explosion of a warm, sensual attraction" that ensures the rapt attention of her troglodyte young neighbor. With the second, much more substantial transformation, Giorgina has "the precise sensation that two different natures coexist within her." She sets off into town with her best hat and ends up in a gambling den with a young hunk: every moral criterion has vanished from her spirit. The bourgeois consciousness has crumbled away within her. She feels herself authorized from within to do everything she pleases, everything that satisfies her desire for diversity. Her third transformation moves Giorgina on from amoral, magnetic sensuality to a harder, more violent energy. Her conventional letter to her absent husband, which begins with platitudes about the weather and the price of fruit, dissolves swiftly into an expression of futuristic poetic desire: "I roam through spaces filled with astral storms and never before witnessed electrical shocks, throwing aside obstacles and destroying distance with dazzling velocity . . . the burden of human weight has fled me, I am a spaceship streaking towards unknown tints and hues in the prism of spectral colours." The professor and his learned colleagues agree on the interpretation of Giorgina's transformations: that they all prefigure in some sense what women will become in the future – amoral (no longer burdened by conventional morality), unsentimental, more male than female, looking out into the mystical infinity of space.

Futurist women nonetheless found themselves in a double bind. Escape from the cloying sentimental femininity so despised by Marinetti, the powerful desire for modernity, the politically progressive attack on the family, were all ideals undermined by the subservience to a masculine ideal. Freedom from traditional womanhood meant conforming instead to the values of a more modern masculinity. Nonetheless, maternity remained the highest ideal, as demonstrated in Enif Robert's *Un ventre di donna: romanzo chirurgico* (A Woman's Stomach: A Surgical Novel, 1919). Based on Robert's own experience of gynecological surgery, the novel equates creativity, art, and poetry, as well as the glorious art of war, with maleness. Yet she celebrates the life-giving womb and female fecundity. Indeed, women such as Benedetta Cappa Marinetti moved from early experimentalism with such novels as *Le forze umane: romanzo con sintesi grafiche* (Human Forces: Novel with Graphic Synthesis, 1924) and *Il viaggio di Gararà* (Gararà's Journey, 1931) to an increasingly traditional view of maternity in line with Fascist ideology.

During the Fascist period, normally considered something of a wasteland for writing by women, there was a further increase in the number of works published by women. Although censorship was in place from the early 1930s, it tended to be haphazard and erratic. Censors ignored most novels so long as they refrained from open criticism of the current regime, of Mussolini, or of the Pope. Ada Negri was admitted to the Italian Royal Academy, and Aleramo found herself praised by the regime. Erratic censorship led to some surprising publications, such as *Monte Ignoso* (Mount Ignoso, 1934) by Paola Masino, which features episodes of sexual violence and infanticide. Masino, part of the literary circle associated with the journal *900* and with her companion Massimo Bontempelli, sought in narratives of hallucinated, "magic" realism an escape from the stifling provincialism of Italian letters, frequently in a feminist key. Masino's extraordinary *Nascita e morte della massaia* (Birth and Death of the Housewife, written in 1938–9, published in 1945) met severe resistance from Fascist censorship, and she was ordered to remove hostile references to the Fascist regime and to maternity. The novel is a comical, satirical exposure of the Fascist and Catholic ideology and social codes that would enclose women within the domestic sphere and tie them to domestic drudgery: the protagonist learns that the average housewife, in one year, washes a hectare of crockery, twelve kilometres of material, and twenty kilometres of floor. After she has spent her early childhood wild-haired and filthy in a trunk, her mother attempts to marry her off, but the scores of men who trail through her room, including the other-worldly philosopher, cannot bear the stench coming from this young child whose refusal to conform leaves her isolated and abandoned – though the linguistic register casts satirical doubt on the desirability as well as the suitability of these suitors. In order to please her despairing mother, she abandons her thoughts of death and matricide, her anarchic difference, pulling the plants out of her hair and transforming herself into the perfect housewife.

The centerpiece of the novel is an elaborate dinner party. The housewife considers all great works of art to be based around food, from Goethe's *Faust* to Shakespeare's *Lear*, Leopardi's *Zibaldone* and Rousseau's *Emile*, while Beethoven's notebooks are packed with details about cooks hired and fired. At the dinner party, stereotypical sections of the middle classes mouth their conformist beliefs even while they chorus the social hypocrisy and be-trayal that underpins the facade of bourgeois marriage. Ladies of a certain age claim to their lovers that their husbands have never understood them, while their married husbands claim to their mistresses that their wives have betrayed and deceived them. Mothers loudly proclaim they are sacred, while the representative of the church, the cardinal, underscores the nexus between women and maternity. The housewife's condition as housewife invades even her dreams – with the declaration of war she sees parachutes floating down like jellyfish, with herself flitting amongst them trying to sort out hankies and underwear. With her eventual death she swaps the fetid, creative trunk of her childhood for an immaculate, sterile tomb that she spends her days cleaning and polishing with a lace hanky. Free time is absorbed in swapping recipes with the spirit next door: "'Oh yes,' they sigh in chorus, 'a woman's work is never done. There's always so much to do in a tomb.'" Masino's surreal, hugely imaginative text is an irreverent and stylistically sophisticated metaphor for the crushing of female creativity under the deadening weight of conformity.

A number of the women writers who were to come to prominence in the postwar period, such as Elsa Morante, Anna Maria Ortese, and Anna Banti, began writing during the last years of fascism. Writing by women after World War II refuses accommodations with prevailing cultural norms and distances itself from current cultural practice. Banti's most famous work, *Artemisia* (*Artemisia*, 1947), presents an imaginative reconstruction of the life of the painter Artemisia Gentileschi (1593 – after 1651). The novel interweaves two narrative voices, the author/narrator and the character/historical figure, offering a text in which Artemisia's dramatic life and that of the narrator mirror and comment on each other across the centuries. *Artemisia* is less a historical novel than a sustained meditation on the woman as artist, past and present, and it explores the splits and fractures between the public and the private, the fracture and sense of loss which marks women's creativity. Banti herself fiercely rejected the label of feminist, seeking, like her characters, equality of mind and liberty of work. Her view of art is elitist rather than democratic, and Artemisia's crowning moment is when she is recognized and acknowledged as a great painter by her father as representative of a male tradition. Like Virginia Woolf, whom she much admired, genius and talent is for Banti androgynous, ungendered. If Woolf weeps for Judith Shakespeare, whose dramatic masterpieces never saw the light of day, Banti regrets the painters and musicians who were distanced, whether by custom or by force, from the realms of creative art. Artemisia's dedication to the pursuits of artistic and intellectual life contrast with her need to love and be loved, the simultaneous urge to take up the roles of wife and mother, and her tragedy is that she must choose: self-affirmation, public recognition, and self-fulfillment are achieved at a high price. Banti's is a passionate claim that women's art should not be regarded in terms of gender, and she makes a powerful plea for an end to the exclusion and seclusion of women as artists.

Other writers, such as Fausta Cialente (1898–1983), Alba De Céspedes, and Milena Milani, who like Banti began publishing before World War II, question and assess women's social roles in the contemporary period rather than past or future worlds. Cialente's early novels, such as the choral narrative *Cortile a Cleopatra* (Courtyard in Cleopatra, 1936) are set largely in Egypt, where she lived with her husband. Later work is more concerned with the pragmatic details of women's lives. *Ballata levantina* (Levantine Ballad,

1962), for example, studies the figure of Daniela who has to achieve financial independence. De Céspedes, daughter of the Cuban ambassador to Italy, was even more intensely involved in politics than Cialente. During World War II she founded *Fronte Unito* (United Front) an anti-Fascist journal, and made regular broadcasts on Radio Cairo for the Allies. She was arrested in Italy in 1935 for a brief time, and her novel *Nessuno torna indietro* (*There's No Turning Back*, 1938), along with a later collection of short stories, was censored by the Fascists. She participated actively in the Resistance, and while her work is imbued with the ideological and cultural climate of the postwar years, her novels also embody the political debates of the 1950s with a decidedly feminist inflection. Women characters dominate her works, but de Céspedes is concerned that women should be depicted in the multiform variety of their complex and various lives. In *Dalla parte di lei* (*The Best of Husbands*, 1949), her protagonist Alessandra explains why she killed her hero husband, Francesco, impelled by her own violence but also by the carefully delineated fractures of a relationship and a society that fails to understand a woman's difference of feeling. Valeria, the protagonist of *Quaderno proibito* (*The Secret*, 1952), is more self-aware than Alessandra: through the act of writing in her secret notebook, she articulates her own disillusionment with life as a married, working woman. But self-knowledge is double-edged here, since it brings Valeria not release, or change, or escape, but a heightened knowledge of her own despair. The domestic drama of *Quaderno proibito* gives way to a broader canvas in *Il rimorso* (*Remorse*, 1962) where the disintegration of a marriage takes place against a backdrop of clearly delineated national politics. While de Céspedes has been taken to task for neglecting the role of women in politics in her nonfictional work, such as her stewardship of *Il Mercurio*, the journal of arts and politics she founded in 1944, her enormously successful novels provide a galaxy of female characters that explore and delineate women's lives within a fast-changing contemporary reality, and their part in moving her readers towards an analysis and understanding of women's lives in postwar Italy should not be underestimated and is only today being reevaluated.

In 1962, Dacia Maraini (1936–), soon to become one of the major figures of contemporary fiction, published her first novel, *La vacanza* (*The Holiday*), and her subsequent *L'età del malessere* (*The Age of Discontent*, 1963) won an important literary prize. The adolescent female protagonists of Maraini's early novels inhabit a world that insists on reducing them to the status of sexual object. Far from the political militancy that was to emerge so strongly in Italy shortly after their publication, these young women live in a state of passive paralysis. These early novels analyse a condition rather than propose a solution, depicting through their almost autistic characters an inchoate sense of oppression that was to find political expression in the feminist movement. In *La vacanza*, Anna spends a summer vacation with her father by the sea, where she becomes a sexual commodity to be used and discarded by the men around her. The novel is set during the last days of the war. This understated social and political crisis forms the backdrop to a crisis that has yet to be named, in which Anna's own identity is submerged into the sexual wishes and fantasies of those around her. Maraini's striking narrative refuses omniscient narration (Anna is literally unknowable) or the confessional register (neither does she know herself). Lingering on the surface of things, Maraini's narrative style gestures to a void and merely increases the sense of isolation and alienation which is Anna's life.

The main character of *L'età del malessere*, Enrica, slowly shifts from passive resignation to increasing self-awareness and self-determination, refusing to merge her identity with the desires of the men who surround her. Rather than offering privileged psychological insight, the first-person narrative registers precisely the absence of self-reflection, marking only the physical immediacy of the present tense. The novel is set in Rome at the beginning of the 1960s, and over a long winter emerging into spring, thus suggesting the beginning of an awakening in the protagonist that was to challenge so many preconceptions about women over the course of the next few decades.

Maraini has written both poetry and drama, but her novels have gained her the widest recognition. Deeply involved in both feminism and left-wing politics as an activist, commentator, and artist, Maraini's prose works set out, in different ways, to expose the violence which patriarchal society wreaks on women's lives and bodies. *Memorie di una ladra* (Memoirs of a Female Thief, 1972) adopts the voice of Teresa Numa, a working-class, semiliterate woman from Anzio, whom Maraini met while investigating conditions inside women's prisons, and the novel gives a voice to those traditionally marginalized by society and culture. *Donna in guerra* (*Woman at War*, 1975) is Maraini's first consciously feminist novel, and it attempts to understand the relationships between men and women from a political and institutional as well as moral and existential perspective. Its adoption of a feminist ideology distances the work from more orthodox left-wing ideological positions, even revolutionary ones, and the novel mirrors a feminist movement growing out of, but away from, the extraparliamentary left. The narrative presents the summer diary of Vanna, a middle-class schoolteacher, who grows to challenge her previously unquestioned assumptions that her role is to service the domestic, material, and sexual needs of her husband Giacinto. The background is a society of persistent poverty and violence, where the hopes of change in the postwar period have stalled and where rapid changes in the economy have led to incremental social change. Vanna encounters the local men on her holiday island who boast of their sexual assaults on women tourists. She meets Suna, a revolutionary feminist, and through her learns to think of gender roles as a product of social and political conditioning rather than biological necessity, while at the same time glimpsing the radical failure of these left-wing groups to challenge the prevailing sexual status quo. Left-wing politics, whether orthodox or revolutionary, are as riddled with patriarchal and paternalist assumptions as their political opponents. It is on the next generation, as Vanna prevents the boys in her classroom from attacking one of the younger girls, that she pins her hopes for reformed and egalitarian relationships between the sexes.

The description of how women's bodies are controlled physically, institutionally, and culturally provides the theme of *Isolina* (Isolina, 1985), in which Maraini describes her attempts to reconstruct the story of the dismembered Isolina whose pregnant, headless corpse was discovered in the river Adige near Verona at the turn of the century. These were the butchered remains of Isolina Canuti, whose affair with Lieutenant Carlo Trivulzio ended when the drunken efforts of his colleagues to effect an abortion with a spoon ended in Isolina's death. Her body was mutilated in an attempt to avoid identification and thus protect the name and reputation of a member of the prestigious Alpine Corps, and of the army itself. Trivulzio was cleared of suspicion, despite the outrage of the local socialist newspaper, *Verona del Popolo*. Isolina herself was accused of prostitution, while doctors were suspected of tampering with evidence as to the stage of Isolina's pregnancy in order to incriminate her and absolve the young officer. The life of an obscure, working-class girl counted for less, concludes Maraini, than the honor of the army and the patriotic ideal that it served. The question of violence done against women but never punished, never accounted for, where women become part of a wider outrageous statistic and their murderers shadowy figures who escape justice and cast a pall of fear and anxiety, is underlined in *Voci* (Voices, 1994) where a local radio journalist, whose young, rather mysterious neighbor has just been found murdered, is given the task of presenting a series of programs on violence against women.

La lunga vita di Marianna Ucrìa (*The Silent Duchess*, 1990), adapted as a play and a film, returns to the question of women's exclusion from culture. The book is set in the eighteenth century, and in the opening scenes the aristocratic Marianna, raped at the age of five by her uncle and left deaf and dumb by this trauma, is taken by her beloved father to see an execution, in the hope that a second shock will eliminate the first and restore her powers of speech. The attempt fails, and when she is just thirteen Marianna is married off to this same rich uncle, bearing him several children in quick succession, learning to submit to his cold embraces. Marianna is not, however, a victim.

Deprived of speech, she nonetheless develops a passion for language, learning to read and write in order to communicate with those around her, and gradually discovering not only the books in her husband's library but the works of some of the foremost and freest thinkers of the Enlightenment, including Voltaire and Hume. With the death of her husband Marianna shows herself to be more philanthropically concerned with the plight of the people who live on her land than are her peers, while she learns to seek out her own pleasure and will in her relationship with her young lover Saro. At the end of the novel, despite the protests of her family, who have not thrown off the trappings of tradition and privilege, and are horrified at her announcement that she will go traveling, Marianna finally asserts her freedom and self-determination. Marianna does not herself become a radical feminist, nor does she seek redemption through literature, but her unorthodox engagement with both classical and contemporary culture leads her to achieve a different and higher goal, the transcendence of the limitations placed upon her and the violence done to her. She comes to view her body as a positive, autonomous value rather than as a fetishistic commodity at the service of others. This is her liberation, and it is at this point that she can leave, to set off on new journeys.

The 1970s saw many writers exploring the condition of women through poetry, drama, and fiction, as the women's movement gained rapid ground and achieved some dramatic social and political successes, including the introduction of divorce and the right to abortion and a whole raft of legislation on women's civil rights. *Negli occhi di una ragazza* (In the Eyes of a Girl, 1971) by Marina Jarre (1925–) tells, in a light-hearted key, of the adolescent Maria Cristina, who refuses to fill the shoes of her dead mother and resolves, despite the opposition of her family, to continue studying and become an artist. An explicit contrast is drawn between Maria Cristina's determination to explore new ways of living and her brother Roberto, who dabbles in student politics but whose thinking is still regressive on personal and sexual matters. In the controversial *Lettera a un bambino mai nato* (*Letter to a Child Never Born*, 1975), Oriana Fallaci (1930–) discusses an unplanned pregnancy, a theme that prompts a poetic and philosophical reflection on the issue of maternity from a social, emotional, legal, and medical point of view. The narrator refuses to transform her identity of an active, working woman into a mother, while simultaneously recoiling from the idea of abortion. Lyrical evocations of the developing fetus are juxtaposed with the headlong disintegration of the narrator's own life, for medical complications require her to remain bedridden. She refuses: the baby dies, and the novel concludes with a hallucinatory trial where accusations of infanticide are countered with a declaration of the woman's rights. Fallaci presents no "correct" position on the problem, and the book's final note underlines her grief for the lost child.

Other novels of the 1970s sought to scrutinize the changing roles of women and the increasingly complex lives of women from the middle classes. *Un quarto di donna* (A Quarter of a Woman, 1976) by Giuliana Ferri articulates the failure of an intellectual woman to fulfill, or to be totally fulfilled by, the role of mother. The protagonist of *L'approdo invisibile* (The Invisible Landing, 1980) by Grazia Livi (1932–) is a weary, thirty-something journalist who leaves Milan on a physical and metaphorical journey to rediscover herself, lost under the pressures of conforming to an ideology that would seek female emancipation through work. *Il bambino di pietra: una nevrosi femminile* (The Child of Stone: A Female Neurosis, 1979) by Laudomia Bonanni (1908–) sees the protagonist employing writing as a therapeutic tool of self-discovery; she consciously compares herself to Svevo's character Zeno, as she too writes for the benefit of her psychoanalyst, thereby exploring through narrative the genesis of her own neurosis in the family and in marriage. The emphasis of the novels of Elena Giannini Belotti (1929–), director of the Montessori Centre in Rome from 1960 to 1980, can be detected from their very titles: *Dalla parte delle bambine* (On the Children's Behalf, 1973); *Prima le donne e i bambini* (Women and Children First, 1980). Belotti's work is preoccupied with the social conditioning received by small girls that she attempts to challenge through both her fiction and her working practice.

Feminism took a different turn again in the 1980s and 1990s. With the end of militant activism and self-assertion in a political and confrontational context, and the achievement of a substantial amount of feminist legislation, including the right to divorce and abortion, and the legal recognition of women's equal status within the family, feminism shifted from the streets into the academies, exploring new ways for women to establish and maintain social links with each other. The attempt by theorists and philosophers to forge a new practice of relationships between women was reflected and refracted in the numerous novels to appear throughout the 1980s that explored the dynamic between mothers and daughters. *Madre e figlia* (Mother and Daughter, 1980) by Francesca Sanvitale (1928–) stages a daughter's struggle to differentiate herself from the mother, even while she feels a powerful sense of identification with the mother's body. *Althénopis* (Althénopis, 1981) by Fabrizia Ramondino (1936–) finds the protagonist searching for autonomy and independence from the mother figure. What is remarkable about these two novels is their development of a language to talk about the female psyche that is no longer the unadorned, antirhetorical prose of the 1960s, but, rather, has become transformed into a tool of baroque complexity and vibrant suppleness. Self-consciously literary, these texts offer a sophistication and complexity sometimes lacking in the previous decade. Literature by women in this period moves away from the plain realism advocated by Anna Franchi and practiced by writers of the 1970s as an extension of political activism, to an exploration of the "female style" adumbrated by Aleramo half a century before and foreshadowed by writers such as Masino.

Two novels from the 1990s suggest a new direction being taken and introduce a new generation. While the protagonist of the picaresque *In principio erano le mutande* (In the Beginning Were the Knickers, 1992) by Rosanna Campo (1963–) is in search of love, a man, and sex, becoming pregnant by a married man who finally returns to her in the eventual self-consciously ironic happy ending, what is striking about the novel is its vigorous affirmation of female sexuality, its vibrant and demotic language, and its self-deprecating humor. Living by herself, with mad and occasionally violent neighbors in a squalid urban landscape, reduced to ill-paid work at a local radio station, the first-person narrator lives her freedoms with *brio*, even while acknowledging the pull of the traditional family unit and the traditional kind of love story women are expected to enjoy. Female desire is here unashamed and refuses reticence, claiming for itself the right to self-expression and self-fulfillment, embracing the disasters of love with resilient good humor.

The recognition of an increasingly cosmopolitan and culturally complex Italy is a common feature between the fiction of Campo and Carmen Covito (1948–), as the realities of diverse immigrant communities figure substantially in both novels. Covito's protagonist Marilina in *La bruttina stagionata* (The Mature and Homely Woman, 1992), like Campo's picaresque heroine, is in search of sexual fulfillment, but hers is a very different path. Covito locates her story more self-consciously against a recent personal and national history of feminism, and what is loosely termed postfeminism. Marilina, single and forty, is horrified to discover that she has grown a small moustache. In the absence of a permanent lover she acquires a toy boy, Berto, through a discreet advertisement. Female friendships, though vital, amusing, important, and sustaining, as in Campo's work, are no longer enough. Marilina makes a living writing university theses for wealthy undergraduates, and this ghost-writing is a fitting metaphor for her invisible way of living, self-effacing and unseen, unable to claim her right to life, to sex, and to love. Her efforts to buy a vibrator, an idea much discussed with her friend Olimpia during their feminist days when ways were sought to dispense with men altogether, end in a hilarious, tragic farce. Gradually her path takes her, via the Algerian Karim, a bisexual nightclub, and other sexual adventures, to a move from invisibility to visibility, to discovering her own sexuality rather than having sexuality circumscribed and defined for her, either by traditional ideology or a more recent feminist discourse. Marilina's openness to sexual experience is not simply a manifesto for plain forty-year-old women to go and get what they really want. Marilina is a woman of culture, a writer of sorts – although her signature is repeatedly erased. Covito is a feminist novelist but, unlike many writers from the previous generation, she seeks not a solipsistic isolation or separatism, whether sexual or cultural, but a recognition that women must emerge from the ghetto. Hers is a cultural practice that aims toward the new century. She seeks not to become like men, following the kind of androgynous ideal espoused by some feminists during the early part of the twentieth century, nor does she want to become lost in sexual difference, as more recent feminist theory would suggest. Instead, she wishes to claim, finally, her subjective self.

This chapter has sought to consider only those writers who self-consciously thematize and problematize the condition of women within their texts. Other writers are dealt with elsewhere in this volume. Feminist writing in twentieth-century Italy follows a path that resonates with progressive political, social, and ethical preoccupations, but does so with a rarely acknowledged energy, verve, and humor. While tracing a development from emancipationism to civic and legal rights, and to the exploration of a female subjectivity no longer in thrall to orthodox social roles, this writing does more than merely reflect the drearily contingent. The resources of imaginative fiction allow for texts that, stylistically as well as conceptually, are both intellectually passionate and strikingly innovative.

Further reading

Aleramo, Sibilla. *A Woman*. Trans. Rosalind Delmar. Berkeley: University of California Press, 1980.

Amoia, Alba. *20th-Century Italian Women Writers*. Carbondale: Southern Illinois University Press, 1996.

Aricò, Santo, ed. *Contemporary Women Writers in Italy: A Modern Renaissance*. Amherst: University of Massachusetts Press, 1990.

Banti, Anna. *Artemisia*. Trans. Shirley Caracciolo. Lincoln: University of Nebraska Press, 1988.

Birnbaum, Lucia Chiavola. *Liberazione della donna: Feminism in Italy*. Middletown, CT: Wesleyan University Press, 1986.

Bono, Paola and Sandra Kemp, eds. *Italian Feminist Thought: A Reader*. Oxford: Basil Blackwell, 1991.

   The Lonely Mirror: Italian Perspectives on Feminist Theory. London: Routledge, 1993.

De Céspedes, Alba. *Remorse*. Trans. William Weaver. Garden City, NY: Doubleday, 1967.

Hellman, Judith Adler. *Journeys among Women: Feminism in Five Italian Cities*. New York: Oxford University Press, 1987.

King, Martha, ed. *New Italian Women: A Collection of Short Fiction.* New York: Italica Press, 1989.

Lazzaro-Weiss, Carol. *From Margins to Mainstream: Feminism and Fictional Modes in Italian Women's Writing, 1968–1990.* Philadelphia: University of Pennsylvania Press, 1993.

Maraini, Dacia. *Woman at War.* Trans. Mara Benetti and Elspeth Spottiswood. New York: Italica Press, 1988.

Marotti, Maria Ornella, ed. *Italian Women Writers from the Renaissance to the Present: Revising the Canon.* University Park: Penn State University Press, 1996.

Miceli Jeffries, Giovanna, ed. *Feminine Feminists: Cultural Practices in Italy.* Minneapolis: University of Minnesota Press, 1994.

Panizzi, Letizia and Sharon Wood, eds. *A History of Women's Writing in Italy.* Cambridge: Cambridge University Press, 2000.

Picchietti, Virginia. *Relational Spaces: Daughterhood, Motherhood, and Sisterhood in Dacia Maraini's Writings and Films.* Madison, NJ: Fairleigh Dickinson University Press, 2002.

Pickering-Iazzi, Robin. *Politics of the Visible: Writing Women, Culture, and Fascism.* Minneapolis: University of Minnesota Press, 1997.

Pickering-Iazzi, Robin, ed. *Mothers of Invention: Women, Italian Fascism, and Culture.* Minneapolis: University of Minnesota Press, 1995.

Russell, Rinaldina, ed. *Italian Women Writers: A Bio-Bibliographical Sourcebook.* Westport, CT: Greenwood Press, 1992.

Testaferri, Ada, ed. *Donna: Women in Italian Culture.* Ottawa: Dovehouse Editions, 1989.

Wilson, Rita. *Speculative Identities: Contemporary Italian Women's Narrative.* Leeds: Northern Universities Press, 2000.

Wood, Sharon. *Italian Women's Writing 1860–1994.* London: Athlone Press, 1995.

PETER BONDANELLA

Italo Calvino and Umberto Eco: postmodern masters

The term "postmodern" raises a number of vexing critical questions, not the least of which concerns the meaning of the "modernism" to which post-modernism must logically be related. Italian literary history departs, in some respects, from the standard treatment of twentieth-century literature in other European literatures and in American criticism because of an important current of Italian critical thought that employed the term *il decadentismo* (decadentism) to define what other literary cultures would have called modernist. The major authors of Western modernism, such as T. S. Eliot, Ezra Pound, Thomas Mann, Marcel Proust, James Joyce, Franz Kafka, or Jorge Luis Borges (to mention only a few) were less influential forces in Italian culture before World War II than elsewhere, although in the postwar period their works were widely read, imitated, and analyzed. While, in the past, Italian critics sometimes overlooked connections between native writers today regarded as modernists (Luigi Pirandello, Eugenio Montale, Italo Svevo, Carlo Emilio Gadda) and their counterparts in the rest of Europe or America, contemporary critics, both within Italy and abroad, have been unanimous in regarding Italo Calvino and Umberto Eco as postmodernist masters. Their works enjoy enormous audiences throughout Europe, the United States, and the English-speaking world, and they have achieved this widespread popularity in large measure because they have been perceived as exemplary expressions of the postmodern bent in contemporary culture, a cosmopolitan literary style that seems to transcend national boundaries.

The careers of Calvino and Eco took very different paths to arrive at a postmodern narrative stance. Calvino's literary fame began with the partisan novel, *Il sentiero dei nidi di ragno* – a book that views the Resistance through the eyes of a young boy. While *Il sentiero* has frequently been cited as a neo-realist novel, there is little of the orthodox nineteenth-century naturalism of Giovanni Verga or Luigi Capuana in this treatment of the war. Subsequently, Calvino created a child-like fantasy world indebted more to Ariosto and the fairy tale than to the canons of European realism in three separate novels released together in 1960 as a trilogy with the title *I nostri antenati* (Our Forefathers): *Il visconte dimezzato* (*The Cloven Viscount*, 1952); *Il barone rampante* (*The Baron in the Trees*, 1957); and *Il cavaliere inesistente* (*The Nonexistent Knight*, 1959). It would be difficult to imagine a more fanciful story than that of a viscount who had been split in half, a baron who had decided to live in the trees, or a knight who consisted of an empty suit of armor. Such characters nevertheless combine a sense of the absurd (typical of the existential literature of the period) with an ideological twist, since they can easily be construed as metaphorical representations of the alienation of the contemporary human being.

This imaginative trilogy was followed by several collections of what English-speaking readers might label science fiction (a genre almost totally alien to the Italian literary tradition): *Le cosmicomiche* (*Cosmicomics*, 1965); *Ti con zero* (*t zero*, 1967); *Il castello dei destini incrociati* (*The Castle of Crossed Destinies*, 1969); and *Le città invisibili* (*Invisible Cities*, 1972). The first collection of stories is recounted from the perspective of a unique narrator named Qfwfq, a cell that eventually evolves from mollusk to dinosaur to space traveler. The other three works show an attention to structure and a playful treatment of narrative that are indebted not only to structuralist theories popular at the time but also to the Oulipo literary group in France, of which Calvino was a member and Eco an admirer.[1] Oulipo's best-known practitioners included Raymond Queneau (one of whose works was translated by Eco into Italian[2]) and Georges Perec. The theory of narrative as a combinative process that Oulipo popularized (and which was indebted not only to their playful experimentation but also to the theories of the folktale linked to Vladimir Propp's writings, Claude Levi-Strauss's structuralist theories, and the writings of the Russian formalist critics) found, in Calvino, a skillful practitioner. *Il castello dei destini incrociati*, for example, employed the shuffling and dealing of illustrated tarot cards, each card being defined as a narrative unit, to demonstrate how a multitude of stories could be created merely by rearranging the order of the narrative units in question. This work may be regarded as Calvino's first postmodernist exercise in a new style of narration. *Le città invisibili*, on the other hand, aimed at a narrative symmetry by organizing the book around a Marco Polo who describes to Kublai Khan the many invisible cities of his enormous empire and, in so doing, provides a great deal of narrative freedom to the reader of the book.

---

[1] See Warren F. Motte, ed., *Oulipo: A Primer of Potential Literature* (Lincoln: University of Nebraska Press, 1986) for an enlightening discussion of this group and a selection of its theoretical writings on narrative, including an important essay by Calvino.

[2] Raymond Queneau, *Esercizi di stile*, trans. Umberto Eco (Turin: Einaudi, 1983; Italian version of *Exercises de Style*, originally published in 1947).

Calvino's last two major novels – *Se una notte d'inverno un viaggiatore* (*If on a Winter's Night a Traveler*, 1979); and *Palomar* – constitute his most openly postmodernist works. They represent the high point of his literary experimentation (a feature common to all his fiction) and, like the novels of Umberto Eco, they are founded upon an implicit theory of literature that is postmodern in its stress upon the participation of the reader in the production of meaning. Calvino's posthumously published discussions of the nature of literature meant to be delivered as the Charles Eliot Norton Poetry Lectures at Harvard University – *Lezioni americane: sei proposte per il prossimo millennio* (*Six Memos for the Next Millennium*, 1988) – are among the most brilliant literary essays produced in Italy during the postwar period and, like similar works by Eco, they shed light on the final destination of Italo Calvino's style.

While Calvino began and ended his career as a creative writer (adding the complementary tasks of literary critic or theorist and journalist to his curriculum vitae during the course of his lifetime), Umberto Eco's path to fiction began in exactly the opposite fashion. After completing a thesis on medieval aesthetics, Eco began moving toward theory, combining an interest in semiotics, information theory, and structuralism. After working for the Italian state television service (the RAI) in cultural programming during its formative years and the Bompiani publishing house in Milan, Eco moved to the University of Bologna in 1971. Like the best of Italian academics, Eco retained close ties with publishers (Bompiani, Einaudi), the world of popular journalism (he began a famous column called *La bustina di Minerva* in the weekly magazine *L'Espresso*), and the literary avant-garde. Many of his contributions to publishing included selecting important theoretical works for translation into Italian, including many of the key texts from the Russian formalists, the Oulipo group, the French structuralists, and European semioticians. Note that these are the same intellectual currents that influenced Calvino's thinking on the nature of literature in general and on prose fiction in particular. Eco's first important essay, *Opera aperta* (*The Open Work*, 1962), was a best-seller and proposed the work of James Joyce – especially *Finnegans Wake*; at the time the novel was unavailable in an Italian translation – as the prototype of the "open" work. Had the critical term been available to him in 1962, Eco would no doubt have labeled what he called an "open" work a "postmodern" work. For Eco, the open work, such as Joyce's last novel, aimed at an indeterminacy of meaning and required the active participation of the reader. *Opera aperta* was followed by an even more popular collection of essays entitled *Diario minimo* (*Misreadings*, 1963), a witty anthology of parodies of various schools of thought or artistic trends (the Frankfurt School, psychoanalysis, Roland Barthes, Michelangelo Antonioni's cinema, cultural anthropology). Parody plays a crucial role in the postmodern fiction of both authors.

Eco's growing interest in culture, especially the relationship between highbrow culture (which is usually associated by Italians with the academy) and the lowbrow variety of popular or mass culture (usually denigrated by Italian intellectuals), led to the publication of a number of very influential theoretical works. In 1964, *Apocalittici e integrati: comunicazioni di massa e teorie della cultura di massa* (partially translated as *Apocalypse Postponed*) offered an influential categorization of two opposing camps of intellectuals: "apocalyptic" intellectuals, the kind typically associated with the European intelligentsia, opposed the very notion of popular culture, while "integrated" intellectuals, more often linked to Anglo-Saxon culture, embraced all forms of popular culture. Typical of Eco's ideological stance in most matters, he stood somewhere in the middle of this lowbrow–highbrow continuum. Calvino's intellectual stance would be most likely categorized as "apocalyptic" or at least highbrow. In the process of providing this useful definition, Eco included reprints of his most interesting essays on American comic strips (*Peanuts, Superman, Terry and the Pirates*). This work was followed in 1976 by *Il superuomo di massa: retorica e ideologia nel romanzo popolare* (the literal translation of the title would be "Superman of the Masses: Rhetoric and Ideology in the Popular Novel"; it was partially translated in 1979 as *The Role of the Reader*). Eco's English title underlined the growing importance of the reader in the production of meaning in literature – a crucial part of postmodern literary theory. This book also reprinted Eco's single most famous essay, "Narrative Structures in Fleming," an earlier analysis of the first James Bond novel, *Casino Royale*, that constituted Eco's first step toward a theory of semiotics.

Eco's contributions to semiotic theory came at a time when the rediscovery of the American philosopher Charles S. Peirce (1839–1914) and his use of the term "semiotics" were beginning to supplant the "semiology" of Ferdinand de Saussure and Roland Barthes. Eco was elected secretary-general of the International Association for Semiotic Studies in 1969, he organized the group's first international congress in Milan in 1974 shortly after receiving the first Italian chair of semiotics at the University of Bologna in 1971, and he published a major summation of semiotic theory in *Trattato di semiotica* (*A Theory of Semiotics*, 1975). Eco embraced Peirce's concept of unlimited semiosis, which claimed to demonstrate how signification operated by a circularity of references from one sign to another and not to object referents in reality, subjective mental states, or Platonic universals. With this approach, Eco finally uncovered a firm philosophical foundation for his own theory of "open" works.

By the time Eco's book on semiotic theory had appeared in print, its author had already become an international academic superstar. He was one of the very few Italian academics at home in many languages and numerous disciplines, while within Italy he wrote widely for *Il Corriere della Sera* and *L'Espresso*, gaining a nonacademic audience that few Anglo-Saxon academics could ever hope to achieve. His cultural theory turned more and more to the consideration of literature. In 1979, he published *Lector in fabula: la cooperazione interpretativa nei testi narrativi* (literally "The Reader in the Story: Interpretative Cooperation in Narrative Texts" but partially translated as *The Role of the Reader: Explorations in the Semiotics of Texts*). The work sets out to define the concept of the Model Reader, something Eco believes every author must construct, and most of the book involves analyzing the presence of the reader in the story. An Author is defined by Eco not so much as a concrete person but as a complex textual strategy establishing semantic correlations and activating the Model Reader. Like so many other postmodern writers, Eco assumes that a text has many levels of meaning and that few of them are "exhausted" by the "intentions" of the Author.

Subsequently, Eco turned to writing fictional literature itself, and with the publication of his first novel, *Il nome della rosa*, he created a blockbuster of monumental proportions, selling tens of millions of copies in every conceivable language. Its astounding success immediately brought the debate over postmodernism outside Italy to the forefront within Italy. Eco's three subsequent novels were less popular but no less postmodern in their reliance upon a pastiche style, combining the most erudite forms of literary theory and arcane information about the past with other generic traits of the mass-market thriller, adventure stories, and mysteries. Each of his four novels reveals a crucial link to literary theory. Eco's own assessment of his first novel in *Postille al "Nome della rosa"* (*Postscript to "The Name of the Rose,"* 1983) provides the most amusing definition of postmodernism found in any literary theory (see the conclusion of this chapter for his definition). In the second novel, *Il pendolo di Foucault* (*Foucault's Pendulum*, 1988), Eco attacked the history of groups of fanatics convinced they have a lock on absolute truth (the Templars, the Rosicrucians, other apocalyptic radicals) and, in the process, satirized the literary theory of deconstructionism, since the novel dealt with overinterpretation and even paranoid interpretation, a topic also analyzed in two works of theory following the publication of the novel: *I limiti dell'interpretazione* (*The Limits of Interpretation*, 1989); and an English volume of Tanner lectures Eco presented at Cambridge University, *Interpretation and Over Interpretation* (1992; the Italian translation appeared after the English original as *Interpretazione e sovrainterpretazione: un dibattito con Richard Rorty, Jonathan Culler e Christine Brooke-Rose*). Eco's third novel, *L'isola del giorno prima* (*The Island of the Day Before*, 1994) is best read against the backdrop of the prestigious Norton Lectures Eco delivered at Harvard University in 1992–3, and they were later published as *Sei passeggiate nei boschi narrativi* (*Six Walks in the Fictional Woods*, 1994). The very form and content of this important book owed a deep debt to Calvino's earlier posthumous Norton Lectures, *Lezioni americane*. Its six chapters echo the six planned lectures at Harvard by Calvino (all but one was completed), and Eco himself draws attention to the fact that Calvino's most important postmodern novel, *Se una notte d'inverno un viaggiatore*, was concerned with "the presence of the reader in the story," while Eco's lectures in *Sei passeggiate* focus upon the same subject. Eco goes on to add that Calvino's novel was published in Italy in the same year that his own book on reader response *Lector in fabula* appeared.[3] Eco's account of an interchange of letters between himself and Calvino on this occasion makes it obvious that both authors recognized in each other a kindred spirit. Eco's latest novel, *Baudolino* (Baudolino, 2000) returns to the Middle Ages of his first best-seller and continues to deal with metaliterary questions with a postmodern bent.

Outlining the careers of Calvino and Eco underscores not only their diverse points of departure – Calvino the literary artist moving toward theory; Eco the academic theoretician turning to the writing of fiction as a means of advancing his theory – but their similar postmodern concerns that override their many personal differences. For the purpose of our analysis, we shall concentrate upon two specific novels generally regarded as the respective masterpieces of each author – Calvino's *Se una notte d'inverno un viaggiatore* and Eco's *Il nome della rosa*. Our discussion of the very different kinds of postmodern expression in Calvino and Eco will be informed by reference to several theoretical works on the nature of literature by the two writers.

Virtually every interesting discussion of the postmodern impulse in contemporary fiction underscores a fascination with metaliterary or metanarrative concerns.[4] In spite of the many obvious differences in the literary styles of Calvino and Eco, Eco's discussion of the Model Reader and the question of how the Reader had to be constructed by the Text created by

---

[3] Umberto Eco, *Six Walks in the Fictional Woods* (Cambridge, MA: Harvard University Press, 1994), p. 1.

[4] A sensible discussion of the problem may be found in Brian McHale's *Constructing Postmodernism* (London: Routledge, 1992).

the Author seems the perfect complement to Calvino's *Se una notte*. In fact, in both *Se una notte* and *Il nome della rosa*, each novelist foregrounds a self-reflexive discourse on books as well as a concern with the response of the Model Reader. As Calvino once wrote, now that "the process of literary composition has been taken to pieces and reassembled, the decisive moment in literary life is bound to be the act of reading."[5] Echoing various theorists of the novel who have argued for the disappearance of the Author as has been traditionally understood in the conventional novel, Calvino goes on to conclude that once focus has shifted from the empirical author to the act of reading, the work of art will "continue to be born, to be judged, to be destroyed or constantly renewed on contact with the eye of the reader."[6] Calvino's experiment with reader response in *Se una notte* produces a sleek, trimmed-down metanovel containing few of the traditional nineteenth-century realist or twentieth-century modernist attributes readers have come to expect in a work of imaginative fiction. His two main characters are an unnamed male reader and a female reader named Ludmilla (usually referred to as Lettore and Lettrice in the Italian text). Calvino is uninterested in creating a fictional world with all its attendant details, historical facts, and local color. In fact, this novel (like so many of his other mature works, such as *Le città invisibili* or *Il castello dei destini incrociati*) has closer affinities to the allegory of the Middle Ages than to the realist novel.

The structure of *Se una notte* should not surprise any reader familiar with the theories of the Oulipo group or with Calvino's own definition of narrative as a combinative process: twelve numbered chapters describing the efforts of a man and a woman to complete a book are divided by ten fragments of ten different novels, all written by different authors. Each of the ten fragments provides a parody of a different kind of novel, ranging from detective stories and Oriental fiction to novels from imaginary countries composed in equally imaginary and exotic minor languages. Each of the ten fragments contains as its chapter heading a fragment of a sentence. The two protagonists engage in a futile attempt to complete a book they purchase in a bookstore, and one discerning critic has quite rightly termed their experience a humorous parody of coitus interruptus, for each time their excitement builds as they begin the act of reading, their expectations are thwarted.[7] The ten fragments added

---

[5] Italo Calvino, "Cybernetics and Ghosts," p. 15, in *The Uses of Literature: Essays*, trans. Patrick Creagh (San Diego: Harcourt Brace Jovanovich, 1986).

[6] Ibid., p. 16.

[7] See Beno Weiss, *Understanding Italo Calvino* (Columbia: University of South Carolina Press, 1993), p. 173, for the description of the novel's structure.

together are brought together to form a single sentence in the concluding chapter of the novel:

> If on a winter's night a traveler, outside the town of Malbork, leaning from the steep slope without fear of wind or vertigo, looks down in the gathering shadow in a network of lines that enlace, in a network of lines that intersect, on the carpet of leaves illuminated by the moon around an empty grave – What story down there awaits its end?[8]

The imaginary readers experience extreme difficulty in moving from the ten very different beginnings of ten different novels to any conclusion – the lack of closure frustrates them as it would any conventional reader. But their very lack of closure – the very lack of a story in any of the ten incomplete novels – constitutes Calvino's completed story. Thus Calvino achieves for the postmodern novel what Luigi Pirandello had accomplished for the theatre in *Sei personaggi in cerca d'autore* (*Six Characters in Search of an Author*, 1921) and Federico Fellini (1920–93) had achieved in his most important film, $8\frac{1}{2}$ (1963). Pirandello creates a theatrical performance in which characters are unable to achieve their dramatic expression and that lack of expression constitutes his drama; Fellini portrays a film director's incapacity to make a film and his completed film chronicles his character's lack of completeness; and Calvino's novel contains successive false narrative starts, whose lack of success constitutes his completed and successful novel.[9] It is not surprising that Calvino's two protagonists eventually decide to marry (since traditional stories end either in the death of their heroes or their marriage, or so the narrator informs us), and in the final brief twelfth chapter of *Se una notte*, we discover them both in their nuptial bed, no longer interrupted by a desire for narrative closure, as Ludmilla turns off her light, asks her husband if he is not tired of reading and receives the witty reply that is also the book's last sentence: "Just a moment, I've almost finished *If on a Winter's Night a Traveler* by Italo Calvino."[10]

Calvino thus creates before our very eyes an engaging portrait of the traditional reader seeking traditional closure in a traditional novel, on the one

---

[8] Italo Calvino, *If on a Winter's Night a Traveler*, trans. William Weaver (San Diego: Harcourt Brace Jovanovich, 1981), p. 256.

[9] While the critics have long recognized the parallels between Pirandello and Fellini, it is less obvious that Calvino's career parallels the intellectual trajectory of both Pirandello and Fellini. For a brief suggestion of ways in which the early career of Calvino parallels that of the early Fellini, and how both men eventually moved from neorealism in literature and cinema toward metanarrative, see my "Beyond Neorealism: Calvino, Fellini, and Fantasy," *Michigan Romance Studies* 16 (1996), pp. 103–20.

[10] Calvino, *If on a Winter's Night a Traveler*, p. 260.

hand, and the postmodern experience of constructing a very different kind of narrative intended for a very different Model Reader, on the other. He manages to draw us into his rather abstract narrative by ingenious beginnings of books that promise much to the naive reader but then fail to deliver, while providing an implicit outline of what a postmodern literature might entail, the source of delight for a more sophisticated brand of reader who is concerned less with the outcome of dramatic plots than with the interplay of ideas. As we arrive at the end of the novel and put together the fragments of the lengthy sentence that served as introductions to each of the successive twelve incomplete novels, we realize that they form a long interrogatory query to us as readers. What story does, indeed, await us as readers when we pick up a book after we realize that our own readers' responses make up such an important aspect of the process of enjoying literature? It is impossible not to agree with the author's own assessment of this novel in *Lezioni americane*, when he calls it a "hypernovel" and declares that his aim was to provide the

> essence of what a novel is by providing it in concentrated form, in ten beginnings: each beginning develops in very different ways from a common nucleus, and each acts within a framework that both determines and is determined... My temperament prompts me to "keep it short."[11]

Eco's *Il nome della rosa* represents another quite different attempt to fashion a Model Reader (or more correctly Model Readers). While Calvino's work aims at a highbrow market and has been received only with great difficulty by a popular audience,[12] Eco's most important novel achieved legendary status as a best-seller and a long seller all over the globe. And it did so not by accident but, rather, by design. A definition of the novel's audience appeared on the dust jacket of the first Italian edition (a jacket written by Eco himself), an important document not included in subsequent Italian editions or English translations. It listed three categories of readers (ideal Model Readers) Eco envisioned for the work: readers interested in the complex plot; readers attracted by the history of ideas who might see connections between the cold war of the twentieth century and the theological debates

---

[11] Calvino, *Six Memos for the Next Millennium*, trans. Patrick Creagh (Cambridge, MA: Harvard University Press, 1988), p. 120.

[12] Calvino's reputation with the general reading public rose only after his experimental works in translation – *Cosmicomics* and *t zero* – were stocked in American bookstores under science fiction rather than general fiction in the 1970s and 1980s. Unlike Eco, Calvino's novels never reached the best-seller lists in the Anglo-Saxon world even though his fiction received numerous accolades from major British and American writers in the pages of the *New York Review of Books*, the periodical that represents the thinking of what passes for highbrow literary taste in America.

in the book; and readers aware of the fact that the novel was a palimpsest of other works, a "whodunit" of quotations, as Eco puts it.[13] Thus, Eco's Model Reader for his work first includes the avid consumers of commercial best-sellers fascinated with storyline and violence (the philistines attacked by modernist writers), so the author chooses to set his novel within a familiar pulp-fiction genre: the venerable detective story. Clear links to this popular and highly lucrative literary form are made by naming his monk-detective William of *Baskerville* (an obvious allusion to one of Conan Doyle's most famous Sherlock Holmes adventure stories, *The Hound of the Baskervilles*) and by providing a Watson figure (a young and naive monk named Adso) who will eventually chronicle William's investigation into the strange events at an Italian monastery in late November 1327 where seven monks die violent deaths (two by suicide, five by murder) and the entire monastery, including its famous library, is destroyed.

The second group of readers for whom *Il nome della rosa* is intended are the sometimes more educated (but not necessarily more intelligent) readers who like reading historical reconstructions of the past as thinly veiled allegories for events in the present or an imagined future. In Eco's account of the genesis of his novel in the postmodern manifesto *Postille a "Il nome della rosa*," the author notes that he began writing in March of 1978 – a date all living Italians will remember as the moment when the Christian Democratic politician Aldo Moro (1916–78) was kidnapped and eventually murdered by Red Brigade terrorists. Since Moro was the man responsible for the "historic compromise" between the Christian Democrats and the Italian Communist Party led by Enrico Berlinguer (1922–84), it was not implausible to see the warring factions supporting Papacy and empire in Eco's novel as medieval reflections of the cold war struggle between American capitalism and Russian communism.

Eco's third Model Reader was the reader closest to its author: the most sophisticated postmodern audience aware of the first two kinds of readings possible with the work but also capable of identifying not only quotations from the philosophical notebooks of Ludwig Wittgenstein or the works of James Joyce but also allusions to the comic strip *Peanuts*, the film *Casablanca*, and other icons of contemporary popular culture. Eco, in fact, flatly rejects the notion (popular among modernist writers and critics) that "popularity" and "lack of value" are synonymous. He and other members of the avant-garde Gruppo 63 had polemically argued this position in their sometimes vicious attacks upon the novels of an earlier generation. Eco would even go so far, in

---

[13] The complete translation of the book jacket may be found in Walter E. Stephens, "Ec[h]o in Fabula," *Diacritics* 13 (1983), p. 51.

a rubric entitled "The Structure of Bad Taste," as to consider *Il Gattopardo* by Giuseppe Tomasi di Lampedusa – arguably the best historical novelist in Italy after Alessandro Manzoni – as virtually a reflection of mass-cult and a kitsch commodity in his earlier *Apocalittici e integrati*.[14] Later, faced with the problems of composing a historical novel himself, Eco would view his commercially successful predecessors far more kindly and would subsequently have kinder words for popular writers such as Ian Fleming or Alexandre Dumas, exactly the kind of novelist he had criticized as too shallow in his youth.[15]

Il nome della rosa is thus the product of serious thought about the role of popular culture in literature, as well as about the development of recent literary history and literary theory. Eco's Model Reader includes a number of literary audiences, and the structure of the novel is consciously intended to appeal to them all on different levels – exactly the kind of "double coding" recent theorists cite as typical of postmodernist fiction. If the world of the traditional detective story reflects ultimately a universe capable of being understood, comprehended, and investigated, Eco's fictional universe overturns these simple expectations. William of Baskerville eventually discovers the evil murderer behind the killings at the monastery (the librarian Jorge of Burgos, a humorous reference to one of Eco's major postmodernist sources, Jorge Luis Borges), but he arrives at this discovery completely by accident. Eventually, as a bookish detective, William believes that the pattern of the deaths follows one found in the Book of Revelation, and the Model Reader(s) Eco assumes for his novel must surely follow William's reasoning. Moreover, the popular detective novel specializes in plots involving complex patterns discerned by the clever detective (Agatha Christie's *The ABC Murders* uses an alphabetical pattern; Ellery Queen's *Ten Days Wonder* follows the Ten Commandments; S. S. Van Dine's *The Benson Murder Case* employs nursery rhymes to form a pattern). Thus the expectations of both the erudite reader who has raced to consult the texts of the Book of Revelation in the Bible and the popular reader who remembers the pattern tradition in the detective novel are equally thwarted at the conclusion of *Il nome della rosa* by William's blundering, accidental discovery of the truth: "There was no plot," William said, "and I discovered it by mistake ... I should have known well

[14] The entire essay is republished in English in *The Open Work* (Cambridge, MA: Harvard University Press, 1989), but is not included in the partial translation of the Italian original, entitled *Apocalypse Postponed* (Bloomington: Indiana University Press, 1994).

[15] This far more generous attitude is particularly evident in his Norton Lectures (*Sei passeggiate*), where Fleming and Dumas are specifically analyzed and praised; or in his third novel, *L'isola del giorno prima*, which is itself a palimpsest of motifs from the swashbuckling novels popular in the nineteenth century.

that there is no order in the universe."[16] Shortly thereafter, this postmodern medieval detective–monk confirms his most nonmedieval belief in the chaos of the universe by referring to a famous passage from the *Tractatus Logico-Philosophicus* of Ludwig Wittgenstein: "The order that our mind imagines is like a net, or like a ladder, built to attain something. But afterward you must throw the ladder away, because you discover that, even if it was useful, it was meaningless... The only truths that are useful are instruments to be thrown away."[17] It is also not surprising, in this book based on so many other books and set in a library, that the cause of the crimes is eventually discovered to be the only surviving manuscript of Aristotle's treatise on comedy – tragically lost in the fire that destroys the entire edifice, engulfs the murderer, and also almost kills William and Adso in the conflagration.

Both *Se una notte d'inverno un viaggiatore* and *Il nome della rosa* reflect the bookishness of postmodern literature: books provide the excuse for each narrative; each narrator creates a peculiarly postmodern Model Reader for his fictional work; each text offers its reader a unique reading experience. Yet, no two literary styles could be further apart, and a comparison of their works demonstrates how flexible the postmodern novel has become. Calvino's style is epitomized by the literary qualities celebrated and analyzed in his *Lezioni americane*, especially lightness, quickness, and multiplicity. As he says about his own prose,

> my work as a writer has from the beginning aimed at tracing the lightning flashes of the mental circuits that capture and link points distant from each other in space and time... Just as for the poet writing verse, so it is for the prose writer: success consists in felicity of verbal expression, which every so often may result from a quick flash of inspiration but as a rule involves a patient search for the *mot juste*, for the sentence in which every word is unalterable, the most effective marriage of sounds and concepts. I am convinced that writing prose should not be any different from writing poetry.[18]

If lightness and quickness characterize both the language and the structure of Calvino's best work, Eco's novels, and especially *Il nome della rosa*, aim at exactly the opposite effect. It often seems as if Eco has read everything, remembered it all, and found some way to insert this knowledge into his first and best novel. His erudition is encyclopedic, and his purpose is to reproduce the world of his medieval monks in every detail (even while maintaining a postmodern attitude toward this recreation). In this respect, Eco follows one of the preoccupations of the traditional nineteenth-century storyteller, as well

---

[16] Eco, *The Name of the Rose Including the Author's Postscript*, trans. William Weaver (New York: Harvest Books, 1994), pp. 491–2.
[17] Ibid., p. 492.   [18] *Six Memos for the Next Millennium*, pp. 48–9.

as one of the requirements for a contemporary best-seller: the recreation of a fictional world. Calvino's *Lezioni americane* identifies two tendencies in literature: that aiming at lightness (his own position), wherein "one tries to make language into a weightless element that hovers above things like a cloud"; and its opposite, an approach that "tries to give language the weight, density, and concreteness of things, bodies, and sensations."[19] Calvino's *Se una notte d'inverno un viaggiatore* embodies the first impulse – that of poetic prose – while Eco's *Il nome della rosa* exemplifies the second impulse. As Eco himself puts it best in the *Postille al "Nome della rosa,"*

> The problem is to construct the world: the words will practically come on their own. *Rem tene, verba sequentur*: grasp the subject, and the words will follow. This, I believe, is the opposite of what happens with poetry, which is more a case of *verba tene, res sequentur*: grasp the words, and the subject will follow.[20]

The fictional works of Eco and Calvino travel along a continuum that ranges between the two poles of the prosaic and the poetic. In entirely different literary styles, their best novels embody the characteristics of the postmodern literary attitude, perhaps best described in the justly famous definition Eco provides in a humorous passage from *Postille al "Nome della rosa"*:

> The postmodern reply to the modern consists of recognizing that the past, since it cannot really be destroyed, because its destruction leads to silence must be revisited: but with irony, not innocently. I think of the postmodern attitude as that of a man who loves a very cultivated woman and knows he cannot say to her, "I love you madly," because he knows that she knows (and that she knows that he knows) that these words have already been written by Barbara Cartland. Still, there is a solution. He can say, "As Barbara Cartland would put it, I love you madly." At this point, having avoided false innocence, having said clearly that it is no longer possible to speak innocently, he will nevertheless have said what he wanted to say to the woman...Irony, metalinguistic play, enunciation squared.[21]

Umberto Eco and Italo Calvino are primarily responsible for bringing contemporary Italian fiction into the postmodern era. Their international popularity has paved the way toward an international audience for a subsequent generation of contemporary young Italian novelists whose intentions have passed far beyond the traditional mimetic concern with merely telling a good story reflecting a slice of Italian life or manners, and who are at home in the

---

[19] Ibid., p. 15. [20] Eco, *The Name of the Rose Including the Author's Postscript*, p. 513.
[21] Ibid., pp. 530–1.

postmodern environment Eco and Calvino were first to introduce into the Italian literary scene.

Further reading

Bondanella, Peter. *Umberto Eco and the Open Text: Semiotics, Fiction, Popular Culture*. Cambridge: Cambridge University Press, 1997.

Bouchard, Norma and Veronica Pravadelli, eds. *Umberto Eco's Alternative: The Politics of Culture and the Ambiguities of Interpretation*. New York: Peter Lang, 1998.

Caesar, Michael. *Umberto Eco: Philosophy, Semiotics and the Work of Fiction*. Cambridge: Polity Press, 1999.

Calvino, Italo. *If on a Winter's Night a Traveler*. Trans. William Weaver. San Diego: Harcourt Brace Jovanovich, 1981.

    Six Memos for the Next Millennium. Trans. Patrick Creagh. Cambridge, MA: Harvard University Press, 1988.

Capozzi, Rocco, ed. *Reading Eco: An Anthology*. Bloomington: Indiana University Press, 1997.

Eco, Umberto. *The Role of the Reader: Explorations in the Semiotics of Texts*. Bloomington: Indiana University Press, 1979.

    The Name of the Rose Including the Author's Postscript. Trans. William Weaver. New York: Harvest Books, 1994.

    Six Walks in the Fictional Woods. Cambridge, MA: Harvard University Press, 1994.

Haft, Adele J., Jane C. White, and Robert J. Whites, eds. *The Key to "The Name of the Rose" Including Translations of All Non-English Passages*. Ann Arbor: University of Michigan Press, 1999.

Hume, Kathryn. *Calvino's Fictions: Cogito and Cosmos*. Oxford: Clarendon Press, 1992.

Jeannet, Angela M. *Under the Radiant Sun and the Crescent Moon: Italo Calvino's Storytelling*. Toronto: University of Toronto Press, 2000.

McHale, Brian. *Constructing Postmodernism*. London: Routledge, 1992.

Ricci, Franco. *Painting with Words, Writing with Pictures: Word and Image in the Work of Italo Calvino*. Toronto: University of Toronto Press, 2001.

Weiss, Beno. *Understanding Italo Calvino*. Columbia: University of South Carolina Press, 1993.

12

ROLANDO CAPUTO

Literary cineastes: the Italian novel and the cinema

Discussing the interrelationships between film and literature, Italo Calvino once wrote: "There remains the fact that the cinema is continually being drawn toward literature. In spite of having such power of its own, the cinema has always been afflicted by jealousy of the written text: it wants to 'write'."[1] There are strands to the respective histories of the twentieth-century Italian novel and the Italian cinema that at times come together to form a kind of Gordian knot, so to speak, so tightly harnessed are they. At such times as these historical strands cross over, literature and cinema can be said to enter into a form of dialogue with one another. This dialogue between the Italian cinema and literature is amongst the most complex, fluid, and multifaceted to be found in any culture. To appreciate its full scope one has to acknowledge it at a number of interrelated levels. First, there is the most immediate and most commonly discussed question of adapting Italian novels to film form. The critical literature contains many detailed analyses of such relationships between novels and directors, the most famous and successful of which were: Alberto Moravia/Vittorio De Sica, *La ciociara* (*Two Women*, 1960); Giuseppe Tomasi di Lampedusa/Luchino Visconti, *Il Gattopardo* (*The Leopard*, 1963); Alberto Moravia/Bernardo Bertolucci (1942–), *Il conformista* (*The Conformist*, 1970); Carlo Levi/Francesco Rosi (1922–), *Cristo si è fermato a Eboli* (*Christ Stopped at Eboli*, 1979); Gavino Ledda/the Taviani Brothers, *Padre Padrone* (*Padre Padrone*, 1977).[2] Aside from their shared narrative content – what the film derives from the story, plot, or

---

[1] Italo Calvino, "Cinema and the Novel: Problems of Narrative," in *The Uses of Literature*, trans. Patrick Creagh (San Diego: Harcourt Brace Jovanovich, 1986), p. 77.

[2] Such classics of novels adapted for the cinema are treated exhaustively by book-length studies listed in the further reading list. Because they are so well known, they will not be discussed in detail here, as more general literary and theoretical questions will be analyzed, giving necessary attention to novels and films that have been unjustly neglected in previous discussions of this question.

representational drama – any film that has its point of origin in a novel – and more so if the novel is part of the literary canon – is first and foremost the record of an encounter between two distinct discursive practices. In the terminology of semiotics, what one apprehends from the adapted work is the literary signifier's degree of resistance under the sway of the cinematic signifier. However, if at all, at the level of expressive style, each can accommodate the other. Second, there have been historical moments in which polemicists and practitioners of the novel and film have entered into a real dialogue regarding the ideological and aesthetic direction to be taken in their respective enterprises. This was the case in the 1940s, for it was the debates around *verismo* and the realist novel that helped shape the early direction of neorealist cinema. Visconti's early films, for example, particularly *Ossessione* (*Obsession*, 1943) and *La terra trema* (*The Earth Trembles*, 1948) – the latter derived from Giovanni Verga's naturalistic novel *I Malavoglia* – cannot be fully divorced from contemporaneous discussions on realism taking place within Italian journals of the era. For example, two names of consequence feature on the screenplay credit for *Ossessione*: those of Mario Alicata (1917–66) and Giuseppe De Santis (1917–97). Both were intellectuals associated with the journal *Cinema*, in which they had published in 1941 an article, "Truth and Poetry: Verga and the Italian Cinema," that had considerable influence among the emergent neorealist filmmakers.[3] De Santis himself would go on to direct *Riso amaro* (*Bitter Rice*, 1949), one of the key works of the period. Third, one finds in the Italian context more so than elsewhere – and the cultural reasons are yet to be fully understood – the recurring figure of what we will call, for convenience's sake, the "literary cineaste," that is, that individual who is equally at home in the world of the cinema and of literature. In that tradition, even a partial list of names would include those of Mario Soldati (1906–99), Pier Paolo Pasolini, Giuseppe Patroni Griffi (1921–), Pasquale Festa Campanile, Alberto Bevilacqua, Tonino Guerra, and Ennio Flaiano. Ironically, this phenomenon of the "literary cineaste" – and the implications which lie behind it – can best be foregrounded with reference to an author who was an anomaly: Italo Calvino.

Calvino's memoir "A Cinema-Goer's Autobiography," in which he recounts his intense fascination with the cinema as an adolescent growing up in the Fascist provincial Italy of the 1930s, is all the more remarkable coming as it does from an individual who was so markedly identified as a man of letters. Furthermore, Calvino's early passion for the cinema seemed not to

---

[3] For an English translation, see David Overby, ed., *Springtime in Italy: A Reader on Neo-Realism* (Hamden, CT: Archon Books, 1979), pp. 131–8.

leave an imprint on him after he, as he put it, "got involved in the world of the printed page."[4] Very few of Calvino's books have been filmed and, unlike so many of his contemporaries, he was rarely tempted to collaborate on screenplays. Surprisingly, in a culture that allowed the free movement between the worlds of literature and cinema, Calvino seemed consciously to keep his distance from the film world, as if he sensed that whole-heartedly to enter into a creative or collaborative dialogue with cinema would result in a kind of Faustian bargain, where one realm would fall under the spell of another, one art form seduced and contaminated by the other, and, of course, as the Faustian allegory well illustrates, there is always a heavy price to pay for such a bargain.

Yet many an author heeded the siren call of the cinema. The Italian silent cinema had already been a first major port of call for literary figures, none more so than that of Gabriele D'Annunzio, whose novels and stories provided a wealth of adaptation sources, beginning in 1911 with the first screen version of his novel *L'innocente* (*The Innocent*, 1892). By 1921, he himself had stepped behind the camera to co-direct (with Mario Roncoroni) *La nave* (*The Ship*), based on his play of the same name published in 1907. More significantly, his name is associated with one of the key films in the history of the silent cinema, *Cabiria* (*Cabiria*, 1914) by Giovanni Pastrone (1883–1959), for which he collaborated on the screenplay and wrote the intertitles. The film represents a typical D'Annunzian melodrama and what can more generally be referred to as a D'Annunzian aesthetic sensibility. This kind of decadent aesthetics had a pervasive influence on Italian cinema, and an arc of influence can be traced from Pastrone's silent epic all the way to Luchino Visconti's version of *L'innocente* (*The Innocent*, 1976) and beyond. There is also the example of the author/filmmaker Mario Soldati. Unlike D'Annunzio, Soldati is a writer whose name falls outside the literary canon. Nonetheless, his case may be more indicative of the kind of cross-fertilization that took place in Italian culture between the worlds of literature and film. Soldati quickly established himself as a scriptwriter of note in the 1930s, principally collaborating on films for directors Alessandro Blasetti (1900–87) and Mario Camerini (1895–1981). By 1939 he had directed his first film, *Dora Nelson*, and continued throughout the 1940s and 1950s to make films in the vein of light comedy and adventure. More significantly, his adaptations of Antonio Fogazzaro's nineteenth-century novels *Piccolo mondo antico* (*The Little World of the Past*, 1941) and *Malombra* (*The Woman*, 1942) placed him in the so-called "calligraphic school," a label

---

4 Italo Calvino, "A Cinema-Goer's Autobiography," in *The Road to San Giovanni*, trans. Tim Parks (London: Jonathan Cape, 1993), p. 61.

that groups together a number of filmmakers who in the early 1940s turned their attention to adapting for the screen works of late nineteenth-century naturalist fiction. Their emphasis on a heightened aesthetic visual style and representations of past worlds, together with a reliance on more classical narrative techniques, placed them at odds with the neorealist movement. While both camps drew inspiration from literary models, the neorealist attention to contemporary social themes and the deemphasizing of classic storytelling conventions resulted in a fairly clear-cut demarcation between these two movements, inspired essentially by different conceptions of the Italian novel. Unlike others of the "calligraphic" school – for example, Alberto Lattuada (1914–) and Renato Castellani (1913–85) – Soldati did not adopt a neorealist orientation in his subsequent films, opting instead to make commercial genre films. At the end of his film career he continued to write novels, some of which were filmed.

One need not look so far back into the history of Italian cinema to discover this recurring figure of the literary cineaste, the man of letters enmeshed in the world of cinema. Of Calvino's contemporaries, or quasi-contemporaries, above all there is the exemplary case of the novelist, poet, and filmmaker Pier Paolo Pasolini, whose use of Roman dialect and slang in his two novels *Ragazzi di vita* and *Una vita violenta* attracted the attention of other filmmakers, notably Federico Fellini, for whom he worked on the script to *Le notti di Cabiria* (*The Nights of Cabiria*, 1957), and Mauro Bolognini (1922–), for whom he worked on the screenplays to *Marisa la civetta* (Marisa the Owl, 1957), *Giovani mariti* (Young Husbands, 1957), and *Il bell'Antonio* (*Bell'Antonio*, 1960), based on the savage satire on Sicilian sexual hypocrisy in the novel of the same title by Vitaliano Brancati (1907–54). Also for Bolognini, he was to adapt Pasolini's *Ragazzi di vita*, released as *La notte brava* (The Brave Night, 1959), and he worked with Alberto Moravia on the screenplay to *La giornata balorda* (The Crazy Day, 1960), drawn from the tales in Moravia's *Racconti romani* (*Roman Tales*) and *Nuovi racconti romani* (*More Roman Tales*, 1959). One thinks also of the author Curzio Malaparte (1898–1957), who wrote and directed from his own original screenplay *Cristo proibito* (*Forbidden Christ*, 1951), a pictorially mannered moral allegory of considerable cinematic merit, and whose famous decadent novel *La pelle* (*The Skin*, 1949) was subsequently filmed by Liliana Cavani (1937–) in 1981. These are only a few of the crossover literary figures in Italian cinema.

Let us return to the young Calvino entranced before the silver screen. His principal passion was the American cinema of classical, genre-coded, stylized, escapist entertainment. What he responded to most were the actors. For him, the cinema meant a gallery of faces and bodies – that is, a recognizable typology of looks. As to character, the more stereotyped the better. He was not looking for individuality or psychological depth but rather the economy of expressive means found in the art of caricature. For Calvino, the imaginary screen world of American genre cinema – precisely because it was subject to the repetition of characters, settings, and events – constituted a cosmology onto itself, a system governed by other rules, different from reality. Calvino recognized and appreciated the "distance" between the screen world and the real world. He did not much like neorealist cinema, precisely because it erased the distance between the two worlds he preferred to keep separate:

> Since the war, cinema has been seen, discussed, made, in a completely different way. I don't know to what extent post-war Italian cinema has changed our way of seeing the world, but it has certainly changed our way of seeing the cinema (any cinema, even American cinema). We no longer have one world within the brightly lit screen in the darkened theatre, and another heterogeneous world outside, the two being divided by a clean break, an ocean or abyss. The darkened theatre disappears, the screen becomes a magnifying glass placed on the routine world outside, forcing us to focus our attention on what the naked eye tends to skim over without settling on. This function has – can have – its usefulness, marginal, more substantial or occasionally very considerable. But it does not satisfy that anthropological and social need for distance.[5]

At the time Calvino entered the literary world, neorealism was very much the prevailing aesthetic. His first novel, *Il sentiero dei nidi di ragno*, falls under its ambit, although one of the book's early reviewers (Cesare Pavese) made note of Calvino's skill for writing fable-like stories, a trait that progressively emerged more fully in his later novels, as he began to seek an alternative to the impasse of neorealism and the insular debates about its status as a populist, national literature (and cinema) of reconstruction. Calvino was soon to see that a literature of national identity responsive only to a given social realism could only curtail the powers of literature's greater potential. It is certainly reductive, yet for the sake of brevity nonetheless valid, to say that his fiction and many of his major essays addressed a single question: what is literature, or, what is literature as a signifying system onto itself? Calvino was not alone in posing such a question, but the quest for an answer found renewed fervor in the twentieth century, and was addressed in one way or another by a range of modernist and postmodernist writers. Some of these writers belonged to the Oulipo group (a French acronym meaning Workshop of Potential Literature). Along with Raymond Queneau and Georges Perec, Calvino was a principal member. Clearly, at one level, Calvino was dissatisfied with the

5 Ibid., pp. 60–1.

Italian literary context and looked abroad to Paris for other literary models. Although tied by bonds of friendship to both Pavese and Elio Vittorini – with whom he co-edited throughout the 1950s and early 1960s *Il Menabò*, a journal of cultural debate – Calvino's novelistic endeavors had little affinity with theirs.

But there was one Italian author Calvino greatly admired, who belonged to his personal pantheon of great writers. In Carlo Emilio Gadda he found an author who shared his conception of "the contemporary novel as an encyclopaedia, as a method of knowledge, and above all as a network of connections between the events, the people, and the things of the world."[6] Evidence of Calvino's high regard for Gadda can be found in his chapter on "multiplicity" in his critical masterpiece delivered as a series of lectures at Harvard University, *Six Memos for the Next Millennium*, a brilliant definition of literature devoted in large measure to discussions of Gadda and other exponents of what Calvino calls the "encyclopedic" novel, such as Robert Musil, James Joyce, Thomas Mann, the Flaubert of *Bouvard and Pecuchet*, and Perec. Such writers, as the terms implies, attempted to include everything in their works, while Calvino himself aimed at simplicity of expression.

As Ian Sinclair's discussion of film adaptations from novels has noted, if a novel "could be effectively translated into this other medium, then it was a failure; because the definition of a valid novel is that it can exist only on its own terms. Anything that succeeds as a film should have been a film in the first place."[7] Two years after the publication of Gadda's masterpiece *Quer pasticciaccio brutto de Via Merulana* came the release of the film version by Pietro Germi (1914–74), *Un maledetto imbroglio* (*A Sordid Affair*, 1959). Director Germi was also the film's lead actor and, together with Alfredo Giannetti and Ennio de Concini, collaborated on the screenplay, which the credits acknowledge as "freely adapted" from the novel. Germi's debut as a director dated back to the period of neorealism, yet his style – like that of his contemporary, Giuseppe De Santis – already evinced a pictorial and dramatic mannerism influenced by Hollywood cinema. This proximity to Hollywood cinematic codes led some critics to call him a "fellow traveler" rather than a mainstay of the neorealist school. A comparison between the novel and Germi's screen adaptation may tell us something about Calvino's fears for literature's corruption at the hands of the cinema.

---

[6] Italo Calvino, *Six Memos for the Next Millennium*, trans. Patrick Creagh (Cambridge, MA: Harvard University Press, 1988), p. 105.

[7] Ian Sinclair, *Crash* (London: British Film Institute Publishing, 1999), p. 11.

Gadda's linguistic experimentation has often been compared to that of James Joyce: "a pastiche – as the title implies – of languages and dialects," as the English-language translator of the book described it.[8] Furthermore, Calvino observed that Gadda's style was characterized by "a dense amalgam of popular and erudite expressions, of interior monologue and studied prose, of various dialects and literary quotations; and in narrative composition, in which minimal details take on giant proportions and end up by occupying the whole canvas and hiding or obscuring the overall design."[9] A question therefore needs posing: how does a novel of dizzying semantic experimentation and modernist ambition result in a generically constrained, causally unilinear narrative film of stylistically conventional orientation?

The tenuous narrative thread of Gadda's novel hangs on the typical elements of a *giallo* (the Italian term for mystery novel). The Italian word *giallo* actually means "yellow," and the word became a popular way to refer to the mystery novels with bright yellow covers popularized in Italy by the Milanese publishing house Mondadori. Gadda's novel presents an intriguing account of the mysterious circumstances surrounding a "double crime" – the theft of one woman's jewelry, the concurrent discovery of another woman's murdered body in a Rome apartment house, and the subsequent police investigation. The novel's generating premise of a "double crime" spins out into an overall doubling strategy: the two apartment staircases; the double cancer that afflicts a character; the double win in a lottery sweepstake, and so forth. So fond is the cinema of generically codified stories that this plot premise alone seems like a ready-made subject for a film. And yet the novel provides no solution to the mystery. Indeed, the detective plot increasingly gives way to the introspective musings on all manner of subjects by Gadda's protagonist, police commissioner Francesco Ingravallo, a most singular literary creation.

Germi's film adaptation is a good example of André Bazin's idea of the "cinema of digest." Bazin (1918–58) argues that popular cinema's function is to produce condensed, summarized, and simplified versions of highbrow novels. Precisely because the cinema is a medium of mass consumption, it addresses a different audience than that of the reader of highbrow fiction.[10]

[8] William Weaver, "Translator's Foreword," in Carlo Emilio Gadda, *That Awful Mess on Via Merulana* (New York: George Braziller, 1984), p. xv.
[9] Italo Calvino, *Why Read the Classics?*, trans. Martin McLaughlin (London: Jonathan Cape, 1999), p. 201.
[10] For his argument, see André Bazin, "Adaptation or the Cinema of Digest," in Burt Cardullo, ed., *Bazin at Work: Major Essays and Reviews from the Forties and Fifties* (New York: Routledge, 1997), pp. 41–51.

Indeed, Germi's film jettisons the philosophical dimension of Gadda's novel and its multiplying plotlines and turns it into an effective *giallo* for a lowbrow audience. Bazin further argues that what is important in the adaptation process is not fidelity to form, but rather the existence of equivalence in style between the two works. And it is precisely on the question of style that the real gaps between the film and the novel open out. To demonstrate the difference, let us quote at length a passage from the novel:

> The body of the poor signora was lying in an infamous position, supine, the grey wool skirt and a white petticoat thrown back, almost to her breast: as if someone had wanted to uncover the fascinating whiteness of that *dessous*, or inquire into its state of cleanliness. She was wearing white underpants, of elegant jersey, very fine, which ended halfway down the thighs with a delicate edging. Between the edging and the stockings, which were a light-shaded silk, the extreme whiteness of the flesh lay naked, of a chlorotic pallor: those two thighs, slightly parted, on which the garters – a lilac hue – seemed to confer a distinction of rank... The tight garters, curled slightly at the edges, with a clear, lettuce-like curl... those legs slightly spread, as if in horrible invitation... A deep, a terrible red cut opened her throat, fiercely. It had taken half the neck, from the front towards the right, that is, towards her left, the right for those who were looking down: jagged at its two edges, as if by a series of blows, of the blade or point: a horror!... The underpants weren't bloodied; they left uncovered two patches of thigh, two rings of flesh: down to the stockings, glistening blond skin. The furrow of the sex...[11]

Leaving aside the eroticism in the description of the woman's corpse, Calvino calls this "one of the virtuoso passages of the book" and likens it to a "Baroque painting of the martyrdom of some saint."[12] The sensuousness of color and form is certainly painterly, yet the clinical exactness also evokes the results of forensic photography. The tableau or photographic suits the cinema, but this passage as rendered on screen fails to produce the desired tableau effect, partly because Germi does not freeze the moment and concentrates only on the plot implications of the corpse's discovery. The film version also fails to do justice to the original because, in Gadda's description, the novelist simultaneously creates the whole tableau and shatters it through the minute focus on detail. Thus Gadda forces his reader to shift constantly from the whole "frame" to the closeup detail, or conversely from the detail back to the whole. Germi's style resists this tendency, uniformly sticking to the outer drama, focusing on incidents that are only of consequence to the story's plot progression. Furthermore, Germi's adaptation

---

[11] Gadda, *That Awful Mess*, pp. 67–70. [12] Calvino, *Why Read the Classics?*, p. 205.

fails to account for the true subject, which is the city of Rome. As Calvino puts it:

> The Eternal City is the book's real protagonist, in its social classes from the most middling of the middle classes to the criminal underworld, in the words of its dialect... in its extrovert nature and in its darkest subconscious, a Rome in which the present mixes with the mythical past, in which Hermes or Circe is evoked in connection with the most trivial incidents, in which characters who are domestics or petty thieves are called Aeneas, Diomedes, Ascanius, Camilla or Lavinia, like the heroes and heroines of Virgil. The noisy, down-at-heel Rome of neorealist cinema... acquires in Gadda's book a cultural, historical and mythical depth that neorealism neglected.[13]

Calvino's assessment of Gadda's portrait of Rome provides an almost exact description of the accomplishment of an altogether different film that has the city of Rome as its basis: Fellini's *Roma* (*Fellini's Roma*, 1972). Indeed, it is Fellini's film – written together with the author Bernardino Zapponi (1927–2000) whose own fiction is strong on oneiric effects of fantasy and imagination – that demonstrates, more than Germi's, a stylistic equivalence to Gadda. For Fellini's film, like Gadda's novel, downplays the linear narrative form and renders a portrait of Rome in all its multilayered guises: historical, mythical, archaeological, fantastical, and imaginary. Nonetheless, Germi's film was a box-office success, and the following year he would virtually repeat his performance of Gadda's protagonist Inspector Ingravallo in the Cesare Zavattini-scripted film *Il rossetto* (*Lipstick*, 1960), another *giallo* melodrama directed by Damiano Damiani which also – not surprisingly, given its derivative basis – deals with the discovery of a murdered woman's body in an apartment house. Zavattini's screenplay mixes the elements of the *giallo* genre with those of the neorealist social problem film, which produces an altogether better film than Germi's. Yet *Divorzio all'italiana* (*Divorce Italian Style*, 1961), Germi's next film also scripted with the same writers (Giannetti and de Concini) who had collaborated on the Gadda adaptation, with its tragi-comic fatalism and baroque visual stylization seems, if nothing else, to capture the tone of Gadda's hybrid novel far more sensitively than Germi's *Un maledetto imbroglio*. In a strange twist to this tale of failed and displaced filmed versions of his novel, Gadda himself had sensed that there was some cinematic potential in his work, for 1983 saw the publication of a document entitled *Il palazzo degli ori* (The Apartment Building of Riches). According to Calvino,

---

[13] Ibid., p. 202.

> This is a film script which Gadda wrote at the same time as the first draft of the novel: either shortly before it, or shortly afterwards, apparently. In it the whole plot is developed and clarified in every particular... The script was never taken up by producers or directors, and no wonder: Gadda had a rather naive idea of writing for cinema, based on continual fade-outs to reveal characters' thoughts and background detail.[14]

Gadda's rather "naive" idea was in fact an attempt to solve one of the more vexing questions in relation to literature and film – that of the narrative voice known as "interior monologue." This crucial narrative voice of modernist literature presented a film director with vexing problems, moving one commentator to proclaim that all "great novels are unfilmable, because they're so interiorised."[15] The literary technique of the interior monologue allows the novel immediate access to a character's interior life, to their thoughts, and the inner recesses of their mind. Cinema's task, on the other hand, is to make thought subject to vision. The relation between exterior and interior life has been a perplexing one for the Italian cinema. If neorealism was the attempt to document the social, materialist conditions of existence, then what followed in the cinema of Federico Fellini, Michelangelo Antonioni (1912–), and Valerio Zurlini (1926–82), among others, was an attempt to discover how the cinema could deal with states of interiority. With $8\frac{1}{2}$ (1963), the story of a filmmaker experiencing a creative crisis, Fellini abandoned any conventional notion of reality. He constantly blurs the distinction between exterior reality and the interior world of dreams, hallucinations, and fantasy, making of them an inseparable synthesis. Like Fellini, Antonioni also believed that neorealism needed to be reshaped to allow for greater attention to the interior life of characters. Unlike Fellini, however, he chose an altogether different formal and stylistic approach to the issue. Where Fellini found narrative techniques to allow him to delve directly into a character's mental states, or their subconscious life, Antonioni was at the forefront of experiments in "objective narration." In analyzing Antonioni's use of the camera in *Il deserto rosso* (*The Red Desert*, 1964), Pasolini spoke of Antonioni's cinematic deployment of the literary technique of "free indirect speech" as a means of representing the female character's neurotic state of mind.[16] Although such a narrative perspective embodying the most salient of literary modernism was a feature of Antonioni's cinema generally, the body of films comprising *L'avventura* (*L'Avventura*, 1959), *La notte*

---

[14] Ibid., pp. 206–7.   [15] J. G. Ballard cited by Sinclair, *Crash*, p. 11.
[16] For his complete argument, see Pier Paolo Pasolini, "The Cinema of Poetry," in *Heretical Empiricism*, trans. Ben Lawton and Louise K. Barnett (Bloomington: Indiana University Press, 1988), pp. 167–86.

(*La Notte*, 1960), and *L'eclisse* (*L'Eclisse*, 1962), together with *Il deserto rosso* – all written in collaboration with Tonino Guerra, an author of fiction in his own right – are exemplary demonstrations of "objective narration" as a means of penetrating the existential, and thereby mental, state of his characters. Normally, both Fellini and Antonioni kept their distance from straight adaptations of Italian novels and most typically employed novels only as a suggestive source of poetic inspiration. Mention should be made of Antonioni's *Le amiche* (*The Girlfriends*, 1955), a fine film version of Pavese's novel *Tra donne sole* (*Among Women Only*, 1949), and Fellini's *La voce della luna* (*The Voice of the Moon*, 1990), based on the novel *Il poema dei lunatici* (The Poem of the Lunatics, 1987) by Ermanno Cavazzoni (1947–).

Zurlini, on the other hand, represents a very special case of adaptation that transcends the typical transposition of a novel into a film and exhibits special affinities to imagery in the plastic arts. In some respects, Zurlini resembles Visconti with whom he shares a deep passion for literature and a masterful skill for screen adaptations. His first feature, *Le ragazze di Sanfrediano* (*The Girls of San Frediano*, 1954), and the subsequent masterpiece *Cronaca familiare* (*Family Diary*, 1962) were both inspired by novels of the same title by Vasco Pratolini. Like Visconti, Zurlini's visual style often expressed a mannered pictorial sense of composition, although the excesses of high melodrama, so essential to Visconti's decadent aesthetics, held little interest for him. While Zurlini's visual style was developed via independent means, the core thematic substance of his cinema touches on what the French philosopher Gilles Deleuze called the grand Viscontian theme of "the too late of lost time."[17] There is in this the idea of the melancholic reflection on time past: the creation of characters who realize too late that they are part of a vanishing world, or who realize too late their fatal encounter with destiny – an idea justly appropriate to *Il deserto dei Tartari* (*The Desert of the Tartars*, 1976), Zurlini's film based on the masterpiece *Il deserto dei Tartari* (*The Tartar Steppe*, 1945) by Dino Buzzati (1906–72). Zurlini's true affinities, however, confessed in many an interview, reside with the cinema of Antonioni. The enigma of interior life pervades the work of both directors, and they document what Antonioni called the "life of the sentiments" that was so important a literary theme of modernist novelists. An existential sadness runs through all of Zurlini's films, including those based on original screenplays such as *L'estate violenta* (*Violent Summer*, 1959), *La ragazza con la valigia* (*The Girl with a Suitcase*, 1961), and the sublimely melancholic *La*

---

[17] Gilles Deleuze, *Cinema: The Time Image*, trans. Hugh Tomlinson and Robert Galeta (Minneapolis: University of Minnesota Press, 1989), p. 96.

prima notte di quiete (*The Professor*, 1972). And like Antonioni's best films, Zurlini's cinema is a stranger to the happy ending. Zurlini looks to authors who already share his worldview, or a certain sensibility about the world, as was the case with Visconti's choice of authors. Zurlini much admired the work of Giorgio Bassani and at one time hoped to adapt *Il giardino dei Finzi-Contini*, which was subsequently made by Vittorio De Sica in 1970. Of De Sica's finely crafted film Italian film historian Peter Bondanella is right to say that the "film captures quite beautifully the elegiac nostalgia of Bassani's portrait of the Edenic garden of this family, an idyllic pastoral oasis where the film's narrator comes of age emotionally and sexually in his ill-fated infatuation for the enigmatically beautiful Micòl Finzi-Contini."[18] Yet De Sica lacks that melancholic, existentialist vision of life shared by Bassani and Zurlini, in whose hands Bassani's novel may have become a far greater film.

Many a director, including Antonioni, had shown interest in Buzzati's *Il deserto dei Tartari* before Zurlini turned his attention to the work, yet it was indeed fortuitous that the project made its way into Zurlini's hands, since he was the director whose films showed a clear predisposition towards certain themes in Buzzati's work. In *Il deserto dei Tartari* he was to recognize a variation on the military life and the approach of death, themes that had frequently engaged his cinema. An early short film by Zurlini is, in fact, entitled *Soldati in città* (Soldiers in the City, 1954), and at least half of his feature films are set in the world of soldiers. But Buzzati's novel was an elusive work containing little narrative action and much interior monologue. Zurlini was to solve the problem by focusing on the pictorial elements inherent in Buzzati's narrative rather than a simple replication of the original's plot. Buzzati's exquisite talent, especially evident in much of his short fiction, for creating fictional worlds that are, at times, metaphysical, oneiric, and situated somewhere between dream and reality, has been justly praised by his most discerning critics. Such a talent forms a principal basis for the many comparisons drawn between Buzzati's fiction and the best works by Kafka or Borges. Buzzati's original title for *Il deserto dei Tartari* was *La fortezza* (The Fortress), a title of self-evident reference to Kafka's *The Castle*. In both works, the structure alluded to in these titles points to a foreboding, ominous, and threatening force opposed to the protagonists. For all its oneiric qualities, we sense the presence of an empirical world, yet a world rendered strange or uncanny by Buzzati's narrative technique behind the universe of *Il deserto dei Tartari*. One cannot but note how the novel

---

[18] P. Bondanella, *Italian Cinema: From Neorealism to the Present*, 3rd rev. edn (New York: Continuum, 2001), p. 324.

consistently dehistoricizes time and deterritorializes space. That the story is set in the "past" is self-evident, but this strange past is one not anchored in a specific historical epoch. From Buzzati's inferences of a not quite real, yet not fully ephemeral or ghostly world, Zurlini takes his inspiration to model the visual design of his compositions on the work of the Metaphysical School of Italian painting, especially the eerie Italian squares and mannequins of painter Giorgio De Chirico, as well as the familiar dreamscapes of surrealist painting. It is to this effect that Zurlini's film introduces one of its most striking image-metaphors. In the novel, the specter of death hanging over the fort finds expression through the idea of the soldiers' slow wasting away of time, and therefore life, awaiting the defining moment of a battle that never takes place. In the film, the character Doctor Rovere, using the analogy of a disease, calls the deathly ambience of the film an "impurity in the walls" of the fort. This deathly ambience has been strikingly prefigured in Lieutenant Giovanni Drogo's approach to the fort's outer walls. The actual fort Zurlini used for the fictional Fort Bastiani was discovered by the filmmakers in the southeast of Iran. Known as the Fortress of Bam, it is an imposing structure, a long-deserted Islamic fort encircled by what resembles the archeological remnants of a dead city. To make his way to the fort, Drogo rides slowly through its silent, ghostly streets, and there at its outer limits he crosses the cemetery occupied by the dead soldiers from the fort. The symbolic effect of such imagery cannot be understated. Fort Bastiani is a lonely sentinel that presides over a netherworld of the living dead. The dead city is sign enough of a lost civilization (perhaps that of the legendary Tartars). The interior space of the fort gives the impression of a catacomb. As the door to the fort opens, two figures greet Drogo's arrival. One stands in the darkness of the entrance, the other in the light of the courtyard. The two figures mirror one another as symmetrical halves of the two realms of light and shade. From a purely pictorial point of view, the image divided in this manner produces an effect not too dissimilar to those mysterious, haunting shadows that cut across so many of Giorgio De Chirico's canvases. Many of the painter's best-known works can be cited as a point of comparison to the film: *La méditation automnale* (1912), *La mélancolie* (1912), and *L'énigme d'une journée* (1914). When asked in an interview to comment on the validity of the term "realismo fantastico" (magic realism) as applied by critics to describe the style of his film, Zurlini was categorical in his preference for the term "metaphysical" and pointed to further examples in the film, such as the repeated use of the mannequin motif his film shared with De Chirico's paintings. The mannequin is one of the most crucial and diffuse icons of the Metaphysical School, found in De Chirico certainly, but also in *La musa metafisica* (1917) and *L'ovale delle apparizioni* (1918) by Carlo Carrà. Some years later, the Paris-based surrealists inherited this icon and made of it another symbol of the uncanny "Other" that resides in the shadow of the real. If Zurlini accentuated the pictorial analogies, he did so not with the intention of adding an extra layer to the novel, but rather because the medium of film is precisely about bringing out of the literary text its visual dimension. Film adaptation at its best, as in the case of Zurlini's *Il deserto dei Tartari*, is not merely a simple process of words turned into pictures. When film adaptation fails, it frequently fails precisely because the film that is produced from a content- or plot-based interpretation of the original novel represents purely and simply a photographic documenting of the novel. The most sophisticated film adaptations involve words filtered through the discourse of the visual. Such was the strategy Zurlini had previously adopted for *Cronaca familiare*, using the paintings of Giorgio Morandi and Ottone Rosai to devise a color scheme for the film that would perfectly express the subdued mood and tone of Pratolini's sad tale of two brothers lost to one another in adulthood because of a barely comprehended childhood. Overshadowed for too long by more famous examples, Zurlini's adaptations are among the finest in the Italian cinema.

Let us conclude with a return to Calvino, the novelist that inspired our examination of the complex relationship between the literary text of a novel and the cinema's visual text. Calvino kept his distance from cinema for good reason. As a child he experienced the power of films and sensed that the twentieth century would belong not to the printed page but to this new "machine of the visible," this new cultural sensorium based on combining sound, image, and narrative in the most seductive of ways. Cinema, Calvino sensed, had the power to rob the novel of its storytelling means. The less radical forms of the novel – and, for Calvino, the less complicated forms of the novel were the so-called psychological novel and the social realist novel or, in effect, any realism – could easily be divested of their expressive conventions by the cinema. Calvino was correct when he declared that the cinema desires to write, but the greatest cinema desired to write in a new fashion faithful to its etymology: it sought a new way of writing – *cinematography* or writing with light – a way of writing that simultaneously erased other forms of writing. Calvino looked to models of literature that could withstand the onslaught of this new writing medium and as a result wrote wondrously unfilmable novels. And yet the final irony of Calvino's "A Cinema-Goer's Autobiography" is that the cinema of Italy's least literary director, Federico Fellini, reflected Calvino's own youth and his literary aspirations better than any other director's work. As he put it,

The autobiography Fellini has been developing without a break from *I Vitelloni* on is special to me not just because he and I are almost the same age, and not just because we both come from seaside towns, his on the Adriatic, mine in Liguria, where the lives of idle young boys were pretty much similar, but because behind all the wretchedness of the days in the café, the walks to the pier, the friend who dresses in woman's clothes and then gets drunk and weeps, I recognise the unsatisfied youth of the cinema-goer, of a provincial world that judges itself in relation to the cinema, in a constant comparison between itself and that other world that is the cinema.[19]

Further reading

Bragaglia, Cristina. *Il piacere del racconto: narrativa italiana e cinema (1895–1990)*. Florence: La Nuova Italia, 1993.

Horton, Andrew S. and Joan Magretta, eds. *Modern European Filmmakers and the Art of Adaptation*. New York: Frederick Ungar, 1981.

Marcus, Millicent. *Filmmaking by the Book: Italian Cinema and Literary Adaptation*. Baltimore: Johns Hopkins University Press, 1993.

Naremore, James, ed. *Film Adaptation*. New Brunswick: Rutgers University Press, 2000.

Testa, Carlo. *Italian Cinema and Modern European Literatures: 1945–2000*. Westport, CT: Praeger Publishers, 2002.

   Masters of Two Arts: Re-Creations of European Literatures in Italian Cinema. Toronto: University of Toronto Press, 2002.

[19] Calvino, "A Cinema-Goer's Autobiography," pp. 64–5.

13

ANDREA CICCARELLI

Frontier, exile, and migration in the contemporary Italian novel

The experience of reading a book written in Italian but conceived in a foreign cultural world is unusual in modern Italian literature. Such an experience, normal in the anglophone, francophone, and the Spanish-speaking world, has become less rare in the past decade thanks to a number of books written, often in cooperation with authors of Italian birth, by foreigners who have immigrated to Italy. Most of these books are in diary form and document the autobiographical struggles of Africans or East Europeans who travel throughout Italy or make Italy their new home. This phenomenon is in the process of evolution, but the literature it has already generated offers the promise of producing a body of work of great interest. Because of the current growth of the multicultural population in Italy, this kind of literature is destined to become a fixture of twenty-first-century Italian culture.[1]

Even though the literary output of these new immigrants might not yet have created an enormous body of work or vast outpourings of scholarly analysis, the cultural impact of this new wave of non-Italian migratory tales written in Italian has provoked rethinking about the concepts of migration, exile, and frontier literature in Italian culture. Up to the 1990s, Italian scholarship had rarely perceived the themes of migration and frontier as two faces of the same literary phenomenon. The sense of estrangement and of otherness experienced in both situations was seldom recognized as an interrelated

---

[1] For discussions of this phenomenon, see: Laura Ruberto, "Immigrants Speak: Italian Literature from the Border," *Forum Italicum* 1 (1997), pp. 127–44; Armando Gnisci, *La letteratura italiana della migrazione* (Rome: Lilith, 1998); Gian Paolo Biasin, *Le periferie della letteratura* (Ravenna: Longo, 1997); and Jean-Jacques Marchand, ed., *La letteratura dell'emigrazione. Gli scrittori di lingua italiana nel mondo* (Turin: Edizioni della Fondazione Agnelli, 1991). For an Italian anthology of some of these new writers, see *La lingua strappata* (Milan: Leocavallo Libri, 1999); some English translations may be found in Graziella Parati, ed., *Mediterranean Crossroads: Migration Literature in Italy* (Madison: University of Wisconsin Press, 1999). For more general considerations of the theoretical implications of this subject, see the works by Said and Kristeva in the list of books for further reading at the end of this chapter.

reflection of a broader condition of exile. For decades, Italian critics maintained a sociological approach to the subject that defined the experience of estrangement narrated by an emigrant turned writer as nothing like that of an expatriate writer.[2] This critical attitude had deep roots in modern Italian history. The century-long tradition of exiled writers and intellectuals that began during the Risorgimento and continued through the decades leading up to the Second World War identified exile with a political condition much more than an existential one. Furthermore, the endemic economic crises between the last quarter of the nineteenth century and the period immediately following the end of the Second World War that forced masses of indigent Italians to leave Italy in search of work abroad tied the idea of emigration to a sense of economic desperation. In fact, until recently, the Italian legal system defined an "emigrant" as somebody who left Italy in search of "hard labor."[3]

Such a definition denied any intellectual choice or activity to the life of the emigrant and excluded anyone with a modicum of education who might aspire to something other than manual labor. Such legal and cultural prejudices produced discussions that focused primarily upon the writer's social origins or the content of the literary works produced. If a writer went into exile or left Italy, because of circumstances other than strict financial necessity, such individuals were rarely seen as encompassed by the general definition of the migrant writer. Moreover, also excluded from such discussions were the literary works produced by foreign-born writers who wrote in Italian or Italian writers who operated in a frontier-like situation at the intersections between different cultures and languages.

Initially, scholarly attention devoted to the presence of foreign-born writers who grew up in non-Italian-speaking countries (North Africa, Senegal), or in areas where Italian is a minority language (Croatia, Albania, Somalia) thus followed a sociological approach, focusing attention upon the content of this literature and the tales of poverty behind their narratives. A few scholars, however, have begun to ponder the theoretical implications and the eventual effects of such a literary phenomenon. Foreign emigrants can write in Italian and can choose Italian as their literary language regardless of the content of their works, and yet, inevitably, they carry within their works a cultural world that cannot be explained by the mainstream of Italian literature. These authors' migratory status, their presence at the crossroads of different languages and cultures, lead them to find their voices in Italian.

[2] For a different view of the dualism between migration and exile, see Joseph Brodsky's "The Condition of Exile," in *On Grief and Reason* (New York: Noonday Press, 1995).

[3] Marchand, *La letteratura dell'emigrazione*, p. xviii, n. 2.

To understand the works of these authors, one must keep in mind the indissoluble union between migration and frontier, between crossing the border and longing to be back on the other side. Such characteristics belong to any writer who crosses a border, who chooses a language other than his or her own to express a world that was conceived in a different idiom, regardless of his or her social background. This is why recent scholars have distinguished between the *literature of migration* and the *literature of immigration*. The latter includes works written on the subject of immigration by nonimmigrant writers, while the former embodies works by immigrant writers regardless of the subject matter of their works. Even when a shift of geographical and national location does not involve a change in the literary language, there is an inevitable exchange of different cultures: an Australian novelist may write in the same language as an Irish author or a writer from Kenya, but he or she represents another world entirely.

The contrast between language and culture is also at the core of the literature of frontier, in which an author writes about his or her daily multicultural experiences for an audience that speaks the same language as the writer. But this audience is far removed from such a diverse cultural condition. Despite the common language, the readers learn about an unfamiliar reality that is as familiar to the writer as the language he or she and his or her audience share. Both the writer and the readers cross an invisible cultural frontier and meet on a bridge that joins two different borders, although the language spoken is the same on both sides of the frontier. But if crossing a border is always a migration of different cultural existences, when a writer chooses a language different from his or her native tongue, the crossing implies the loss of a secret world that is now transposed into a new idiom. Such an operation implies the alienating experience typical of the expatriate writer who writes in a language that is not his or her native tongue, no matter how well it may eventually be learned. On the other hand, it may well be true that when an immigrant writer is established abroad but continues to write in his or her native language, this may be an equally alienating experience, since the chosen literary language corresponds to an old, not a new, existential reality. Writing in a nonnative language indicates an awareness of having migrated from one place to another, but it also infers an internal frontier between the old and the new languages. The migrant writer knows that to fuel his or her works, he or she must travel back and forth across the border.

A number of interesting writers deserve to be analyzed for their eloquent expression of a multicultural experience. They include Swiss-born Fleur Jaeggy (1940–); Hungarian-born Giorgio Pressburger (1937–) and Edith Bruck (1932–); and Enzo Bettiza (1926–), born in what was once called Spalato (today Split) on the Dalmatian coast of Croatia. Another equally interesting group of writers operate at the crossroads of cultures: Claudio Magris (1939–) from the border city of Trieste; and Paolo Maurensig (1943–) from the border city of Gorizia. These writers were formed either within a culture different from that reflected by the Italian language (for example, the Hungary of Pressburger and Bruck) or in a bilingual or even trilingual situation (the case with Jaeggy, Bettiza, Magris, and Maurensig).[4]

It is not my intention to minimize or eliminate the cultural and intellectual differences between these authors who have achieved both critical and public success at different stages of their careers and in dissimilar ways. They are all still active and may yet produce their most important works. Furthermore, not all of them are primarily novelists: some are poets (Bruck), playwrights (Magris, Pressburger), and almost all produce short fiction of high quality, in addition to being novelists. But they are united by the fact that the themes of frontier, migration, and, therefore, exile, characterize each of their lives and works. They all cross borders in one direction or another and often seem to be aware that the frontier is an ambiguous symbol. As Magris puts it, the frontier can serve either as a bridge or as a barrier.[5] Crossing a border implies a linguistic choice: Italian becomes the linguistic vehicle to interrogate their original world (Bruck, Bettiza, Pressburger) or to reach out to geographical dimensions other than the ones usually represented in that language (Jaeggy, Magris, Maurensig). Fleur Jaeggy's works play around the inner despair of a superficially perfect but psychologically shaken Switzerland in a language (Italian) that seems far removed from the original German-speaking environment scrutinized by her eye. In her books, Edith Bruck treats the perpetual refugee status of Holocaust survivors who never feel at home anywhere. Pressburger draws his narrative from the solid roots of Budapest's Jewish district as the only place where his characters may feel at home, despite the international setting of many of his works. Magris moves from Trieste and its multilingual history to explore the intellectual intersections

---

4 Other foreign-born writers who have achieved a certain critical success are the Iraqi-born novelist Younis Tawfik (1957–) and the Slovak Jarmila Ockayovà (1955–), but space prohibits an in-depth examination of their works here. Tawfik lives in Turin and is both a journalist and a scholar of Arab literature. He is active in the Italian Islamic intellectual community and his novel *La straniera* (The Stranger, 1999) describes two very different Arab immigrants who meet in a multiethnic Turin. One is a young architect from the Middle East who has studied in Italy and has found a good job; the other is a young woman, also from the Middle East, who is forced to prostitute herself to survive. Ockayovà lives in Reggio Emilia, another northern Italian town with a large multiethnic population. She has written several novels and the most successful one is her first, *Verrà la vita e avrà i tuoi occhi* (Life Will Come and Will Have Your Eyes, 1997), a story of the friendship of two young women who meet in a train. Her recent novel, *Requiem per tre padri* (Requiem for Three Fathers, 1998), is set in the former Czechoslovakia in 1969, one year after the Soviet invasion.

5 Claudio Magris, *Utopia e disincanto* (Milan: Garzanti, 1999), p. 52.

of a *Mitteleuropa* formed around and by the River Danube on the one hand, and by the Adriatic on the other. Bettiza stresses the ideological simplicity and cultural intricacy of the Italian-Slavic-Austrian-Venetian environment of his Dalmatian childhood. Maurensig explores the racial tragedies that have shaken Austria and Germany in the first part of the twentieth century.

The works of Fleur Jaeggy, born in Zurich and a resident of Locarno before moving to Italy, are often written in a fragmented style that seems translated into Italian. This style does not derive from a lack of syntactical structure but from its implicit connection to the environment depicted, usually German-speaking Switzerland with its Lutheran Protestant culture. For instance, the first ten lines of her opening tale in the short story collection *La paura del cielo* (*Last Vanities*, 1994) are broken into thirteen sentences. Such a fragmented style is atypical of Italian prose, but it is well suited for a story that narrates the life of a frustrated person unable to achieve her dreams without destroying them or the dreams of others. Often the author employs biblical language and images to emphasize the conflict between the simple natural setting of the narrated events and their anthropological complexity. She also emphasizes a contrast between the external search for order (symbolized by Switzerland's perfect gardens, clean roads, and smiling people), on the one hand, and the turbulence and unhappiness underneath the individual lives of her various protagonists. Her fragmentary style unveils a tension between the supposedly idyllic exterior life and the internal conflict of her characters. They are either broken by the weight of this search for normality at all costs, or wounded by their difficult status as outsiders in a society that does not easily accept difference.

In Jaeggy's most important novel to date, *I beati anni del castigo* (*Sweet Days of Discipline*, 1989), the reader is surrounded by a direct and precise narrative style, as incisive as the scalpel of a surgeon. Its plot follows the memoir of an alumna of a Swiss boarding school. It is a typical Swiss boarding school in its severity and its hypocritically democratic discipline that supposedly shapes the lives of spoiled children. Indirectly, the narrator recounts the life of one of these children, Frédérique, who stands out from her other schoolmates because of her unusual search for perfection, as well as her secretive and fascinating character. Frédérique is very independent, a leader who does not care for the material and psychological support that other teenagers usually need. She aspires only to what is essential in life and will do so to the point of renouncing anything which is not necessary to her keen aesthetic sense. The novel's conclusion is consistent with Jaeggy's belief that life makes no sense, is an irrational race against time, and is, indeed, consumed by time. What we think we learn and can use to shed light upon the contradictions of life ultimately results in the absence of light, or blindness. The boarding school, an institution that should provide the knowledge and wisdom to deal with life, becomes transformed into an institution for those who cannot see on more than merely a physical level. In fact, all Jaeggy's characters seem to look for darkness or seem to prefer to live and operate in the shadows. The only light that is disclosed and allows the characters to see reality is twilight, the light that appears just before darkness falls, which allows her protagonists to see only the surface or silhouette of things without revealing their interior dimensions. The repetition and imitation that surround life are manifested in the protagonist's love for cinema and for the movie theaters with their dark rooms that open up to the light of the screen, where life is depicted on the silver screen as though it were real. What makes this novel extremely interesting is its extraordinary prose, marked by short and segmented sentences that embody Jaeggy's concept of life as a broken, repetitive, and useless fight against the consuming passage of time. These stylistic characteristics are also visible in Jaeggy's last work, *Proleterka* (Proleterka, 2001). The title derives from the name of a cruise ship carrying German-speaking tourists from Venice to Greece. It recounts the difficult relationship between a daughter and her father, expressed through the fiction of a secret diary that witnesses the frustrations and the aspirations of the protagonist. Once again, Jaeggy's disjunctive prose serves the construction of such a tormented character well. Jaeggy develops her plots and characters by entrusting them to an essential prose that distills her images and the ambience of her protagonists while magnifying the contrasts between her language of choice (Italian) and the non-Italian atmospheres of her narratives.

The feelings of estrangement, alienation, and of not belonging that pervade Jaeggy's works can also be detected in the works of Giorgio Pressburger and Edith Bruck. Jaeggy's depiction of the frustration of life's contradictions – the contrast between the overstructured Swiss society and the shadowy uncertainties that devour individual lives – is greatly complicated in the two Hungarian-born writers by their Jewish origins. Both Pressburger and Bruck treat the Holocaust in many of their works, but they do so differently. An Auschwitz survivor, Bruck was born Edith Steinschreiber in a small town in Hungary. She was deported at the age of twelve, and after the war she left Hungary and lived in Israel for a few years before moving to Italy in 1954. Pressburger grew up in Budapest's vibrant eighth district, the title of his first book *Storie dell'ottavo distretto* (*Homage to the Eighth District: Tales from Budapest*, 1986), a work co-authored with his twin brother Nicola. The brothers escaped from Hungary after the Soviet invasion of 1956 and came to Italy, entering the peninsula like many other expatriates from Eastern Europe through the border city of Trieste.

Survival is the main theme of Bruck's novels, a theme she investigates in all its anthropological ramifications. The Holocaust is obviously central to her autobiographical works, such as *Chi ti ama così* (*Who Loves You Like This*, 1959), but it also fuels her fictional works, even when this historical tragedy seems far removed from them. This is the case in two novels – *Nuda proprietà* (Naked Property, 1993) and *L'attrice* (The Actress, 1995) – that slowly unveil the sense of dislocation and alienation caused by the trauma of the Holocaust. *Nuda proprietà* describes an eviction and its consequences: its protagonist, Anna Wolf, is a Jewish journalist who has lived in Rome most of her life. She is forced to leave the beloved rented apartment in which she has lived for decades, causing in her the return of the perennial idea of being rootless, the fear of reliving what her family went through during the Second World War, and what her people have experienced for centuries. To overcome these feelings, she decides to buy a house from an elderly antisemitic German lady, Frau Kremer. Anna agrees to live in one part of the house while the other part will remain Frau Kremer's until the old lady dies. When Anna moves in, she reveals her ethnic and cultural identity, but Frau Kremer pretends not to hear or to understand. The protagonist of *L'attrice*, Linda Stone, is an actress in decline attempting to return to the spotlight by unveiling her painful secret. She is a Holocaust survivor who has changed her name: for her, the fiction of acting represents the only way to remove the reality of her terrible past. After she reveals that she is a camp survivor, she is offered a part in a film shot on site at Dachau. She accepts but as she returns to the spot that feeds her memories with nightmares, she realizes that returning is a mistake that will cost her her identity. Both *Nuda proprietà* and *L'attrice* deal with the multiple personalities caused by a forced and traumatic relocation. Paradoxically, this traumatic event provides the protagonists with an identity – so long as they do not challenge it. Both novels stress the otherness of being a foreigner, an outsider continuously recognized by his or her name or by his or her unfamiliar accent. Bruck's protagonists have an additional and secret motive to feel "elsewhere" – their link to the Holocaust. Similar themes may be found in what is the most intense of Bruck's works, *Transit* (Transit, 1978). The protagonist of this short novel, Linda Weinberg, is a Hungarian Holocaust survivor living in Italy, who works as a consultant for a film on the concentration camps. When she goes to a Communist country near the border of Hungary for the shooting of the film, everything seems to fall apart. She finds it extremely difficult to communicate with the American film crew, who want to alter the reality of the events that occurred in the camps. The local population attack her for her ethnicity, but this time not because she is Jewish, but because she is from Hungary, a country that collaborated with the Nazis during the Second World War. Insurmountable barriers exist everywhere, even between her and the Jewish doctor who seems eager and capable of assisting her. Even her knowledge of several languages is of little use to her and makes her appear to be an imposter attempting to conceal her true identity. By the novel's conclusion, Bruck makes it clear that her protagonist does not even belong in Italy, the country in which she lives. She is merely a person in transit. Bruck's novels display the anxiety of a writer who has chosen a language (Italian) in which to express her own inner world, a world that cannot find a home in any language. Her choice to write in Italian, and not in her native tongue (Hungarian) or in the learned language of her ethnic background (Hebrew), suggests that her choice is motivated by an attempt to find a linguistic and cultural balance to counter, and at the same time to filter out, the agonizing memories caused by her forced migrations.

Budapest and its eighth district, mostly inhabited by Jews, are at the center of many of Pressburger's works, especially his tales and short stories. Pressburger's books are written in an elegant Italian, but they always convey the feeling that they have been conceived elsewhere, in a different intellectual universe. This diverse linguistic dimension is as ambivalent as his Habsburg birthplace, with its mixture of Slavic and Austrian qualities. This already multicultural territory is enriched by the Jewish experience, sometimes expressed within autobiographical boundaries, and this locale serves as a literary source to be recounted and narrated, while on other occasions Pressburger's settings explore an existential condition typical of many central European intellectuals. Pressburger is equally at ease and at home in narrating episodes based upon Jewish folkloric tradition and other stories connected to the scars of the Holocaust. One of his constant themes is the dream. His characters, as is often found in the Jewish tradition, dream and consume their time trying to interpret or to follow the dreams' messages, even when the dreams sometimes have a devastating effect on the characters' lives. Dreams transport the mind into temporary realms that differ from life; they are a metaphor of the human condition rebelling against reality. Dreams make up part of the literary process that opposes the linguistic center of Pressburger's works: he chooses the daily language of his contemporary reality – Italian, a language not his own – to recover his own lost reality in his past, a world as remote and fragile as a dream. The migration from Budapest is an open wound that bleeds images of a past that was never without its problems and that hides the tragedy of the Holocaust in the background. Nonetheless, the departure from Budapest is the main event that changed the writer's life, an event that brings the past to life through a new language. For Pressburger, writing in a different language is the only way the author can describe the world of his childhood, a world that fuels his entire narrative, as his prose balances between the will to narrate and the desire to explain the double diversity of his Hungarian and Jewish world. In addition to this cultural ambivalence, Giorgio Pressburger has the biographical complication of another double – his twin brother Nicola, a financial journalist and analyst who died in 1985. Giorgio left Hungary with Nicola, the co-author of Pressburger's first two books: *Storie dell'ottavo distretto*, and the novel *L'elefante verde* (*The Green Elephant*, 1988). These two works, along with *La legge degli spazi bianchi* (*The Law of White Spaces*, 1989), *I due gemelli* (The Twins, 1996), *La neve e la colpa* (*Snow and Guilt*, 1999), and *Di vento e di fuoco* (Of Wind and Fire, 2000), confirm the suspicion that Pressburger's literary reference points are derived from a world that precedes his arrival in Italy. Even keeping Nicola's name on his books signals how strongly Pressburger's writing clings to the contrast between the "before" and "after" of his emigration, an experience he shared with his brother. Between editing and revising, in the case of the early works, or later when Pressburger attributes to Nicola some of the stories he recounts more than a decade after his brother's death, one may well wonder how much of Nicola's hand can be detected in Giorgio's literary production. More than co-authorship, then, the discerning critic can envision almost a double personality, the trace of the presence of the other half of a set of brothers that functioned as an integral part of an intellectual process experienced and debated together. This double presence is evident in *L'elefante verde*, an intense autobiographical novel, which tells the complicated story of twins – Samuele and Beniamino – who are destined to succeed. The green elephant appears in a dream to their grandfather who hears from the rabbi that it is a sign of peace and prosperity in the family. The prophecy never comes to pass for the twins' grandfather or for their father, Isacco, who manages to survive the Holocaust and to pass the torch of the prophecy to his sons. Far away from home, the twins achieve their dreams of success: one becomes a banker, the other an actor and a director. When the father is able to travel and visit his children, he discovers that the one who was destined to be an economist, Samuele, is now the actor, and Beniamino, predisposed to be an actor, is now the banker. The prophecy was fulfilled but in an unexpected fashion. The migration, the acquisition of a new culture, and the use of a new language have reversed the anticipated roles of the twins. As the novel draws to a close, during the funeral of the father, the narrative voice of the novel – never previously associated with the twins – suddenly changes to the first-person voice of Beniamino. Beniamino claims that he also speaks on behalf of Samuele who is too busy acting and staging plays, and could not participate in the writing of their story. This finale substantiates the ambivalent relationship with the double and its implicit ties to the duplicity and divisiveness of migration. The autobiographical subject invites us to surmise that the economist Nicola, and not the artistic Giorgio (as one may have expected), was the driving force behind Pressburger's writing. The transposition of roles underlines the twisted truth about writers who cross the frontier but continue to write about the same fears and pleasures of a world they have lost and that, when commuted into a different language, becomes like a dream. That world, when recounted, may be good or bad, truthful or not.

The desolation of the Holocaust and the inconveniences of nomadic life imposed upon the wounded psyche of a survivor shape the structure of Pressburger's last novel, *Di vento e di fuoco*. Sara, a young Italian woman on the verge of giving birth to her first child, asks her mother (after whom she is named) and the other three women who lived with him about her father Andreas, a Holocaust survivor obsessed by the search for the "truth" of life. The four women send her faxes, letters, and emails that describe their relationships with her father. Unexpectedly, through one of the women, Sara's father contacts his daughter from a Jerusalem Hospital where he is recovering from burns and multiple fractures – perhaps a casual victim of the violence that rules the "sacred land" – and where he dies the day his daughter gives birth. From the messages Sara receives, we learn that her American father was actually born a Jew in a central European city that can only indirectly be identified with Budapest. Having barely escaped death during the Second World War, after a few years in Israel, he leaves to look for his mother, who has apparently survived the Holocaust, and he is then adopted by an American family. He later joins the American Air Force and he is sent to Italy, to Sicily where he meets Sara's mother. They marry and move to the United States but, when he suddenly disappears, the pregnant young woman moves back to Italy, where ten years later Andreas reappears with another woman and child. He then disappears again and again until he makes the final contact from Israel. From the letters, Sara learns about her mother and the tormented lives of the other three women. Two of them – Rachele and Rivcà – were born in the multilingual territories of the former Yugoslavia; the third woman – Lia – is an Italian Jew.

Di vento e di fuoco is a dense epistolary novel, and, at times, the various letters are like autonomous tales that need to be reconnected to the simple plot and to the general fabric of the book. The book is permeated with symbolism, and its main theme is the search for the truth, for a Promised Land of knowledge where everything makes sense and can be explained. As in other Pressburger books, dreams, visions, and names are fundamental elements of the narration. The alienation and estrangement of the father is enclosed in his name. There is a passage in the book in which Andreas, in line with Jewish tradition, mentions the importance of words, and how they create and share the meaning of life. Ironically, the adoptive family renames him Andreas, in German, the language of the people who oppressed and destroyed his family. But his real name was Gershon, the name of Moses' first child, a name meaning "stranger in a strange land." Both names are perfect omens. Andreas is an omen in reverse because, according to its Greek roots, the name captures all the attributes that define masculinity as virile and brave. Pressburger's novel informs us, however, that his character Andreas is perpetually running away, never accepting responsibility for his relationships, and cries incessantly for help. Unlike his father Moses, Gershon did reach the Promised Land, as does the new Gershon who dies in Israel, but the meaning of the name, tied to the exodus of his people, underlines his status as a constant foreigner. He is, indeed, a stranger in a strange land. He does not belong to the European country where he was born and that violently rejected him and his people, nor does he belong to his adopted country, the United States. He cannot find rest in Italy, where he lives for many years as a nomad without a fixed residence, and even Israel, where he dies, seems to be a temporary shelter, as he requests to be buried in Italy. The names and the number of the women – four like the four elements – are also extremely significant for the symbolism of the novel. Sara is Abraham's wife, the mother of Isaac, father of Jacob, founder of the twelve tribes of Israel. Jacob married two sisters, Rachel and Leah – in Italian Rachele and Lia – and had two servant-wives, Bilhah, Rachel's maid, and Zilpah, Leah's maid: a total of four wives. We know that Jacob, self-exiled from his own homeland, before returning wrestles with an angel who renames him "Israel" (this name means "he who wrestled with God and with men and won"). Andreas–Gershon, not unlike his ancestor Jacob, escaped from Israel and wrestled all his life to make sense of humanity and of the divine, and went back to Israel after many years to complete his journey. Perhaps it is not a coincidence that the last letter Sara receives is from Rachele, mother of Sara's half-brother, whose name, we learn in this last letter, is Gabriel – the same as the archangel of the Annunciation. Pressburger's "stranger in a strange land" speaks many languages, including the Hebrew of his ancestors, but he requires Italian to communicate the results of his search. He exposes the instinctual world of his cultural roots through the learned language of his second existence.

The same inner knowledge and passionate will to defeat memory and bring forward one's own past characterize the works of Enzo Bettiza. Born in the Dalmatian city of Split, but a city he calls by its Italian name of Spalato, Bettiza has a mixed ethnic background: his mother was Serbian, while his father was of Italian descent. As Bettiza puts it, Dalmatia was the Mediterranean counterpart to the continental *Mitteleuropa*, and he lived in Spalato for the first eighteen years of his life before going into life-long exile in June 1945, when most of the last Italian families of the region were forced to leave their land forever. In his autobiographical memoir, *Esilio* (Exile, 1996), Bettiza highlights the historical and cultural complexities of a city where, before the beginning of the Second World War, one could hear people speaking Italian, Venetian dialect, Croatian, Serbian, and German, according to the speaker's ethnic or cultural background. Bettiza did not originally conceive *Esilio* as a novel but as an account of what led up to the senseless ethnic war of the early 1990s. However, the book reads like a historical novel with a strong autobiographical twist. Bettiza's use of oral sources, as well as his narration of the endless adventures and episodes describing the family's history from the Napoleonic Wars to the Second World War, broaden the perspective and the scope of what might have remained a personal memoir into a novel with historical dimensions. Bettiza maps out the intellectual story of the region, weaving family events throughout, and singling out relatives, friends, and private and public figures as if they were characters in a novel. The writer explores the cultural and linguistic intricacies of the Adriatic region, which was an important center of the Roman Empire and which, in more modern times, belonged to the Republic of Venice, to the Napoleonic empire, and then to the Austrian Empire until 1918. Although it is difficult today to grasp the numerous linguistic solutions and cultural contradictions of a multicultural world with such strong ethnic identities and very different languages, Bettiza touches upon some of these contradictions and colors them with irony – an irony masking his pessimism. Typical of the paradoxes of life in this region was the case of Bettiza's father and uncles during the First World War. While they grew up thinking of themselves as Italians, they were Austrian citizens who served in the Austrian army against Italy. After the collapse of the Austrian Empire, they opted for Italian citizenship, becoming practically foreigners in their own land, which by then had become part of Yugoslavia. In fact, after the war, one of Bettiza's uncles became openly pro-Italian despite the fact that, during the war, he had been wounded by an Italian bullet that had left him with badly damaged lungs.

Bettiza's book is really a novel about exile, about the feeling of estrangement of a person growing up as a member of an ethnic minority in a land that he calls home but where other languages prevail. The resulting feelings of alienation become even more complicated when he is forced to leave his multicultural birthplace forever. Bettiza concludes that the contradictions of the Austrian Empire, with its enlarged citizenship that did not deprive a Dalmatian or a Hungarian or a Czech of his ethnicity, was preferable to the distinct sense of nationhood later introduced, a nationhood that attempted to eradicate cultural differences and led to the violent suppression of minorities. Bettiza's book is a welcome fresco that demonstrates the necessity to shed one's own monolinguistic and monocultural approach to the world in which one lives. While a book may be written in Italian, Bettiza reminds us that the book may also depend upon a world that relates to another culture and that did not find its primary expression in Italian, as is the case with Bettiza's Dalmatia.

The subtle mixture of cultures and languages in Pressburger's and Bettiza's works is also evident in the works of Paolo Maurensig and Claudio Magris. Neither author was born outside Italy, but within its most northeastern boundaries. They belong to the class of writers who examine the clash and blend of different cultures with the eyes of those who observe a foreign territory from the other side, through the lens of a powerful telescope. This keen observation of movements, customs, and habits of the people on the other side of the border helps us realize and understand that their actions and ways of life are not so dissimilar from ours after all.

Maurensig's two best-known novels, *La variante di Lüneburg* (*The Lüneberg Variation*, 1993) and *Canone inverso* (*Canone Inverso*, 1998), cut across the territory of the former Austrian Empire throughout the twentieth century. Both novels enter the intricate subterranean vessels of the cultural fabric that first produced the Holocaust and later sought to normalize life all too quickly after this horrific crime. The conflict between this guilty normalization and the painful need to remember makes up the theme of both narratives. Maurensig was born in the border town of Gorizia, a town strongly imbued with Austrian and Slovenian culture. His novels' plots and atmospheres cross the border with ease and reconstruct both the historical Austrian environment and the contemporary setting with equal grace and precision. The first novel, probably his best, opens with the apparent suicide of a rich German industrialist who lives between his apartment in Munich, where he works, and his elegant farm near Vienna. The deceased, a healthy sixty-eight-year-old man, was a chess expert, and near his body lies a strange chessboard made of rugs, a chessboard abandoned in the middle of a game. From here, the story develops through the tales of two characters, one young and one old, who share a passion for the game of chess. The intriguing plot narrates a chess duel between two prominent young players, a Nazi and a Jew, which began in Germany and Austria before the last world war and went on through the inhumanity of the initial campaigns of racial discrimination and later through the horror of the concentration camps. This eerie competition had two similar conclusions diluted by time, one during the war, and one many years later with the suicide that opens the novel. In both cases, the duels were surrounded by death. The reason for the title of the book is not revealed until the very last line of the novel. Maurensig acutely portrays the contrast between the elegance of the world of chess and the vulgar antisemitism penetrating even that intellectual environment. But his narrative also contains dense descriptions of the Holocaust seen through the tormented thoughts of a survivor.

Canone inverso begins with an auction: there, a man buys a splendid violin that mysteriously belonged to a street musician named Jeno Varga. From this opening event, the narrative passes in a descending spiral that dissects the class-biased and racist world of music in 1930s Vienna. At the core of the plot there is the friendship between two young violin students – the rich Kuno and the poor Jeno – a friendship that sours. Varga's violin conceals a secret that causes turmoil, bans the talented musician from the world of grand music, and renders him a wandering street musician in Vienna for the rest of his life.

Both novels have the typical allusive language of a thriller, but they also convey an elegant and detached style that is perfectly capable of recreating the Austro-Germanic world of the stories. In fact, Maurensig's novels have a twofold character: while they are written in Italian, they deal with non-Italian subject matter with the knowledge of an insider, a native speaker. This insider's vision of another world outside that of the novel's language is not only evident in the skillful depiction of the characters and of their environment, but it is above all clear from the sophisticated psychological analysis of what lies beneath the historical behavior of an entire society. The writer is aware of his privileged position: he takes full advantage of his post near the frontier boundary that allows him to look over at the territory there and to appreciate all the details of the other side of the border. He narrates like an insider even though he stays on his side of the border. He is perfectly conscious of belonging, linguistically, to the Italian tradition, but he is also aware of being a part of a broader intellectual zone that permeates both edges of the frontier. Maurensig's ability to move back and forth between the contemporary world and the period before the Second World War is matched by his gifted shift between cultures inside himself, as he moves from one dimension of the border territory to the other. In his hands, Italian becomes the perfect tool to scrutinize the historical and cultural spaces that he observes and discovers through his telescope.

A well-known scholar of Austrian and German literature, Claudio Magris uses his hometown of Trieste as his outpost, as a lighthouse with which he sheds light on the darkness of the other side. Magris may be the major Italian essayist to treat the subject of frontier, exile, and migration. He is certainly the Italian writer who has most discussed the importance of studying geo-cultural communities as a whole, regardless of the different languages with which they are composed. His works analyze the laceration of the Holocaust, the cultural conflicts and affinities of the German-speaking populations of the Austrian Empire, the Italianate instability of the people of the former Yugoslavia, and the general inclusiveness identifiable in specific intellectual traits forming what Italians call the culture of *Mitteleuropa*. Emblematic of these themes is *Un altro mare* (*A Different Sea*, 1991), a short novel treating a geographical area that now belongs to Italy, Slovenia, and Croatia but that was still Austrian during the novel's unfolding. It is the story of a young scholar of ancient Greek, Enrico Mreule, who follows the premises of a pact established with two other friends: to live according to one's own free spirit. Enrico migrates to Argentina and comes back many years later to spend his last days on a small island, little more than a sea-rock, in the Istrian Adriatic Sea. Enrico's life traverses the collapse of the Austrian Empire as well as the horror of the Second World War. The ambivalence of Enrico's life – formed by a mixture of different cultures – is captured by the book's title as well as the very beginning of the book. There is the "other sea" – the immense ocean that stands in contrast to the enclosed wedge of the upper Adriatic – but there is also the other culture and the other language. The novel opens with an inscription, in Greek – "virtue brings honor" – translated into German. This epigraph is on the door of the Imperial Lyceum of Gorizia, the school Enrico and his friends attended. It is in this gray building that Enrico's destiny sets its course. Such a beginning integrates and responds to the oceanographic image of the title: there are two seas, but there are also two lands, actually a mixture of lands and languages that will come apart during Enrico's absence. It is at an Austrian Lyceum that Enrico develops his love for the Greek classics, his Western cultural roots that come from only a few hundred miles south, and it is in this same Lyceum that he decides to leave its multifaceted roots in search of new and open spaces. The last pages of the book are probably the best, with the figure of the elderly Enrico who scrutinizes the horizons of the suffocating Adriatic Sea of his childhood, a sea that, after two cruel wars, is now indeed another sea.

Many of Magris's works analyze the disquieting and restless representation of the variegated cultural stratification inherited by the Austrian Empire. *Danubio* (*Danube*, 1986) is a meditation and exploration of the historical memory, of the intricate correlation between places, figures, and the geographical and geological course of the river. Magris crosses and cuts through the heart of *Mitteleuropa*, of that series of cultures and languages shaped by Austrian rule, but molded, above all, by its majestic river, the Danube. It is a journey that touches well-known places and that discovers the importance of forsaken plains or riverbeds that have witnessed the ferocity and the benevolence of human events. From the Black Forest to Vienna, from Budapest to

Belgrade, from Bucharest to the estuary in the Black Sea, the river embraces and marks the limits of the old Habsburg world just as the Mediterranean marks and demarcates the ancient world. Magris's eye digs out of the waters of the river legends and historical facts imaginary and real figures, weaving them all together. Cultural history and events are respected, but they become part of a fluid narrative. Famous and obscure people, as well as the cities, the places, the geographical entities of the river come alive like the characters of a novel. One of the work's most intriguing aspects is the conflict between the unity of its subject (a geocultural examination of the River Danube) and the diversity of the themes and places narrated. This conflicting aspect is the key to the book: the unity of the river, its incessant creation of civilization with its share of wars and tragedies, corresponds to the broad unity of the Austrian Empire, while the diverse landscapes correspond to the cultural differences that enrich such an entity. Ultimately, the Danube is a pole that attracts and explains different cultures. Literature is seen as the navigation and exploration of the self and of the reality in front of us in which the national tradition gives way to a geographical itinerary. The quest and the journey are symbols of the otherness represented by the author's language, because it is the only point of reference to the other side, to his original point of departure. After a few pages the reader forgets that the author has to go back occasionally, that this long journey cannot be a continuous trip, but that it, too, must have its rests, its pauses, its episodes, its delays caused by the necessity of setting the experience down on paper.

In the last pages of the book, the itinerant narrator reaches the end of the Danube and observes the manmade estuary that channels the river toward an official, visible, and useful entry into the sea. The Danube port authority imposes rules and regulations that create a specific structure and a precise code imposed upon the free-flowing river. But if we look at the other side of the delta, not yet manipulated by human hands, we do not see strict rules or a defined human grammar of what a delta should be. Everything is mixed up, as it should be. It is almost impossible to distinguish the point where the estuary becomes the sea or river, or where the river becomes delta. This contrasting image between an inclusive and extended view and one that defines and channels is an image that explains, better than any other metaphor, the role and the place of the authors analyzed here in the Italian literary scene of today.

Further reading

Brodsky, Joseph. *On Grief and Reason*. New York: Noonday Press, 1995.
Bruck, Edith. *Who Loves You Like This*. Trans. Thomas Kelso. Philadelphia: Paul Dry Books, 2001.

Jaeggy, Fleur. *Sweet Days of Discipline*. Trans. Tim Parks. New York: New Directions, 1993.

Last Vanities. Trans. Tim Parks. New York: New Directions, 1998.

Kristeva, Julia. *Strangers to Ourselves*. Trans. Leon Roudiez. New York: Columbia University Press, 1991.

Magris, Claudio. *Danube*. Trans. Patrick Creagh. New York: Farrar, Straus and Giroux, 1989.

Inferences from a Sabre. Trans. Mark Thompson. New York: Braziller, 1991.

A Different Sea. Trans. M. S. Spurr. London: Harvill, 1993.

Maurensig, Paolo. *The Lüneburg Variation*. Trans. John Rothschild. New York: Farrar, Strauss, and Giroux, 1997.

Canone Inverso. Trans. Jenny McPhee. New York: H. Holt, 1998.

Pressburger, Giorgio. *Homage to the Eighth District: Tales from Budapest*. Trans. Gerald Moore. Columbia, LA: Readers International, 1990.

The Law of White Spaces. Trans. Piers Spence. London: Granta and Penguin Books, 1992.

The Green Elephant. Trans. Piers Spence. London: Quartet, 1994.

Snow and Guilt. Trans. Shaun Whiteside. London: Granta, 1998.

Teeth and Spies. Trans. Shaun Whiteside. London: Granta, 1999.

Said, Edward W. *Reflection on Exile and Other Essays*. Cambridge, MA: Harvard University Press, 2000.

14

The new Italian novel

While during the closing decades of the twentieth century the Italian novel was relatively successful, not so long ago, in the 1980s, critics were lamenting the allegedly bleak future of the genre. At the center of this polemical argument about new "young writers" was the controversial statement by Edoardo Sanguineti (1930–) that the style and content of these new writers constituted a useless elegance. Some of the writers under attack were Antonio Tabucchi, Pier Vittorio Tondelli (1955–91), Daniele Del Giudice (1949–), Andrea De Carlo (1952–), Aldo Busi (1948–), and Roberto Pazzi. Paradoxically, to outside observers of the Italian scene in France and Germany, the Italian novel at that moment and in the following years seemed so healthy that foreigners were envious of its successes at home and abroad, and translation of the works of not just Umberto Eco but also of Tabucchi, Alessandro Baricco (1958–), Susanna Tamaro, Paola Capriolo (1962–), and many others began to attract readers from around the world.

It is a puzzling characteristic of the Italian literary scene that contemporary fiction is criticized for its lack of social or political awareness. For example, some academic critics have attacked Umberto Eco's best-selling fiction and those who imitate postmodern pastiche on these grounds. Negative comments appear periodically in the cultural pages of newspapers questioning the validity of the "pulp" or "trash" fiction of so-called literary "cannibals," such as Aldo Nove (1967–), Niccolò Ammaniti (1966–), and their followers. Recently, critics have questioned a complex novel such as *Q*, written by four co-authors answering collectively to the name of Luther Blisset. This unusual book was named one of five finalists for the Strega Literary Prize in 1999 and is a long, intricate and engrossing postmodern historical novel about Martin Luther, the Vatican, papal politics, the Holy Inquisition, and the Counter-Reformation. It recalls, in many ways, Pynchon's *Gravity's Rainbow* (1973), Eco's *Foucault's Pendulum* (1988), and DeLillo's *Underworld* (1997).

Since 1985, several great masters of Italian fiction whose careers began in the first half of the century have died, including Italo Calvino; Elsa Morante; Alberto Moravia; Paolo Volponi (1924–94); Leonardo Sciascia (1921–89); and Goffredo Parise (1929–86). Critics who were accustomed to the novels written by these writers, most of whom were intimately engaged in the social and political life of the peninsula, found it much easier to criticize new writers who had yet to be accepted into the canon, particularly because of what the critics saw as their lack of any ideological message. New writers (Baricco in particular) have sold well with the general public but may well have to wait for some time before academic critics take them seriously enough to include them in their historical scholarship. Perhaps the contemporary Italian novel requires time for conservative critics to abandon their prejudice not only against best-sellers[1] but against all fiction that blatantly reflects a postmodern style in which writers and the public alike are influenced, educated, and conditioned by the media – especially film and television – or by American culture.

In the last decade, Antonio Tabucchi has been the subject of numerous essays, lectures, interviews, translations, international conferences, and doctoral theses. Several of his works have been adapted for film. Tabucchi appears to have escaped the irate comments of conservative critics who have little appreciation of what Roland Barthes has termed the "pleasure of the text," a pleasure that Barthes believed was based in large measure on the author's ability to exploit various elements of literariness in constructing playful fictional worlds. When Sanguineti made his derogatory remarks about writers whose style exhibited a useless elegance, Tabucchi had already published *Il gioco del rovescio* (The Backwards Game, 1981); *Donna di Porto Pim e altre storie* (*The Woman of Porto Pim*, 1983); and *Notturno indiano* (*Indian Nocturne*, 1984). However, these three important texts, as well as his first two novels – *Piazza d'Italia* (1975) and *Il piccolo naviglio* (The Little Vessel, 1978) – had received moderate success with the general public, and Renato Barilli was among the first Italian critics to speak of and to praise Tabucchi's "minimalist" technique, a style associated more often with American than with Italian novels. Nonetheless, from these early texts it was clear that

---

[1] The polemical debate that arose from the commercial success of Elsa Morante's *La Storia* provides an excellent example of how Italian critics regard best-sellers with great suspicion, often considering them as mere marketing ploys by the publishing houses. They look askance at almost any book that sells large numbers of copies. This attitude marked the critical reception not only of Lampedusa's *Il Gattopardo* but also *Il nome della rosa* by Umberto Eco, as well as the novel that rivaled Eco's in sales figures, Susanna Tamaro's *Va dove ti porta il cuore*.

Tabucchi was not primarily concerned with social or political issues. The publication of Tabucchi's *Piccoli equivoci senza importanza* (*Small Misunderstandings of No Importance*, 1985) and *Il filo dell'orizzonte* (*Vanishing Point*, 1986) in the midst of the controversial debates on Italy's "new" writers offered further evidence that Tabucchi's works were not primarily aimed at social commentary.

Tabucchi's playful open-ended metafictional stories certainly contain minor allusions to Italian politics and society. Yet his clever psychological and delightfully ambiguous stories may give the impression of advancing metaliterary and intertextual arguments rather than focusing upon a "message." In *Requiem* (*Requiem*, 1992), a novel Tabucchi wrote originally in Portuguese and had translated into Italian by another hand, there are interesting ironic comments about "minimalism" and "postmodernism." The entire discussion between its narrator and the fictional "Guest" becomes even more revealing if we consider that the author may be talking about himself as being "partly to blame" for the emergence of postmodernist trends in Italy. But given the author's clever and elaborate use of popular media (especially movies), and his constant use of paratextual and intertextual strategies, it is legitimate to wonder whether Tabucchi's criticism of such contemporary literary trends is serious or whether it is merely part of an elaborate critical game – itself part of postmodern style.

Piazza d'Italia and *Il piccolo naviglio* mark Tabucchi's debut as a narrator. These two short picaresque novels deal with the lives, dreams, frustrations, and disillusionments of individuals who stand in sharp contrast to the social, political, and historical events surrounding them and their families. The historical scope of *Piazza d'Italia* covers a period from Italian Unification to the Fascist era. Volturno Banarchist, its protagonist, is a rebel, and, at times, a clairvoyant, and he remains the model for the characters in Tabucchi's work who express a social awareness, individuals that emerge occasionally in his brief theatrical compositions *I dialoghi mancati* (Missed Dialogues, 1988) and in the novel *Marconi, se ben mi ricordo* (Marconi, If I Remember Correctly, 1997), where Tabucchi employs a chorus from the Greek classical theatrical tradition to emphasize a social message.

In *Piazza d'Italia*, characters such as Quarto, Volturno, Garibaldi, or Anita allude to famous protagonists or places during the Risorgimento. In spite of these historical allusions, the author seems not to take any ideological stand on the issues surrounding these historical events. After the interesting portrayals of anarchist and anti-Fascist characters such as Garibaldi and Volturno in *Piazza d'Italia*, we have to wait from 1975 until 1994 for the characters Monteiro Rossi and his girlfriend Marta in *Sostiene Pereira* (*Pereira Declares*, 1994) before we meet real *engagé* characters with clear political concerns. With a few exceptions – such as in the story "Bitterness and Clouds," where we find a left-wing student contrasted to a pro-Franco professor – we have only brief allusions to repressive political regimes in Tabucchi's works.

Thus it is safe to say that Tabucchi's references to social, political, or historical events in *Sostiene Pereira* function primarily as background, framing the private life of the characters. Tabucchi certainly does not overlook the role of history, nor does he tolerate social injustice. Nonetheless, what interests him the most is the construction of the inner turmoil, the anxieties, the doubts, the obsessions, the need to search, the dreams, the existential malaise, and the psychological states of his protagonists.

Several critics have remarked that with Tabucchi's fiction we usually begin and end with an open text. Indeed, more often than not, we begin and remain in the middle of the narrative during the entire story. The author himself underlines for us this particular feature of his fiction, as he prefaces his texts with remarks about the ambiguous relationship between fiction, writing, dreams, and reality, or between ambiguities and truths, or light and darkness. He is careful to suggest that: "stories do not begin, they happen and do not have a beginning...the beginning is only the continuation of another beginning."

In the opening note of *Notturno indiano* Tabucchi links "insomnia" with "traveling." He also extends the realm of the journey to the narrator, the protagonist, and the author in such a way as to suggest autobiographical allusions. In the introductory note of *Piccoli equivoci*, after connecting baroque aesthetics to ambiguity, the author confesses something that could very well provide a summary of his narrative vocation: "I am driven, rather, to seek them out. Misunderstandings, uncertainties, belated understandings, useless remorse, treacherous memories, stupid and irredeemable mistakes, all these irresistibly fascinate me, as if they constituted a vocation, a sort of stigmata...I might be consoled by the conviction that life is by nature ambiguous and distributes ambiguities among all of us." In like manner, the narrator of *Requiem* speaks of writing a nonconcluding story: "I was writing and wondering why I was writing the story I was working on...it was a strange story, a story without a solution...how did I come to be writing it? More than that, the story was changing my life." And in the story "A Riddle," Tabucchi's narrator declares: "I shouldn't be here telling a story proposing a riddle that has no solution." This art of exploiting riddles, puzzles, unsolved mysteries, or ambiguities and uncertainties in general, has become a trademark of the author's remarkable talent for leaving his readers with more questions than answers about the story they have just read.

Among the most important intratextual elements of Tabucchi's fiction we must consider the theme of a quest – the search for someone or for one's own self. In *Notturno indiano*, the connections between the characters Roux, Xavier, and Nightingale, as the narrator clearly suggests, are different aspects of the same self. And in the suspenseful mystery story *Il filo dell'orizzonte*, we again notice how Spino, in searching for the identity of the murdered person, cleverly called Nobodi (echoing the English word "nobody"), may in essence be searching for his self. Just as important are the metaphoric allusions to the sense of guilt or remorse and of *saudade* – a Portuguese word that stands for a nostalgic melancholy defined in *Requiem* as a category of the spirit. *Saudade* and remorse are two key motifs that resurface, unexpectedly, over and over again in several of Tabucchi's characters. Remorse, as we are reminded by the copyist in *Requiem*, is like a virus: "I think herpes is a bit like remorse, it lies dormant within us and then, one fine day, it wakes up and attacks us, then goes to sleep again, only because we've managed to suppress it, but it's always there inside us, there is no cure for remorse."

Postmodern narratives often have links to the detective genre, and Tabucchi's works often contain an element of mystery. Tabucchi's narratives contain a mystery woman named Isabel, who makes her first appearance in *Notturno indiano* when the narrator mentions her name as he states that he has written a letter to her explaining about his trip and how "feelings flower again with time." In *Piccoli equivoci senza importanza*, in the story "Anywhere out of the world," Isabel is discussed clearly in terms of betrayal, remorse, and guilt. And, most interesting, in *L'angelo nero* (The Black Angel, 1991), Isabel is discussed in relation to a mystery novel. In *Requiem*, Isabel is again mentioned but makes no appearance; however, we learn that she has killed herself. Furthermore, in the introductory "Note" to this text, the author speaks about a story that belongs to a novel written a long time ago but put aside for various reasons.

Piccoli equivoci and *Requiem* share several leitmotifs in spite of the years separating their publication. In addition to their definitions and discussions of guilt and remorse, there are also the different definitions of "life" that appear to be related to the author's stories. A few samples from *Piccoli equivoci* should suffice: "life is by nature ambiguous and distributes ambiguities among all of us"; "Life is an appointment... An appointment and a journey"; "[life is] like a woven fabric in which all the threads cross, and what I want one day is to see the whole pattern"; "life's gearbox, a wheel here, a pump there and then the transmission, which links it all up and turns power into movement, yes, just the way it is in life"; "life can't be measured in moral terms, it simply happens." Moreover, in *Gli ultimi tre giorni di Pessoa* (*The Last Three Days of Fernando Pessoa*, 1994), Tabucchi discusses life in similar terms: "life is indecipherable"; "life is a theater of images." And such definitions must be linked to Tabucchi's discussion of literature's relationship to dreams in *Dove va il romanzo?* (Where Is the Novel Going?, 1995): "Literature which is a mirror of life, a reflection of life, evidently is more dream than life. And thus, it is a dream of a dream"; "it is also a projection of desire, to say it with Freud . . . it is a return of the unconscious"; "as Breton has taught us, literature is a unique oneiric space."

Tabucchi enjoys this type of narrative and this kind of textual pleasure explains in part why he has chosen Fernando Pessoa (1888–1935) as his muse. Tabucchi likes the way Pessoa plays with autobiography and fiction and toys with his fictional characters that are essentially different aspects of his own personality. In *Gli ultimi tre giorni di Pessoa*, Tabucchi has the great Portuguese writer commenting on the practice of living through his characters: "to live my life has been like living one thousand lives." Furthermore, Tabucchi admits in *Dove va il romanzo?* that he sees himself as a double of Pessoa and of his characters because "Pessoa is not an author, he is a literature, and this is why I fell in love with him, he has constructed a universe." Writing fiction for Tabucchi is mainly a question of how to create credible possible worlds with repetitions, redundancy, returning characters, leitmotifs, intertextuality, and intriguing paratextual strategies.

Italo Calvino, Jorge Luis Borges, and the French "New" novelists (Alain Robbe-Grillet, Natalie Serraute, and Michel Butor) paved the way for writers such as Tabucchi who are interested in the phenomenological and sensorial perception of reality and in a narrative that is essentially a cognitive process. By the same token, a number of young Italian novelists have been encouraged to follow in Tabucchi's footsteps and to engage in what is essentially postmodern metanarrative by influences from mass media or from such American postmodernists such as Thomas Pynchon, John Barth, Barthelme, and Don DeLillo. The narratives of Aldo Nove, one of the original leaders of the so-called "cannibals" mentioned earlier, have attracted a cult following in Italy. The success of the hilarious *Woobinda* (Woobinda, 1996), *Puerto Plaza Market* (Port Piazza Market, 1997) and *Super Woobinda* (Super Woobinda, 1998) launched a successful career from which young readers began to quote phrases and expressions. Nove is a master at the depiction of contemporary pop culture, television, and film characters, as well as scenes and lines from all sorts of commercials, and his characters never fail to identify themselves with an opening statement about their horoscope sign. In 1996, the anthology *Gioventù cannibale* (Cannibal Youth) appeared, containing works by young writers called "cannibals" by the critics. They presented life in the rawest and most unpretentious fashion possible. A few of these writers whose novels stand out include: Rossana Campo, whose novel

In principio erano le mutande is an account of a southern Italian girl's rebellion against restrictive traditional customs; Giuseppe Culicchia (1964–)
with his account of generational rebellion in *Tutti giù per terra* (We All Fall
Down, 1994) and *Bla bla bla* (Bla Bla Bla, 1997); and the vivacious Silvia
Ballestra (1969–), with her poignantly humorous tales about university life
in *La guerra degli Antó* (The War of the Anthonys, 1992), *Gli orsi* (The
Bears, 1994), and *Compleanno dell'iguana* (The Iguana's Birthday, 1991).

Pier Vittorio Tondelli's two anthologies of writers under twenty-five years
of age called *Giovani blues* (Youth Blues, 1986) and *Belli perversi* (Beautiful
Perverts, 1987) may have started a trend toward searching for new talents
among young authors with this particular "cannibal" style. Tondelli, Andrea
De Carlo, and Enrico Palandri (1956–) are several of the key forerunners of
the youth-oriented new writers that emerged in the 1980s and 1990s. They
popularized the so-called "romanzo generazionale" ("generational novel")
that focused above all on the relationships and activities of young people
conditioned by mass media, video music, advertising, consumerism, and the
Americanization of the Italian language and overall lifestyle. In Tondelli's
early novels, such as *Altri libertini* (Other Libertines, 1981) and *Camere separate* (Separate Rooms, 1989), an uninhibited naturalness treats homosexual
love stories and relationships among friends. *Pao Pao* (Pao Pao, 1982), *Rimini*
(Rimini, 1985), and *Un weekend postmoderno* (A Postmodern Weekend,
1990) show Tondelli's talent for painting loud and dynamic images of a pop
rock culture that includes all its jargon, nightlife, and crowded scenes in disco
bars and vacation spots so popular in the 1970s and 1980s. Throughout
his work, Tondelli focuses extensively on the concerns, actions, sexuality,
behavior, and linguistic "tics" of a restless generation of young people always
moving, traveling, searching, partying, engaged in idle discussions, and, yet,
usually bored with their lives.

Andrea De Carlo captures similar images of youth culture, relying primarily on visual and auditory effects to magnify his realism. His links to the
cinema are crucial to his prose (he once worked with Federico Fellini). In discussing De Carlo's first two novels *Treno di panna* (*The Cream Train*, 1981)
and *Uccelli di gabbia e di voliera* (Birds of Cage and Aviary, 1982), Italo
Calvino rightly identified the influence of American hyperrealists upon the
young novelist's work, and De Carlo is certainly knowledgeable about Jack
Kerouac and the "beat" or "on the road" generation of American writers, as
well as being an expert on rock music, cinema, pop culture, and the minimalist tendencies in the arts during the 1980s. Novels such as *Macno* (Macno,
1984) illustrate his skillful reliance upon cinematic and photographic montage techniques. Moreover, Mexico, California, Los Angeles, and New York
are places that he knows from experience, having lived there for extensive

periods of time, and the colorful details of these places that he includes in his works add to the realism of his fast-moving narrative in novels like *Yucatan* (*Yucatan*, 1986) and *Tecniche di seduzione* (Techniques of Seduction, 1991). In some of De Carlo's novels, such as *Due di due* (Two of Two, 1989), social and political themes become more prominent in stories about close friends who drift apart as their ideologies and lifestyles change after student unrest in 1968 and 1977 causes upheavals in Italian society. Recently, in *Nel momento* (In the Moment, 1999), De Carlo seems to have returned to a more intimate brand of narrative, focused upon existential problems and private relationships.

Enrico Palandri's short stories collected in *Boccalone* (Big Mug, 1979), the postmodern manifesto of a young generation, won the author high praise, and this critical favor continued in *La via del ritorno* (The Way Back, 1990), and *Allegro ma non troppo* (1993). Palandri's style, his lively colloquial dialogues, and his depictions of situations from the daily lives of university students and their friends became popular with new writers, such as Silvia Ballestra and Paolo Nori (1963–), who also began to compose novels and short stories about the youth culture of the 1980s and 1990s.

New women writers

Women novelists have become more prominent in the literary scene of the past two decades. Paola Capriolo, Susanna Tamaro, Silvia Ballestra, Marta Morazzoni (1950–), Rosanna Campo, Laura Cardella (1966–), Carmen Covito, and Pia Pera (1956–) have all enjoyed success with readers in a publishing industry previously dominated by men. Paola Capriolo is a refined narrator whose talent was immediately recognized by critics such as Maria Corti when she published her first collection of short fiction entitled *La grande Eulalia* (The Grand Eulalia, 1988) and her novel *Il nocchiero* (The Steerman, 1989). Her popularity among the general public was consolidated with *Vissi d'amore* (*Floria Tosca*, 1992), an exquisite melodrama using Puccini's *Tosca* as its inspiration. Capriolo treats her readers to suspenseful stories, elegant style, unusual love relationships, solitary characters, rich symbolism, and unmistakable metanarrative strategies. Echoes of Franz Kafka, Dino Buzzati, Gabriel Garcia Marquez, and Jorge Luis Borges enrich her consistent use of magical, allegorical, symbolic, and oneiric elements. Her skills are best demonstrated in *La spettatrice* (*The Woman Watching*, 1995), a novel that reconfirms her love for nineteenth-century Gothic narratives dominated by light and chromatic effects, slow-moving action, and a sophisticated intellectualism in treating time frames. From the opening pages of *La spettatrice*, its omniscient narrator offers to the reader foreshadowings about the fate of the characters and the progression of the story. Mirrors, masks, costumes, theatrical performances, anxieties, uneasy feelings, and a sense of death are the recurring symbols and motifs of the novel. Vulpius, the main protagonist, gradually shuts out the whole world as he continues to imagine how he looks in the eyes of the mysterious woman he saw in the audience staring at him in the theater. He will go on feeling the gaze of the woman wherever he goes, and in this obsessive awareness will reveal the dark side of his existence that leads him to lose his friends and his own life.

Carmen Covito made her debut with a small masterpiece entitled *La bruttina stagionata*. The private life and love misadventures of Marilina, a homely, intelligent, and middle-aged woman of letters, provide the ground for Covito's irony through which she attacks hypocrisy and a myriad of stereotyped themes about single, plain-looking, middle-aged women and their relationships with men. Throughout Marilina's metamorphosis, as she learns to accept her body, gain self-confidence, and affirm her sexual freedom and independence, Covito makes sharp, ironic comments on prejudices and antiquated views that have kept Italian women, especially in the South, prisoners of old social customs and moralistic taboos at home, at work, and in public. The author's ability to treat even the most delicate or unsettling topics, such as sex changes, homosexuality, and fetishism lies, in part, in her excellent control of a vivid language full of ironic allusions to today's fast-changing society.

In *Benvenuti in questo ambiente* (Welcome to This Place, 1998), Covito's wit and her metafictional narrative skills become even more noticeable as the author exploits the world and vocabulary of computers and the internet in an unusual story that verges on the grotesque and the surreal. Saladino, an illegal immigrant from Tunisia, works as a housekeeper for two wealthy individuals: Marco, a lawyer, and his sister Sandrina, a programmer of software and artificial intelligence. Saladino takes his orders from the image of a woman on a computer. Midway through the novel he discovers that the voice coming from the monitor is that of Lucia, the mother of Marco and Sandrina. Lucia hides in the basement because she has become a freak as a result of her wish to have extra breasts implanted. Lucia's sinful past is juicily narrated to Saladino, as we also learn about the scandalous private life of her two children. Racism, body-piercing, wild parties, and drugs are just a few of the ingredients that spice up this postmodern, parodic cyber-detective story filled with themes from the news, commercials, films, the internet, and mass media.

Pia Pera's narrative debut was a collection of short stories: *La bellezza dell'asino* (The Beauty of the Donkey, 1992), and its literary language and descriptions of its youthful characters remind the reader of the popular fiction of Campo and Ballestra. Pera's postmodern metafictional rewrite of Nabokov's *Lolita*, entitled *Il diario di Lo* (*Lo's Diary*, 1995), won her notoriety in the editorial world. This diary-novel exploits the usual postmodern devices of found manuscripts and intertextual parodies. The author gives a voice to the famous teenager whose name has become a metaphor for precocious sexuality. She presents a Lolita much more bratty and foxy than her model, and Pera imagines how Lolita must have thought, felt, and schemed. Pera's Lolita uses a language that may be overly literary, just as her behavior may be a bit too mature than her age would permit. Pera's model forces the reader to ask questions. What if Lolita had voiced her real views in the original novel? What would she have said about her lustful relationship with an older man?

New voices of Italian fiction

Fiction dealing with the postmodern notion of remakes or revisitations of classic narratives has been popular since the 1980s in Italy. To mention only a few examples, Tabucchi's *Sogni di sogni* (*Dreams of Dreams*, 1992) presents a playful metaliterary fiction based on dreams that famous people might have experienced, while *Itaca per sempre* (Ithaca Forever, 1998) by Luigi Malerba (1927–), a retelling of Homer's *Odyssey*, shows the reader Penelope in the central role of the novel as she duels psychologically with her husband. She forces Ulysses to explain why it took him so long to get back home and why she was the last person to be told the true identity of the old beggar who slaughtered her suitors. Did Ulysses, Malerba asks, not trust Penelope as much as he trusted her son and his old wet nurse? Is Ulysses now ready to leave home once again, following the prophecy that condemned him to a life of wandering? Malerba's eloquent dialogues and his beautifully rendered interchange between Penelope, Ulysses, and their son Telemacus make *Itaca per sempre* a most enjoyable metafiction.

From the early 1990s Alessandro Baricco, an expert on classical music, has enjoyed the spotlight as one of Italy's most promising and most commercially successful new authors. His first two works, *Castelli di rabbia* (Castles of Anger, 1991) and *Oceano mare* (*Ocean Sea*, 1993) enjoyed good sales figures from readers who enjoyed Baricco's talent for narrating parallel stories about unusual characters in strange and surreal settings, usually with the sea as their background. In *Oceano mare* the sea and the Pensione Almayer serve as converging points for the interaction of eccentric and mysterious characters, such as a young girl who runs the *pensione*, a painter who thinks he can paint the ocean with the ocean, a scientist who wishes to know where the ocean ends, a sailor with a dark past, a dying baroness, an adulteress, an invisible man in room 7, and a priest who writes unusual prayers. Each character is looking for something different from the power of the sea. Stimulating reflections on nature versus science, on writing, art, and dreams are intermingled with the brief dialogues that take place between the characters in their occasional encounters on the beach or in the hotel.

City (City, 1999), one of Baricco's most popular novels, takes place in an unnamed American city. The story begins with Shatzy Shell on the phone from a TV station, conducting a poll to ascertain whether or not a certain character should die in a popular soap opera. The intentional allusions to the media hype that surrounded the "Who shot JR?" incident on the American television serial *Dallas* (an enormous hit in Italy) are obvious. The main characters of the three parallel stories are Gould, a child prodigy who comes from a divorced family, and who attends university classes; Shatzy Shell, who is writing a western and who ends up looking after Gould; and a boxer, Larry Lawyer, whose legendary fights date back to the days of radio. *City* is an outstanding manifestation of Baricco's great facility for the presentation of several stories that cross and merge at different points in the novel. The author excels in fusing past and present, fiction and metafiction, adding witty discussions on art, film, and literature and the contemporary obsession with consumption. He also employs flashbacks and stop-action framing similar to techniques employed in the cinema. Shatzy's western, about a sheriff who chases after the bad guy in a town where time has stopped after its clock mysteriously stopped ticking, links the lives of Gould and Shatzy. Baricco's remarkable talent is such that even with all the stop-action framing, interruptions, flashbacks, and the constant alternation of stories, the reader never loses track of the suspenseful plots being developed.

Widely translated and well reviewed abroad as well as within Italy, Baricco's *Seta* (*Silk*, 1996) is his best-known and most acclaimed work to date. It is a slim book translated into more than fifteen languages, the fictional story of a nineteenth-century French merchant of silkworms, Hervé Joncour, who, when an epidemic disease decimates European and Middle Eastern silkworms, leaves for Japan to buy more of them. In Japan, he finally buys his precious merchandise, but, above all, he falls in love with a mysterious young woman to whom he never even speaks. The hidden irony of the book is that Joncour's wife has, on the contrary, a beautiful voice, but it is the silent Japanese woman who attracts the French merchant. The lack of verbal communication between the two represents a diagram of life: what we like and desire very rarely belongs to our daily life. *Silk* cannot really be called a novel or a novella. It is probably more a variation of the two genres. There is a plot, a narrative scheme, and the development of the few characters, but there is also the enthusiasm for discovery, the mystery of a non-speaking main figure, the fascination for the unknown, all elements that, at the same time, stand out and melt together with the narrative structure. The book is written in a lyrical style, with sentences that intend to capture or underline the sense of estrangement of the protagonists, as well as the fascinating and unsettling freshness of a new world. *Silk* represents an exception in Baricco's production, especially because of its thin but effective plot, which does not intertwine with other subplots, as in some of his other books.

Niccoló Ammaniti, along with the previously mentioned Aldo Nove, was one of the early "cannibals" who began to exploit pulp, splatter, and trash fiction in their depiction of sex, violence, and heavy metal rock. Ammaniti's debut came with the publication of a collection of short fiction entitled *Fango* (Mud, 1996), a work that brought him immediate fame. Non-Italian readers of this collection will have little difficulty in recognizing the striking connections between *Fango* (especially its opening story, "L'ultimo capodanno," ["The Last New Year's Eve"]), which is filled with the kinds of violence and explosions that characterize films such as *Fargo* (directed by the Coen brothers), and a number of recent American movies such as *Donnie Brasco*, *Pulp Fiction*, or *Reservoir Dogs*. More recently, Ammaniti's *Ti prendo e ti porto via* (I Shall Come and Take You Away, 1999) shares some similarities with Baricco's *City* in terms of masterfully interrupting, merging, and overlapping parallel stories. The lives of a tiny and shy teenager, Pietro Moroni, who is frequently bullied by his schoolmates, and of a forty-year-old playboy, Graziano Biglia, a legendary stud in disco bars and the beaches around the summer resort town of Rimini, converge for a few moments in a small town north of Rome. A woman named Flora Palmieri is the catalyst that brings together the two characters, as well as other peculiar or shady characters, all of whom seem to come from dysfunctional families. Flora is a middle-aged virgin who teaches in Pietro's school. She is seduced and abandoned by Graziano. At the end of the novel Pietro kills Flora for having failed him. Pietro, Graziano, and Flora all learn the hard way that promises are made to be broken.

While in *Fango* Ammaniti capitalizes on graphic descriptions of violence, *Ti prendo e ti porto via* employs the frequent use of obscenities and pornographic depictions, especially as it follows Graziano's steamy amorous adventures. However, in Ammaniti's style, such graphically explicit elements are expressed with a naturalness that reflects the high level of desensitivity contemporary readers have when confronted with violence or what only recently was still considered to be obscene language. Thus Ammaniti demonstrates to his reader how explicitly violent and sexual images from comic books, cartoons, the cinema, and mass media in general have saturated our literary language.

Italian mystery writing

In the contemporary literary scene, mystery writing deserves special mention. Despite notable exceptions such as Gadda, Sciascia, or Eco, Italy has never produced a strong literary interest in the mystery. Most criticism has, in fact, snubbed such genres as popular fiction. It is therefore somewhat surprising that in more recent years Enrico Brizzi (1972–), Andrea Camilleri, and Carlo Lucarelli (1960–) have acquired national and international fame with their mystery novels and stories and have also attracted the attention of major literary critics. Camilleri lives in Rome but was born in Porto Empedocle, a coastal town in Sicily, while Lucarelli was born in Parma but lives near Bologna. The regional origins of the two authors play a major role in their writings, as most of Camilleri's works take place in Sicily, and many of Lucarelli's in Bologna. Despite their interest in the mystery, Camilleri and Lucarelli have different professional backgrounds. Camilleri taught stage direction at the Art and Drama School of Rome, has been a successful screenwriter, and has worked as a director for both the stage and television. Lucarelli is the anchorperson of a television program on unsolved murders, works for the publishing industry, edits a literary internet site, and sometimes sings for a punk rock group.

Camilleri began publishing fiction in 1978 (*Il corso delle cose* [The Order of Things]), when he was already in his fifties, and, after more than a decade of being unknown, he suddenly acquired fame thanks to his novels centered on the investigations of Inspector Salvo Montalbano. Salvo is an astute Sicilian policeman who operates in the fictional town of Vigàta, a fictitious name for Camilleri's own birthplace, Porto Empedocle. Camilleri's experience as a screenwriter and as a director was certainly useful in his narrative approach. His books are always lively and visual, even when dealing with philosophical issues or with serious historical or political situations. Camilleri's style is characterized by complex but clear plots, by a balanced mix of Sicilian dialect and standard Italian – a trait that confers a realistic and fresh tone to his novels – by fast and intense dialogues, and by his ability to depict a character in just a few lines without depriving the reader of the pleasure of unveiling the characters' nature as his plots evolve.

Camilleri's production to date has been intelligently divided between historical novels that take place in Vigàta or in Sicily in the late nineteenth century, on the one hand, and his short stories and novels about the contemporary Detective Inspector Montalbano's investigations, on the other. The first group of works includes: *Il birraio di Preston* (The Brewer of Preston, 1995), *La concessione del telefono* (The Telephone Contract, 1998), *La mossa del cavallo* (The Knight's Move, 1999), and *La scomparsa di Patò* (The Disappearance of Patò, 2000). The novels following the adventures of his hero Montalbano are *La forma dell'acqua* (*The Shape of Water*, 1994), *Il cane di terracotta* (*The Terra-Cotta Dog*, 1996), *Il ladro di merendine* (The Snack Thief, 1996), *La voce del violino* (The Voice of the Violin, 1997), *La gita a Tindari* (The Trip to Tindari, 2000), and *L'odore della notte* (The Fragrance of the Night, 2001). Montalbano seems to be modeled on George Simenon's Inspector Maigret. He shares with his French counterpart a true love of good food and wine, an ability to fake ignorance when facing his superiors, and an innate instinct for uncovering hidden murderous trails. But, in contrast to Maigret, Montalbano is more educated, more familiar with wide-ranging works of philosophy and literature, and above all more rebellious against the corrupt establishment in which he lives, contemporary Sicily. This last characteristic is not surprising, as Montalbano lives and operates in a region dominated by the Mafia, while Maigret deals primarily with bourgeois crimes of passion in Paris and is rarely at risk of losing his life in his investigations.

La gita a Tindari is a good example of Camilleri's narrative skills and of the reasons for which Inspector Salvo Montalbano has become such a popular character. The plot is apparently simple: three people who live in the same building, a young Don Juan and an elderly couple, are killed, with no apparent connection between them. Montalbano senses that the murders are actually linked, and his investigation brings him to the heart of a diabolically well-planned Mafia scheme profiting from illegal organ transplants. Camilleri's slow plot development from suspicion to certainty tantalizes the reader, from the possible innocence of a suspect to the guilt of an apparently extraneous person, from the unveiling of inadmissible evidence to the theatrical finale staged by the inspector and his men, who need to apprehend the murderers without triggering the rage of their superiors, who wish to avoid serious confrontations with the Mafia. At the same time, this novel displays Camilleri's stylistic originality in full. The mix of comic and tragic elements that compose our daily life is conveyed through the dialogues between the inspector and the suspects, as well as between him and his faithful but sometimes recalcitrant underlings. The events are all well inserted into the Sicilian cultural and geographical landscape, itself a necessary part of the plot, thanks to Camilleri's magisterial portrait of the relationship between the novel's characters and their homeland.

In *L'odore della notte*, Camilleri presents Montalbano as more poised, less tense, less eager to get involved with the inevitable action inherent in his job. The plot itself is less defined, more focused upon psychological rather than dramatic developments. In this work, the case under investigation is not even assigned to our hero: Montalbano investigates on his own the disappearance of a dishonest financial investor. While only in his early fifties, Montalbano is already contemplating his possible retirement while he meditates upon the intricacies of this puzzling case. This novel confirms Camilleri's best writing qualities, which allow him to write mysteries with the same protagonist over and over again, while preserving a freshness that makes each book and each story distinct.

This last characteristic is also typical of his historical novels. Despite their common Sicilian background and their focus on the fictional reconstruction of actual or presumed criminal events – a trait that marks Camilleri as indebted to Sciascia's example – the historically based books reflect very different narrative solutions from those that foreground Inspector Montalbano. In *La mossa del cavallo*, for instance, the book's surprising ending is entrusted to a clever linguistic game. In the late 1800, Giovanni Bovara, a Genoese born to a Sicilian father, is sent to Sicily as an inspector for the Department of Agriculture. Giovanni is seen as an outsider because, despite his Sicilian origins, he speaks and acts like an "Italian," that is, a stranger ("forestiero") in the island, and because he shows no intention of ever accepting any favors from the local corrupt political establishment. When he uncovers the illegal plans of a Mafia boss who controls the mills of the area, he becomes a target of organized crime. During one of his inspections, Bovara witnesses the murder of a dishonest priest, Father Carnazza, but stands too far away from the crime to recognize the assassin: before dying, Carnazza reveals the name of the murderer. Bovara runs off to look for help and offers his testimony to the police, only to find out that he has become the accused, as the body of the dead priest is found in his house. While in custody, Giovanni, who has not spoken Sicilian dialect since he was a child, intuits that his only chance of survival is to reacquire his linguistic heritage, the only key to penetrate the alien world that surrounds him. Bovara's return to the Sicilian dialect allows him to offer a new, ambiguous explanation of what the priest told him before dying. If interpreted in dialect, and not in Italian, the priest's words, in fact, accused three different people – the same people who were actually involved either with the murder or with the fake incrimination of Bovara. This linguistic escapade allows Giovanni to persuade the magistrates of his innocence, and, at the same time, triggers a war between the accused and their co-conspirators.

In another novel, *La scomparsa di Patò*, Camilleri resorts to an open experimentalism that goes beyond such linguistic boundaries, and it directly involves the narrative structure. The entire book is constructed upon the fictional transcription of the documents generated by the disappearance of a banker in a small Sicilian town in the nineteenth century. The reader learns of the plot and of the events surrounding the disappearance of Patò through a clever concatenation of newspaper articles, private and public correspondence, blackmail letters, and police reports. Many different accounts and unofficial truths emerge from the reading of these documents. As in most mysteries dealing with Sicilian reality, the official truth will not correspond to the actual solution of the enigma, which is presented to the reader in the form of a police report later retracted. In this original book, Camilleri confirms his writing qualities and his profound knowledge of the complex historical and political background of Sicily, as well as his stylistic ability to keep the reader interested in his mysteries, even when the narrative events need to be deduced from both fictional and actual reports, as well as from historical documents.

Like Camilleri, Carlo Lucarelli has published both historical novels and works centered around specific inspectors or investigators. If Camilleri's historical books take place in the nineteenth century, Lucarelli's deal mostly with the Fascist period, an era on which Lucarelli is an expert. Two books in particular show Lucarelli's skills as a writer who can restore the general historical ambiance without overlooking the aspects of the daily life of the epoch: the short novel *Guernica* (Guernica, 1996), and *L'isola dell'angelo caduto* (The Island of the Fallen Angel, 1999). The first, republished with a different ending in 2000, takes place in Spain at the height of the Civil War in 1937. Its plot is simple: a young Italian officer is sent to the front to recover the fallen body of his best friend. This enterprise becomes far more complicated than it seems and exposes the naive young officer to a world of deception, ferocity, loyalty, and pain. Lucarelli gives a vivid image of the brutality of the war, with its consequences of devastation and corruption, as well as a refreshingly original description of both major characters. He stresses the ambiguous environment that produces and absorbs, at the same time, all the actions and the ideas surrounding his protagonists.

In *L'isola dell'angelo caduto*, a novel that takes place on a island where the Fascist regime sends its political prisoners into exile, the tone is, instead, more descriptive, more pensive, and the general mood is best described by the anxiety of the main characters, all but one of whom are unhappy living in such a remote and timeless place. The windy and ambiguous island seems to be the real key to the mysterious murders that have suddenly shaken the community. The moody climate of the secluded island, with its unpredictable weather, illustrates the uncertain destiny of all the protagonists. The contemplative police inspector who will solve the crime almost by chance, the ironic anti-Fascist doctor, the delusional wife of the inspector, the primitive but clever chief of the Fascist militia, are all representations of the garrulous life on the perennially wind-swept island.

Lucarelli's investigators, contrary to the mainstream mystery tradition, are not always characterized by wise or refined intellects. In a few cases, in fact, they are very average people who reflect contemporary mass culture. This is the case, for instance, of Coliandro, the protagonist of *Falange armata* (Armed Militia, 1997), and of *Il giorno del lupo* (The Day of the Wolf, 1998). By his own admission, Coliandro is merely a simple policeman, intolerant and incapable of understanding and accepting the rapid changes contemporary Italian society is undergoing. He often has excellent intuitive insights but he never really grasps the subtle details of the events taking place around him even when he actually solves his cases. Exactly the opposite is true of Inspector De Luca, protagonist of several of Lucarelli's mysteries that are set in the chaotic period between the collapse of Italy's Fascist government in 1943 and the immediate postwar period, when policemen with connections to the fallen regime are suspected by every political faction associated with the triumph of antifascism. Like Coliandro, De Luca considers himself a mere policeman and never questions the political links of the police to the Fascist regime. He is an astute and intelligent investigator. He anticipates the moves of his suspects and understands all too well the machinations of his superiors. He tenaciously determines to solve his cases even if the pursuit of his investigations causes him to risk his life in the last years of the war in *Carta bianca* (Carte Blanche, 1990) and *L'estate torbida* (The Turbid Summer, 1991), or moves him to risk his entire career after the war in *Via delle oche* (Goose Street, 1996).

One other protagonist of Lucarelli's stories is Inspector Grazia Negro, who, unlike Coliandro, is intelligent and has fine intuitive reasoning powers. Both share the same regional origins (Apulia) and both entered the police force after graduating from high school without attending a university. Inspector Negro is very sensitive to the people involved in her investigations. At the beginning of the stories in which she appears, she does not emerge immediately as the main investigator, but she soon becomes crucial to the solution of the cases that always deal with serial killers. In the three novels in which she appears – *Lupo mannaro* (Werewolf, 1995), *Almost Blue* (*Almost Blue*, 1997), and *Un giorno dopo l'altro* (One Day after Another, 2000) – Lucarelli's writing produces an admirable psychological analysis of his characters. His productivity has raised concerns about the overly commercial intentions of some of his works; in addition, he has been criticized for his sensational endings and repetitive narrative sequences. Nevertheless, most Italian critics admit that Lucarelli maintains an unusual stylistic clarity and rhythm, supported by the rare ability to reveal to the reader the intricacies of the inner world in which the characters of his books move and operate.

A new literary language for a new millennium?

Italy's new narrators love to exploit obscene language and colloquialisms, as well as the use of English words and names of famous people. They frequently cite the brand names of all sorts of products, ranging from toothpaste to television monitors, automobiles, washing machines, cellular phones (providing the specific model number in question), and fashionable designer clothing. Some of these authors (Covito, Capriolo, or Baricco) write in a sophisticated literary style, while others (Nove, for example) excel in dialogue derived from rapid exchanges made up, for the most part, of banalities and expressions from the world of advertising and mass media. In short, these so-called "new" novelists focus more often upon linguistic effects than upon elaborate plots typical of traditional realistic fiction.

The condition of the Italian novel in the first decade of the new millennium poses several questions to the reading public or the literary historian. For example, are their entertaining parodic and ironic postmodern creations a form of criticism of today's consumer society or an unfortunate product of such a world revolving around mass media? Are their literary playfulness and postmodern style both a comic vehicle that moves the reader to laughter as well as a serious form of literature that uncovers the social and moral values underpinning contemporary society? Following the example of Tabucchi's fiction, the pleasure of the text of such new novelists is not limited to the linguistic and metaliterary elements that enrich the literariness of their possible worlds. There is also another pleasure to be derived from their parodic or ironic depictions of a society in which everything is recycled – not only garbage but also history, literature, art, and, above all, the cinema. Our postmodern society is not merely mirrored or reproduced in these works. In general, entertaining and stimulating parodies also deconstruct the world. These works emphasize the fact that our contemporary lifestyle has been reduced to a state of imitations and superficialities. They encapsulate very well the message embodied by the narrative of many "new" Italian novelists, even if only indirectly: today, life imitates, above all else, the world of media and entertainment, reducing everything, including death and tragedy, to one enormous spectacle.

Further reading

Barański, Zygmunt G. and Lino Pertile, eds. *The New Italian Novel*. Edinburgh: Edinburgh University Press, 1993.

Baricco, Alessandro. *Silk*. Trans. Guido Waldman. New York: Vintage, 1998.

Ocean Sea. Trans. Alistair McEven. New York: Vintage, 2000.

Benni, Stefano. *Terra!* Trans. Annapaola Cangogni. New York: Pantheon, 1985.

Brizzi, Enrico. *Jack Frusciante Has Left the Band: A Love Story – With Rock 'N' Roll*. Trans. Stash Luczkiw. New York: Grove, 1996.

Busi, Aldo. *The Standard Life of a Temporary Pantyhose Salesman*. Trans. Raymond Rosenthal. New York; Farrar, Giroux, Strauss, 1988.

Seminar on Youth. Trans. Stuart Hood. Manchester: Carcanet, 1989.

Sodomies in Elevenpoint. Trans. Stuart Hood. London: Faber, 1992.

Camilleri, Andrea. *The Shape of Water: An Inspector Montalbano Mystery*. Trans. Stephen Santarelli. New York: Viking, 2002.

The Terra-Cotta Dog: An Inspector Montalbano Mystery. Trans. Stephen Santarelli. New York: Viking, 2002.

Capriolo, Paola. *Floria Tosca*. Trans. Liz Herron. London: Serpent's Tail, 1997.

The Woman Watching. Trans. Liz Heron. London: Serpent's Tail, 1998.

De Carlo, Andrea. *The Cream Train*. Trans. John Gatt. London: Olive Press, 1987.

Del Giudice, Daniele. *Lines of Light*. Trans. Norman MacAfee and Luigi Fontanella. Harmondsworth: Viking Penguin, 1989.

Takeoff: The Pilot's Lore. Trans. Joseph Farrell. New York: Harcourt Brace, 1997.

Lucamante, Stefania, ed. *Italian Pulp Fiction: The New Narrative of the "Giovani Cannibali" Writers*. Cranbury, NJ: Fairleigh Dickinson University Press, 2001.

Lucarelli, Carlo. *Almost Blue*. Trans. Oonagh Stransky. San Francisco: City Lights Books, 2001.

Pazzi, Roberto. *Searching for the Emperor*. Trans. Margaret J. Fitzgerald. London: Deutsch, 1989.

The Princess and the Dragon. Trans. Margaret J. Fitzgerald. London: Deutsch, 1990.

Adrift in Time. Trans. Vivien Sinott. London: Deutsch, 1991.

Pera, Pia. *Lo's Diary*. Trans. Ann Goldstein. New York: Foxrock, 2001.

Tabucchi, Antonio. *Letter from Casablanca*. Trans. Janice M. Thresher. New York: New Directions Book, 1986.

Little Misunderstandings of No Importance. Trans. Frances Frenaye. New York: New Directions, 1987.

Indian Nocturne. Trans. Tim Parks. New York: New Directions, 1989.

Vanishing Point. Trans. Tim Parks. London: Chatto and Windus, 1991.

Requiem. A Hallucination. Trans. Margaret Costa. New York: New Directions, 1994.

Pereira Declares: A Testimony. Trans. Patrick Creigh. New York: New Directions, 1996.

Dreams of Dreams and the Last Three Days of Fernando Pessoa. Trans. Jancy J. Peters. San Francisco: City Lights Books, 2000.

Tamaro, Susanna. *Follow Your Heart*. New York: Dell, 1995.

INDEX

CAMBRIDGE COMPANIONS TO LITERATURE